MW01039246

Kabbalistic Writings
on the Nature of Masculine & Feminine

Kabbalistic Writings on the Nature of Masculine & Feminine

Sarah Yehudit Schneider

A STILL SMALL VOICE

JERUSALEM

KABBALISTIC WRITINGS ON THE NATURE OF MASCULINE & FEMININE
Published by *A Still Small Voice*
Copyright © 2001 by Sarah Yehudit Schneider
PAPERBACK EDITION, 2020

A Still Small Voice Publishing Group is a division of the Still Small Voice
Correspondence School that has been providing teachings on classic
Jewish wisdom to subscribers around the world since its inception in 1991.

5 7 9 8 6 4

All rights reserved. No part of this book may be used or reproduced
in any manner whatsoever without written permission from A
Still Small Voice except in the case of brief quotations in reviews
for inclusion in a magazine, newspaper, or broadcast.

This work was originally published in hardcover
in 2001 by Jason Aronson, Inc.

Set in Arno Pro by Raphaël Freeman MISTD, Renana Typesetting

Library of Congress Cataloging-in-Publication Data

Kabbalistic writings on the nature of masculine and feminine / [compiled,
translated, and introduced by] Susan (Sarah Yehudit [Idit]) Schneider.
  p. Cm
Annotated English translations of selections from Hebrew texts. Included
bibliographical references and index.
ISBN-10 965-92818-0-3   ISBN-13 978-965-92818-0-0
1. Cabala. 2. God-Omnipresence. 3. Mysticism-Judaism.
1. Schneider, Susan, 1951-
BM526 .M64 2000 296.1'6-dc21 00-038964

Printed in Israel
A Still Small Voice
Chabad St. 90/16 Jerusalem 97500 Israel
(+972-2) 628–2988

news@astillsmallvoice.org
www.astillsmallvoice.org/

"קול ה׳ יחולל אילות...".

"The voice of God causes the hinds to bear ... "

(PSALMS 29:9)

בס׳ד

הרב לוי יצחק הלוי הורוויץ

דער באסטאנער רבי

Grand Rabbi Levi Y. Horowitz

"I feel that this endeavor is very worthwhile. Even the person with greater background will find new thoughts to contemplate and study in this work through the author's focus on how to use the practices of Torah, prayer, and mitzvot to enhance one's relationship with Hashem."

Rabbi Levi Y. Horowitz (The Bostoner Rebbe)

"I hold Ms. Schneider in very high esteem and can verify that she is highly respected, reliable, and that she approaches her work with an exceptional intellectual motivation which constantly inspires...It is rare to find someone with such depth of knowledge and commitment to bringing back the pride of our heritage."

Rabbi Noah Weinberg, Dean

"...she enables the serious student to taste the vibrant spirituality of Judaism that permeates even its most basic principles of faith and practice through her creative treatment of the subject, and emphasis on internalizing the information... I warmly recommend A Still Small Voice to anyone who is interested in enriching their lives with the spiritual content of Judaism."

Rabbi David Refson, Rosh Yeshiva

RABBI MEIR SCHUSTER
FOUNDER & DIRECTOR

RABBI AVRAHAM EDELSTEIN
EXECUTIVE DIRECTOR

"Of all our staff in the women's hostel over the years, Susie has stood out as the person most capable of answering the wide range of questions that have come up. She has worked hard both to acquire the necessary knowledge and to find ways of translating this into the language of the unaffiliated."

Rabbi Meir Schuster

כפר חב״ד, טל׳ — 03-9607351
מנדל־עזר, גוש־עציון, ד.נ. צפון יהודה
טל׳ — 02-9327204

"I have been impressed by Susan Schneider's knowledge of Torah in general and Chassidut in particular, as well as her command of the English language and ability to deftly convey even very abstract ideas clearly... I trust her ability to develop and elaborate raw ideas into cogent, well-researched expositions."

Rabbi Yitzchak Ginsburgh

"This course draws on mysticism and mainstream Judaism, and covers a wide range of essential issues and practices. It is not pushy, but it demands time, and thought and commitment... You will be challenged and stimulated... It is very provoking for the beginner and advanced alike."

Rabbi David Zeller

בס"ד

December 11, 2001

TANENBAUM COLLEGE

PRESIDENT
Bernard Hochstein

CHAIRMAN OF THE BOARD
Howard P. Ronson

DEAN
Rabbi Dr. David Refson

PRINCIPAL
Rabbi Moshe Chalkowski

MICHINA
Rabbi Eliezer Liff

SHALHEVET
Rabbi David Kass

NEVE SHOSHANA
Rabbi Chaim Metzger

NEVE NERLITZ
Rabbi Gerald Ackerman

NEVE RUSNIA
Dr. Anya Essas

ZAIDNER INSTITUTE
Rabbi Noson Geisler

ENOS CHAVA
Rabbi Dovid Abramov

ADMINISTRATOR
Abraham Stefansky

ASSOCIATE DIRECTOR
Irene Wexler

To Whom it May Concern,

I have had the pleasure and privilege of knowing Sarah Yehudit Schneider for over a decade. During this time, she has done what so few of us ever do; she has broken down the borders that keep so many of us from ever experiencing that elusive something called excellence. From a serious student of spirituality who was just beginning to investigate Jewish studies in a serious way, she has become an author. Additionally she is the editor of "Still Small Voice" a magazine that has opened the doors for hundreds of students by providing them with an individualized study plan. This is but a small portion of what her spiritual and intellectual outreach represents.

Sincerely
Tziporah Heller,

Senior Lecturer, Neve Yerushalaim

Gal Einai

נ	ל	ע	נ
ח	ש	ב	ו
ת	א	ל	ג
ם	ת	י	ר

גַּל־עֵינַי

ת.ד. 545, רחובות 76100. טל: (08) 936-5947 ; פקס (08) 947-3843
P.O. Box 545, Rechovot 76100, Israel; tel: +972-8-936-5947; fax: +972-8-947-3045
E-mail: inner@inner.org   Web page: http://www.inner.org

בס"ד
י"ח שבט היתשי"ס

To Whom It May Concern,

I have known Sarah Yehudit (Susan) Schneider of Jerusalem for approximately
eighteen years. During that time I have been positively impressed by her
knowledge of Torah in general and *Chassidut* in particular, as well as her,
command of the English language and ability to articulate even very
abstract ideas clearly and succinctly. In addition I trust her ability to
develop and elaborate concepts into cogent, well-researched expositions.
She has written several articles an a book for Gal Einai and I was very
satisfied with her work each time.

I am confident that her present work reflects her established scholarly
reputation.

Sincerely,

Yitzchak Ginsburgh
Yitzchak Ginsburgh

YG:mw

CONTENTS

EXPANDED CONTENTS

2. **Two Great Lights – A Cosmic Vision of Equality**
   Babylonian Talmud *Chullin* **6ob** presents a three-step
   sequence of relationship between male and female that
   appears whenever gender exists. It proceeds as follows:

   - initial equality between masculine and feminine
   - diminishment of the feminine
   - re-attained equality (that is even more consummately equal
     than was possible before).

   These three stages comprise a single moon cycle. They apply
   on all scales, from the span of an individual woman's life to

the history of creation (for the entire period of existence from the beginning of time to its end is but a single circuit of the moon).

The moon symbol introduced by the Talmud refers to the feminine archetype, and is synonymous with the kabbalistic term, *woman*. These names are used interchangeably, and the proof of their equation appears in the following chapter.

3. **The Small Light to Rule by Night – The Seven Stages of Feminine Development**

An excerpt from *The Diminished Moon* by R. Isaac Luria identifies seven (really eight) stages in this feminine life cycle of waning and waxing. He describes *woman*'s recovery from diminishment and her path of attaining full-statured equality. In the end, *woman* stands equal and opposite to *man* and they meet for the first time as spiritual, intellectual, and emotional mates. Until then, *woman* needs *man* to pull down her transcendent lights, for she cannot reach them on her own. In the final and seventh stage she becomes self-sufficient in that regard. Only when perfectly equal in stature, intellect, and access to resources can *man* and *woman* unite in consummate union. When they meet on every level, from the crown of their heads to the soles of their feet, every part of each finds its match in the other.

This is the Jewish vision of how *man* and *woman* should and will relate when they have healed themselves and fixed the world. The joy of their consummate union underlies all the anticipated pleasure of messianic times.

4. **Constriction Precedes Expanse**

The Woodgatherer Was Tslofchad **– R. Yehuda Ashlag's Commentary on *Zohar* III 157a** explores one fascinating implication of this seven-stage cycle of feminine development. Each step does not proceed smoothly from the one before. Rather *woman* first develops a kind of false equality, collapses again quite suddenly, and starts a new push toward growth and full stature which she eventually attains at the end of her effort. R. Ashlag explores the difference between the false equality of her first phase of development and the true equality that prevails in the end. His teachings have intriguing implications for feminism today.

5. **Disparities of Gender Are the Cause of Evil**

   An excerpt from *The Diminished Moon* by R. Shlomo Elyashev (The *Leshem*) cracks the whole subject open and proves that gender disparities are the ultimate cause of evil in the universe. The question of why G-d would design a world with gender inequalities is the same question as why he purposely incorporated evil into creation. R. Elyashev addresses these questions in profoundly satisfying ways. It becomes manifestly clear that the elimination of evil requires the elimination of all disparities between *man* and *woman*.

6. **Transformation Is Only Possible after a Fall**

   Perfection and Perfecting by R. Avraham Yitzchak Kook explores the cosmic function served by *woman's* ordeal. He shows that positive transformation cannot happen except via the jerky motion of one step back for two steps forward. There seems to be no other way to improve except by stumbling and recovering from that fall. This two-step sequence, as inefficient as it seems, eventually ends with the net gain of progress made. The moon's cycle of waning and waxing, of diminishment and re-attained stature, is the prototype for this cosmic truth and the means by which an absolutely perfect G-d manifests the elusive joy of perfecting.

ACKNOWLEDGMENTS

This book would not have happened without the help of many, so it gives me great pleasure to pronounce my thanks:

First to my parents, Gene and Betty Schneider, for their unconditional love and support, and for holding a positive vision of my life through thick and through thin.

For my teachers: R. David Refson, who provided me (and countless others) with the opportunity of *teshuva* as a free (and priceless) gift with no strings attached. R. Yitzchok Ginsburgh, a pure spring of living Torah, whose spiritual guidance and modeling of inner work inspires the world to otherwise unimagined possibilities. R. Tsipora Heller, a living Torah on the women's side of the *mechitza*, who is humbly available to generations of students as teacher, counselor, and even as friend. R. Yitzchok Berkowitz, my *posek*, whose integration of mind and heart turns the Torah's *yoke* into blessed wings.

To the rabbis and rebbitzins who reviewed chapters in their area of specialty and made invaluable corrections: R. Moshe Shatz, who read the *Ari*, Ashlag, and *Leshem*; R. Yehuda Gelman and Ruchi Ebner, who read R. Kook; R. Meyer Sachs, who read R. Schneur Zalman of Liadi.

To Myriam Tova Millhauser for her tireless encouragement and critical suggestions; Karen Dubb for her careful reading, pointed questions, and consistently helpful advice; Andreas Burnier, an accomplished Dutch writer, who appeared, like an angel, and critiqued the manuscript from a feminist perspective; Pamela Clamen for her loyal and generous friendship, which helped me dedicate time to this work; Maurice Kirshenbaum for his faithful encouragement *of A Still Small Voice*; and Devorah Nov for being a soul-sister on the path.

To my students, *chavrutot*, and subscribers to *A Still Small Voice*: these teachings are the fruit of our shared encounters with the text of books and the text of life.

And last but certainly not least, to Sara Lea Handelsman, the Office Manager *of A Still Small Voice*, and her gracious husband, Yossi, for piloting the office with unfailing good spirit and skillfully managing its contacts with the outside world.

כל הנשמה תהלל י־ה הללוי־ה

1

PRELIMINARIES

WORDS FROM THE HEART

It is impossible to encounter the vast and awesome wisdom of kabbalah, and not feel ashamed of one's own limited capacity to hold even a fragment of its light and not tremble before the unavoidable distortions of truth inherent in those limitations. And yet, God assigns each person, from the most erudite to the most dull-witted, a spark of Torah to birth into the world, which can surely be recognized by one telltale sign: it is always the Torah that is closest to heart.

The purpose of this work is twofold:

- To publicize Jewish texts that are indisputably authoritative and that present a spacious and enlightened vision of the evolving relationship of masculine and feminine through time. They are teachings with practical implications that can help to guide our life choices and religious expressions along paths that serve God and good and truth.

- To enable a direct encounter with kabbalistic source material for persons who lack the skills or resources to access this experience on their own. Its luminous wisdom is sure to inspire a respect and affection for the Torah and its traditions.

It is my hope that readers will take these teachings to heart, for they are truly food for the soul. Yet a wise student must also be wary of hidden premises that color the way information is presented and distort its conclusions.

One solution is to recite a prayer before study that includes within it the following element:

> I seek truth and do not want to be limited by my own narrow-minded conception of what it should look like. I will open myself to these teachings with one condition: Whatever is true should enter my life and take root; whatever is false should pass through and leave no impression. With Your help, God, I trust that it will be so. Let me embrace truth and deflect falsehood.

I recommend this practice as a reliable method of learning deeply and with an open mind, but only taking truth to heart.

GOD LANGUAGE

The most essential term for God in Judaism is the Tetragrammaton, or four-letter ineffable name, that appears throughout scripture and prayer (ה/ו/ה/י). A Jew often refers to Divinity as *HaShem*, which means literally *the Name*, and alludes specifically to this most sacred appellation.

These four Hebrew letters contain all the permutations of the verb *to be*. Tradition teaches that when speaking *the Name* (*HaShem*) in prayer or study, one's intention should be toward THAT WHICH WAS, IS, AND WILL ALWAYS BE.[1] While there are

---

1. Yosef Caro, *Shulchan Arukh*, OC, 5.

more essential levels of Oneness that defy description, the Tetragrammaton provides a simple and accurate working definition of the Jewish concept of Divinity. God becomes the point of eternity that lies within each moment and each object, that which preceded creation, permeates creation, and will endure beyond its passing. God and *HaShem* are used interchangeably to indicate this notion of Eternal Presence.

It is commonly misconstrued that the Jewish God is a male God. In fact, Judaism's concept of Divinity transcends gender, as the Bible attests when it recounts the creation of Adam and Eve: "God created humankind ... in the image of God ... male and female...."[2]

This teaching is further conveyed by the Tetragrammaton itself. Of its four letters, two are masculine (ו/י) and two are feminine (ה/ה). Many kabbalistic discourses elaborate on this premise that God incorporates both male and female attributes in equal measure.[3] While there are levels of Divinity that transcend gender, when *HaShem* chooses to engage with creation He dons the cloak of duality and manifests both male and female polarities.

The conventions of gender in kabbalah echo the physical differences between men and women. When *HaShem* assumes the role of transcendent, active bestower and outward, extending principle, He is referred to in the masculine case. When expressing the role of indwelling presence and receptivity, the feminine is used.

While all these teachings about the bi-gendered nature of Divinity are profoundly true, a dilemma still remains: What pronoun should be used when referring to God? In Hebrew there is

---

2. Genesis 1:27.

3. R. Moshe Cordevero (Ramak), *Pardes Rimonim (Pomegranate Orchard),* *Shaar Shem ben Dalet (Gate of the Name Comprised of Four Letters),* 3:4; R. Yosef Gikatilla, *Shaarei Ora (Gates of Light),* Shaar 5.

no neutral option; one must choose either *He* or *She.* Since *he* is less exclusive than *she,* for it also refers to mixed groups (which is not so for *she*), nearly all writings employ it for this purpose.

In English the neutral pronoun *It* also becomes a possibility, yet its impersonal tone carries a derogatory connotation since it often implies something *less* than human. For all of these reasons, the author chooses to follow the tradition of using the pronoun *He* when referring to *HaShem,* despite the danger that unalerted readers could mistakenly conclude that God is male.

May the light of truth soon dissolve all of our false beliefs and distorted conceptions. May *"the land be filled with knowledge of God as the waters cover the sea"* (Isaiah 11:9).

THE WRITTEN TORAH
AND ORAL TORAH

Tradition teaches that the Written Torah was revealed along with its entire body of commentary, called the Oral Torah.[4] All the teachings that would ever unfold from those Five Books were included together in that first moment of revelation.[5] The bare bones summary of its communication was scribed by Moses, though *HaShem* directed the recording of each word down to its spelling.[6] This prophetic work constitutes the Written Torah. Its words are fixed and final. An error in even a single letter disqualifies the entire scroll.[7]

The Oral Torah is more complex and includes two primary cat-

---

4. TB, *Brachot* 5a.
5. *Sifra* 105a; TB, *Megillah* 9b; TY, *Peah* 2:4; *Torat Kohanim* (end of *Behukotai*); *Midrash Tehillim* (*Mizmor* 12).
6. TB, *Bava Batra* 15a.
7. R. Moses Maimonides (Rambam), *Mishneh Torah,* Laws of *Sefer Torah* 7:11; TB, *Menachot* 30a.

egories. The first is the authoritative chain of tradition that started with Moses and passes from mouth to ear, master to disciple, from Sinai until today.[8] The second is the accumulated wisdom of individual Jews from that point onward, no matter what their standing in the community or level of religious observance.[9] Tradition teaches that Moses spent his forty-day post-revelation retreat atop Sinai, studying Torah with *HaShem* and receiving all the levels of implication intended by each word. In his prophetic state Moses beheld all the moral, legal, and mystical commentaries concealed within the text, some of which are known and some of which remain to be discovered.[10] Moses then selected the seventy most distinguished elders and trained them in these mysteries for the next forty years.[11] Under Moses' watchful eye each man became a living Torah. His instinctive and reflexive way of responding to a question was corrected and recorrected until it came to reflect the Torah's truth and God's will on a consistent basis.

Each one of these elders replaced himself with his own prized student, trained over the years. This transmission of instruction that passed through the generations, from mouth to ear, master to disciple, constitutes the Oral Torah. In 180 C.E., R. Yehuda HaNasi compiled and wrote the Mishnah, a compendium of the Oral Torah's legal precedents and principles. For 1,490 years, from Sinai until then, this body of explanatory teachings was only transmitted by word of mouth. For reasons beyond the scope of this work, R. Yehuda HaNasi ruled that the survival of the nation required that

---

8. *Sifra* 105a; Rambam, *Mishneh Torah*, Introduction to *Pirkei Avot* 1 and commentaries.
9. R. Tsadok HaKohen, *Pri Tsadik* (Fruit of the Righteous), *Chankha* 2 (p. 142); Ibid., Chodesh Adar, essay 1; *Likutei Maamarim*, pp. 80–82; *Yisrael Kedoshim*, p. 152.
10. *Sifra* 105a.
11. Exodus 18:17–27; Numbers 11:16–17.

it now be rendered into written form. The gates opened and from that point onward, the recording of these oral teachings flourished and continues to do so in an unfolding chain of tradition extending to the present.

Each generation makes its contribution, though not all writings are equally authoritative. A general principle applies that correlates the authority of a commentary to the time period that it was written: the closer a text is to Moses' direct instruction, the more authoritative the work; the further, the less so.

The Oral Torah is a hybrid of creative insights emerging from the heart of its author, illuminating the traditional explanations received from teachers who received them from teachers...who received them at Sinai. Tradition teaches that every Jewish soul experienced the revelation of the Torah at Sinai and that its divine truths engraved themselves on the hearts of all present.[12] The authority of an oral teaching derives from the presumption that it is truly one of the implications that shone at Sinai. Though it is first being *written* now, it was already revealed back then.

Each new insight must pass a consistency test before it can integrate as a full status portion of the Oral Torah: It must be consistent with the entire body of teachings explicated thus far, and it must be consistent with a more intangible property, the indefinable gestalt of the Tradition. The acceptance of something as Oral Torah in the authoritative sense of that word is a consensus process that occurs informally over time. The Jewish people as a collective unit have a special sense that guides them to accept or reject certain teachings. Though they often err in the short term and resist innovations that are truly Torah, they eventually come

---

12. Deuteronomy 29:14; *Midrash Rabbah, Shmot 28:6; Pirkei de Rebbe Eliezer* 41; R. Shlomo Elyashev (*Leshem*), *Leshem SheBo V'Achlama, Drush Olam HaTohu (HDYH)*, 2:p. 46: top/rt.

round, though it may take a generation or two for them to catch up. The Torah's home is the Jewish people, and eventually all of its sparks will find their way in.

The second category of Oral Torah is the accumulated body of insights pressed from the hearts of Jews striving to live with integrity to the truths they absorbed at Sinai.[13] This is so, even when the individual has no conscious relationship with the Torah and its practices. The Talmud boldly asserts, "There is no truth except Torah."[14] This means that whenever a person discovers a truth, he or she generates a new piece of the oral tradition, for if it is true, then it is Torah.

The essays translated here are all part of the authoritative unfolding of the oral tradition. The first piece, called "Two Great Lights," is from the Talmud (500 C.E.), which, besides the Torah itself, is the most authoritative text in the Jewish tradition.[15]

The second essay, by R. Isaac Luria, is a much later commentary (≈1570). The kabbalistic body of implications, because it comprises the deepest layer of the Oral Torah, was the last to be explicated. Consequently, although R. Luria's writings are relatively recent in the larger scheme of Jewish scholarship, they are second only to the *Zohar* in the authority of their kabbalistic teachings.

The rest of the essays are more contemporary still, and these later writings do not hold the same weight of authority as the first two pieces. Nevertheless, each of these rabbis was a giant in his time, divinely inspired, whose life and teachings embodied the Torah to an impeccable degree. With one exception, these writings have passed the test of consensus and are fully accepted teachings of the oral tradition. R. Kook's works are still controversial in cer-

---

13. R. Tsadok HaKohen, ibid.
14. TY, *Rosh Hashanah* 3:8.
15. R. Yitzchak Alfasi (Rif) on TB, *Eruvin* 35b.

tain communities, though the majority of observant Jews embrace his prolific contributions without reservation.

PaRDeS

PaRDeS, which means literally "orchard," is an acronym for the four levels of biblical interpretation. Every story, sentence, and even word of the Torah has all these layers of implication within it.

1. "P" (*Pshat*) is its literal meaning and narrative intent, the plot or story line.
2. "R" (*Remez*) is the level of *hint* whereby peculiarities of grammar, spelling, syntax, and structure indicate deeper levels of meaning and hidden interrelationships within the text. An unusual word that appears in one context and again in unrelated context *hints* to a relationship between these passages even with no obvious connection between them.
3. "D" (*Drash*, or *Midrash*) is the homiletical level of interpretation, in which the entire Bible is understood as a metaphor for each individual soul's unfolding. Everyone has an aspect of Abraham that must be willing to sacrifice Isaac, everyone must receive the Torah at Sinai, and so on.
4. "S" (*Sod*) is the secret, mystical, or kabbalistic level of interpretation that hints to the inner worlds, angelic kingdoms, realms of soul, and mathematical intricacies of Divinity.

The pieces that follow focus primarily on the fourth level of interpretation, called kabbalah. Consequently, they presume a familiarity with the three layers beneath them, for each higher level builds on the ones below. It is always good to know where in the scheme of PaRDeS a commentary derives, and how these four threads weave through a text. The synopses and annotations accompanying each essay will provide this information.

KABBALAH

I

Kabbalah is the mystical interpretation of the Torah and its precepts. It explores *HaShem*'s deepest intentions for creation. What purpose does the universe serve? Why did the Creator fashion it this way and not another? What is the point of each detail and how does it support the larger vision? If God is good and perfect, then why isn't the universe likewise so? What is the significance of the 613 religious practices that *HaShem* requests from the Jewish people? What is God communicating by each turn of events in our personal and collective histories? What does it mean that human beings are created in the image of God? The questions unfold and reduce to one, single-pointed quest: *How do I bring body, heart, mind, and soul into perfect harmony with spiritual law?*

Kabbalah derives its answer to this question (and the others) from its extremely detailed and complex description of the universe. Just as physics explains how the world works based on its vast database of patiently acquired technical knowledge about natural law and physical structure, so is this true for kabbalah, which is a *meta*-physics in the most literal sense of the word. The parallels between these two pursuits are numerous.

Kabbalah examines the most subtle patterns of the spiritual world with mathematical precision. And, just as science evolved a specialized lexicon of formulas and terminology to describe its observations, so is this true for its mystical counterpart.

Kabbalah is advanced study. Just as a physicist must invest at least ten years of undergraduate, graduate, and postgraduate training to master the knowledge base of his or her chosen specialty, likewise for the student of kabbalah. It, too, requires decades of patient effort to begin to crack its codes and extract a hint of sweetness from its abstract formulations, and further effort still to enjoy practical benefit from its teachings.

Consequently, the project of rendering kabbalistic writings accessible to an audience unversed in its fundamentals becomes extremely challenging. Two divergent imperatives must be honored and the tension between them is not easily contained. On one hand, it is critical that the presentation stay true to the letter and spirit of the original works. The power of kabbalistic teachings is intricately linked with its language and thought forms. On the other hand, it must be accessible to a general readership.

In most educational frameworks, teachers are responsible for bringing their lessons down to a level that suits the pupil. For subjects counted among the basic requirements of literacy, the burden of "stretch" rests with teachers to translate their higher wisdom into a form that inspires their students. A skilled pedagogue is one who meets each student wherever he or she is.

Kabbalah is the opposite. Its teachings are hidden, and intentionally so. The burden of "stretch" rests with its disciples to prove their devotion by forgoing the immediate gratification of instant understanding and instead meet the subject matter on its terms. This stretch from below to above is part of the experience and the initiation of kabbalah.

And yet, the whole point of this book is to make kabbalistic teachings available to the general public because they are profoundly relevant to the dilemmas that we currently face as individuals and as a nation. Their messages reframe contemporary events in paradigm-shifting ways and bring healing, illuminating, and guiding lights to bear on the issues at hand. The fact that people are asking the questions to which these esoteric teachings are the answer means they are ready to hear them and to begin digesting their implications.

To honor these conflicting interests, the book is organized along two parallel tiers, as will be explained in the section entitled "Structure and Technical Notes."

II

Kabbalah is the "science of correspondences."[16] This is its literal definition, as well as a description of one primary form of kabbalistic meditation. The Hebrew language is built from three-letter roots, each of which burgeons into a constellation of meanings based on the range of words that derive from its three-letter base. The place where a root first appears in the Bible defines its core meaning and all other significations become secondary to that first sense. The three-letter root for Kabbalah appears only twice in the entire Torah, each in the same context, and both times it means "to correspond." Although the simplest usage of the root קבל is "to receive," this form only appears in later prophets and biblical writings. Its primary sense, as conveyed by the Torah itself, is "to parallel or correspond."

> "You shall make fifty loops on one curtain, and you shall make fifty loops on the second that is to join with it. The loops of each *shall be opposite and corresponding to* the other."[17]

Two important teachings derive from this linguistic fact. The first is immediately relevant to the writings that follow, the second a useful bit of information that is sure to be relevant in further study.

1. The definition of *kabbalah* as "the science of correspondences" also contains within itself a teaching about its primary method of inquiry. Kabbalah employs conceptual maps that cut through appearances and identify the bare-boned organizational patterns inside the universe. The

---

16. R. Yitzchak Ginsburgh, Unpublished Lecture Series on "The Fifty Gates of Understanding."
17. Exodus 26:5.

Tree of Life, with its ten *sefirot* and twenty-two connecting pathways (introduced and diagrammed in the chapter entitled "A Preview of Terms to Come"), is the model most commonly employed. The world is observed through the lens of these maps, and correspondences are made between this and that: between the world and the map, or between two maps, or even between two aspects of the world. One identifies an equivalence based on logic, similarity of attributes, similarity of position, or even numerology (*gematriot*). This entire book is based on two such equivalences, the correspondence of sun with all things masculine, and moon with all things feminine.

When two elements are equivalent, it is possible to extrapolate back and forth between them and discover hidden truths about each from the other. Details and generalizations that apply to one also apply (perhaps with qualifications) to the other. For example, if A and B are equivalent, then if *this* is true about A, it is also true about B (even when not explicitly mentioned in relation to B). And, if $A = C$, then also $B = C$. The two partners (A and B) of a kabbalistic equivalence form the vertical poles of a ladder and each implication of their correspondence becomes a rung.[18] Sparks fly and insights abound from the exchange of information generated inside an equivalence. With each new layer of implications the ladder extends upward and inward.

Piercing the formless expanse, this stairway of light can eventually transport its travelers to the heart-of-all-things.

---

18. All this connects to Jacob's famous ladder dream. One could speculate that this is also a reason for R. Yehuda Ashlag's choice of the title *Sulam (Ladder)* for his commentary on the *Zohar*.

Without the ladder and its carefully crafted rungs, there is no way to pass from here to there. In this sense, kabbalistic study is a meditation. The essays that follow employ its technique.

2. Perhaps the most classic focus of correspondence meditation is called the "Fifty Gates of Understanding." These are fifty levels of integrating what it means that God is one, and each portal leads to a more rectified state of consciousness. When the Torah describes "one set of fifty loops corresponding to and opposite a second set," it alludes to this meditation. Every gate has at least three parallel correspondences: it correlates to one of the fifty times that the phrase "exodus from Egypt" appears in the Torah;[19] to one of the fifty rhetorical questions that God asks Job at the end of his ordeal;[20] and one of the fifty anthropomorphisms that the Torah employs in relation to *HaShem*.[21] These three systems of correspondence create a triangular equivalence.

    One who meditates diligently on these Fifty Gates of Understanding will acquire a wise and knowing heart.

III

There is a new branch of mathematics called fuzzy logic. Its innovation, and its goal, is to formulate a mathematical language that accurately reflects the ambiguous nature of reality. In the real world things are rarely black and white. Most of our conceptual categories place artificial lines of demarcation between things that really overlap or are just two points on a gradual continuum of grays. For

---

19. *Tikunei Zohar* 76b–77b; Ramak, *Pardes Rimonim, Shaar* 13.
20. Raavid, Introduction to *Sefer Yetzirah*.
21. R. Ginsburgh, ibid. There he elaborated upon the fifty nouns that appear in *smichut* (construct) relationship to *HaShem*'s name in the Bible.

example, the statement that "men are taller than women" is both true and false. As a generalization, it is mostly true, but there are many exceptions to its rule. There are tall women and short men who violate its prediction. Comparing Scandinavian women to Japanese men might produce the exact opposite result.

Classic logic is bivalent, which means it can only answer *yes* or *no*. It does not allow for *yes, but...*, or *mostly*, or *sometimes*. That is fuzzy's innovation. Its aim is to get computers to accurately reflect the complex nuances of the real world, which are nearly always partial truths.

Kabbalah is an old hand at fuzzy logic. It knows that the world is holographic[22] and that every piece contains aspects of the entire universe inside itself. Consequently, a black-and-white assertion about *A* as opposed to *B* is never perfectly true. For since *B* also contains *A*, the assertion about *A* is also always partially true about *B*. There is no statement in kabbalah that is absolutely, flatly, and simply true. There is always another context or angle of perspective where the relationship between elements shifts or even flips upside down. Every assertion has qualifications.[23]

Yet one must not lose sight of the forest for the trees. One can still make statements that are true, despite their qualifications. Men *are* generally taller than women, and one *can* make useful distinctions about the world based on that rule of thumb.

Similarly, one must not lose sight of the trees for the forest by getting fixated on generalizations that don't accurately reflect the fuzzy nature of the real world. One who gets overly attached to a principle that was only meant as an approximation will have to keep his eyes half-closed to avoid all the fuzzy contradictions to his belief.

Kabbalah forces its disciples to keep their minds nimble, for

---

22. See Glossary under Holographic Structure.
23. R. Isaac Luria (Ari), *Etz Chaim* 1:1:5.

each circumstance is unique and there is never a pat answer. Any moment could be an exception to the rule. A kabbalist is constantly reminded that the world is a fuzzy place and truth is a fuzzy commodity.

All this applies to the essays that follow, particularly the teachings of R. Isaac Luria. There is no end to the qualifications that attach to each sentence. The moon's odyssey is infinitely more complex than described, and her path of development does not perfectly follow the smooth course outlined in that short passage. And yet, if one were to include all the qualifying statements on the subject, its larger message would get lost in a mass of minutiae. A decision was made to include the minimum level of detail to produce meaningful statements that still remain accessible to readers unversed in its larger body of teachings. The conclusions presented are at least as true as the assertion that "men are taller than women."

STRUCTURE AND TECHNICAL NOTES

I

The implications of these teachings are exciting and relevant to all. The original texts are the heart of their communication. Though not everyone is equally motivated to delve into the source material and follow its careful development of thought, its authoritative voices remain central to the work. As proof texts they will verify the statements made in their name; as holy texts they will transform all who take them to heart.

To accommodate readers with varying interests in the technical underpinnings of these ideas, the book is organized along two parallel tracks.

- Whoever wants the gist of its content without delving into its kabbalistic details can read the synopses before each piece and the debriefings that follow, and obtain a thorough overview of the subject matter.

- Whoever wants to encounter the original sources directly, and experience, firsthand, how the teaching develops from the inside will find each essay presented in both Hebrew and English and clearly explicated.

The author's recommendation is to first survey the larger picture of the entire work by reading the synopses that precede each piece and then delve into the denser material at a more careful pace. This book follows a definite developmental sequence, whereby each chapter builds on the ideas and vocabulary of the ones before. This is true for the preliminary writings as well as the source texts themselves. Consequently, it is recommended that the reader follow the natural development of the book.

II

One way to express love of God is to passionately aspire to know the innermost depths of the Divine Beloved. When this is so, study becomes solely for the sake of celebrating God's beauty and all personal benefit loses its allure. Tradition calls this *the study of Torah for its own sake*, and all of these original sources were written from that place.

One of the features that often characterizes such writing is a reverie of associations that are more poetic than linear. Whenever there is a scenic detour, it is always taken, for if the whole point is to celebrate God's glory, then *the means are the ends*, and what's the hurry if you can catch a glimpse of some rare beauty along the way?

This is hard for people whose minds are trained in linear, goal-oriented analysis. The problem is exacerbated by a technical complication. In the original Hebrew text the scenic detour can be a single word or phrase that conjures a whole gestalt of associated ideas, emotions, and contexts, but that is so concise that it does not disrupt the larger flow of thought. Since an annotated translation must also unpack the whole constellation of associated ideas triggered by that word or phrase, it unfortunately *does* disrupt the flow to a much more significant degree.

To minimize the disorientation created by these digressions, an outline of the essay's linear sequence appears along the margin as a clear indicator of where each idea fits into the essay's overall flow of thought.

III

Each chapter begins with a Bare Bones Literacy page that presents a several-sentence summary of the piece and the vocabulary essential to its comprehension.

The Hebrew appears as a block of text on each page, followed by an annotated translation. The bolded words are its literal rendering, though sometimes loosely phrased. Priority was given to the clear conveyance of an idea over a precisely literal (though awkward) translation of each word.

The italicized terms *man, woman, mother,* and *father* refer to kabbalistic archetypes (called *partzufim*) and, by extension, to the masculine and feminine attributes found in both men and women. Similarly the English names of the *sefirot* are indicated by italics.

A glossary appears at the back of the book with technical terms clearly defined. Most of the specialized vocabulary is introduced in the upcoming section entitled, "A Preview of Terms to Come."

A PREVIEW OF TERMS TO COME

When kabbalah describes the universe, it employs a specialized vocabulary that draws heavily upon anthropomorphism. This image-based terminology might seem inappropriate, given the abstract subject of its inquiry. In fact, its choice of language is deliberate and reflects a methodology of analysis that permeates Jewish tradition.

> In the Talmud, as in most areas of original Jewish thought, there is deliberate avoidance of abstract thinking based on abstract concepts. Even matters that could easily be discussed through abstraction are analyzed by other methods.... The Talmud employs models in place of abstract concepts.... The model is utilized in accordance with a series of clearly defined steps, approved by tradition....
>
> ... The weakness of all abstract thought lies in the fact that it is constantly creating new terms and concepts, and since they cannot be defined except by use of similarly abstract terms we can never know whether they constitute a departure from the subject or are still relevant. Therefore we almost never find abstract terms in the Talmud, even when they would seem to be vital to the discussion and when any other legal system would have introduced them.... The Talmud very rarely employs such terms, although it frequently deals with the problems defined by these words in ways that differ greatly from those of other philosophical or legal systems.[24]

One could substitute the word *Kabbalah* for Talmud and the previous statement would still be true. Kabbalah employs an anthropomorphic model, called the Tree of Life, which serves as its map of reality and provides a concrete focus for its teachings. The Tree of Life is a specific arrangement of ten points called *sefirot*, which combine into six archetypal personages called *partzufim*.

---

24. Adin Steinsaltz, *The Essential Talmud,* trans. Chaya Galai (New York: Basic Books, Inc., 1980), pp. 228–230.

The ten *sefirot* are ten channels of Divine flow and revelation that link the Transcendent Light with Its evolving (and apparently finite) creation. Each has its unique character and is hierarchically organized and interrelated with every other. They bring into being the entirety of existence from the superconscious regions beyond human thought, through mind and emotions, to the physical world. While the pure essence of Divinity is beyond attribute, number, and categorization, when *HaShem* chooses to communicate with creation He lowers Himself (so to speak) and assumes one of these ten guises to provide a "handle" of apprehension, to present a familiar *face* within the vast expanse of pure abstraction that is His natural state. The *sefirot* include within themselves all facets of reality. They are not discrete, but systematically interconnected and interincluded to form an organic whole that is greater than the sum of its parts.

The Tree of Life comprises three vertical pillars. The right is the pillar of expansion and has a masculine association; the left is the pillar of contraction and is feminine in expression; the central pillar is theoretically androgynous, though each of its three lower *sefirot* "lean" toward the right or the left and so has a masculine or feminine tendency despite its positioning on the center line.

Sometimes these ten *sefirot* are organized into six groups, each of which is called a *partzuf*, an archetypal personage constructed in the image of a human being. Kabbalah then arranges these *partzufim* into an archetypal family unit and uses this model to ground its metaphysical inquiries. Each of the six *partzufim* plays a different role in the family system:

- *Atik Yamin (Ancient of Days)* is the great -grandfather
- *Arikh Anpin (Long Countenance)* is the grandfather
- *Aba* and *Ima* are *Father* and *Mother*
- *Zeir Anpin (Short Countenance)* is *Man* (also *Son*)
- *Nukva* is *Woman* or *Wife* (also *Daughter*)

Tree of Life

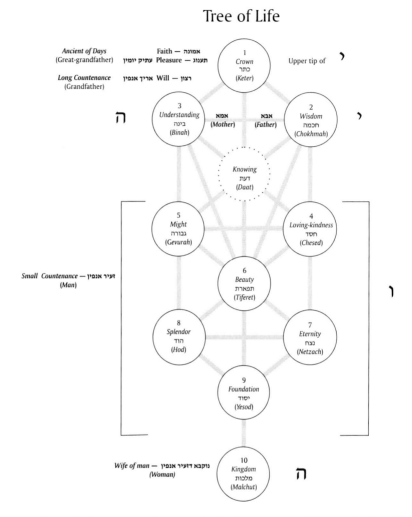

Equally frequently, these *partzufim* function as different "voices"
or sub-personalities within a single individual. When the translation employs the terms *father* and *mother* or *man* and *woman* as
referring to *partzufim*, they will be italicized.

Each of the ten *sefirot* and six *partzufim* have a distinguishing
trait that is their contribution to the soul (whether of the individual
or family unit). A person's nature and level of spiritual development
determines which of those traits are integrated in strong and healthy

ways, and which are under- or overdeveloped. The Tree of Life marks a ten-step path from below to above that each soul follows in its journey toward perfection and reunion with its Creator.

The flow of lights from above to below, from *keter* to *malchut*, is the sequence of creation, both originally and continually. The reciprocal current from below to above, from *malchut* to *keter*, is the path of creation's perfecting and aspiring to reunite with its Source. The *sefirot* are traditionally counted from above to below.

The first *sefirah* depicts the superconscious will of God tucked at the heart of each point of reality. It is called *keter* (*crown*) for just as a crown rests *upon* the head, so does God's will direct each detail of the world's unfolding though it itself remains apart, hovering outside the actual "body" of creation itself. All of the *sefirot* on the central pillar unify polarities. *Keter* joins God's will with man's will. It includes two *partzufim*: an upper one called *Atik Yamin* (*Ancient of Days*) and a lower one called *Arikh Anpin* (*Long Countenance*). The trait associated with *Atik Yamin* is spiritual bliss (תענוג), and the trait associated with *Arikh Anpin* is *will* (רצון) for it is the source of all motivating impulses within the personality. In the family system, *Atik Yamin* is great-grandfather, *Arikh Anpin* is grandfather.

The next three *sefirot*, *chokhmah* (*wisdom*), *binah* (*understanding*), and *daat* (*knowing*), encompass the faculties of mind (ours literally and God's metaphorically). *Chokhmah* is the flash of insight, the lightening bolt of intuition that, for an instant, illumines the brain; yet its discovery will be lost unless captured and elaborated by *binah* (*understanding*), the analytical faculty of mind. The thought as it appears in *chokhmah* is a dense point of light with a myriad of details locked inside its intensely compacted form. *Binah* unravels this thought in breadth and depth, elaborating its implications and applications, constructing a kind of visionary landscape that provides an extended context for the original seed idea.

Daat (knowing) is the mirrored reflection of *keter* (crown) operating now *within* the conscious realms. Therefore, in counting the *sefirot* in relation to the totality of creation, *keter* (crown) appears instead of *daat* (knowing), while in relation to the conscious universe, *daat* replaces *keter* in the scheme of emanations. They cannot both be included at once, for the *Sefer Yetzirah* stipulates that the Tree of Life contains "…ten [*sefirot*] and not nine, ten and not eleven."[25] The traditional counting includes *keter* instead of *daat*. This is because *daat* is more a "state of integration" than a proper vessel like the other *sefirot*. The gestalt of the integration of the other ten becomes something greater than the sum of its parts and assumes an identity unto itself that kabbalah calls *daat*. Since it sits on the central pillar, *daat* unifies polarities and has two modes of expressing that trait: Higher *knowing* integrates the right brain with the left brain, *chokhmah* (wisdom) with *binah* (understanding). Lower *knowing* integrates the brain with the heart. *Daat's* capacity to integrate knowledge is so total that it can dissolve the existential chasm between knower and known, subject and object, heart and mind. For this reason, Hebrew employs the word *daat* as a euphemism for sexual union (And Adam *knew* Eve…), because such is its counterpart in the physical world. Since *daat* is not really a *sefirah* unto itself, it does not assume the role of *partzuf*.

The next six *sefirot* are the emotional attributes (called *middot*). They are:

chesed (loving-kindness),
gevurah (might),
tiferet (beauty),
netzach (victory),
hod (splendor),
yesod (foundation).

---

25. *Sefer Yetzirah*, 1:4.

The first, *chesed* (*loving-kindness*), is the outward-directed and expansive impulse of unconditional generosity. This is tempered by *gevurah* (*might*), the force of restraint and contraction. *Gevurah* expresses itself in several ways. It meters the impulse to give, forcing it to adapt to the "vessel's" capacity to receive, and so prevents *chesed* from smothering (and even annihilating) its recipient with an overabundance of beneficence; it negates all that opposes the will of God; and it is the boundary-making, form-building power within creation. *Tiferet* (*beauty*) is the "heart" of the ten *sefirot*. Situated on the central pillar, *tiferet* unites the selfless generosity of *chesed* with the self-preserving boundaries of *gevurah*. It harmonizes these two opposing impulses in accordance with the attribute of mercy and compassion. Its perfectly just, though sensitive, application of generosity and restraint is motivated, above all, by an abiding empathy with the innermost realities of one's fellow creatures and a genuine desire for their highest good.

Netzach (*victory, eternity*) and *Hod* (*splendor* or *thanksgiving*) are usually discussed as a pair, and are often called the "kidneys that advise" about practical matters. *Netzach* is the power to overcome obstacles to the implementation of truth (which it conceptualizes in absolute terms) while *hod* (*spendor*) is the strength of wholehearted commitment to one's goals, even when their truth is beyond comprehension. *Hod* negotiates with all "parties" involved and, employing the relative face of truth, obtains a consensus to support *netzach*'s goals. Together, they determine how best to express the "compassion" of *tiferet* in a way that is maximally productive, considering the practical limitations imposed by concrete reality.

Yesod (*foundation*) is the bond, or channel, that actually joins the giver with the receiver or the person to the world. It collects the mental and emotional influences that percolate down through the preceding *sefirot*, condenses them into tangible form, and transmits them, in logical sequence, to the receiver. Situated on the central pillar, *yesod* unites self with other. All of these six *sefirot* together comprise the *partzuf* man.

Malchut (*kingdom*) is the tenth and last *sefirah*. It is the culmination of the above sequence of emanation as it takes physical form and actually bears fruit. *Malchut* has no lights of its own except what it receives from the nine above her. Yet this dark and lowly endpoint of Divine emanation actually becomes the *keter* (*crown*) of the reflected or returning light, the point where a sun ray becomes a moonbeam. Consequently, it is both the lowest and the highest of the *sefirot*: "*Keter* is in *malchut* and *malchut* is in *keter*, but after a different matter."[26] The entire unfolding of creation is the process of perfecting *malchut*, of bringing the physical revelation of Godliness to a point where it precisely mirrors the transcendent glory of its heavenly prototype, the celestial paradise called the Garden of Delights. The completion of this process is called the "dwelling of *HaShem* below," the messianic era, and the "redeeming of the *Shekhinah* [God's feminine Presence] from exile." *Malchut* corresponds to the *partzuf woman* who is the wife of *man*. Situated on the central pillar, *malchut* possesses the mysterious power to bind soul to body and spirit to matter.

The Tree of Life, with its roots above (*keter*) and fruits below (*malchut*), is ubiquitous. Present as the heart of every piece of reality, from the most subatomic particles of matter to the most sublime extremities of the universe, from the world of nature to the world of angels and beyond, this holographic unit is the fundamental building block of creation. Its universal map presents the elements that are always present in any point of focus, from pinhole to cosmos, though while all ten are always there, not all are equally apparent. Many or most may lie dormant, exerting a less direct and

---

26. R. Moshe Cordevero (Ramak), commentary on *Sefer Yetzirah*, 1:14:6.

perceptible influence. Nevertheless, a complete description of any *thing* must identify these ten elements as they are interincluded within that particular object, idea, or field of study.

This model of *sefirot* and *partzufim* is the lexicon of kabbalah. A small investment of effort in the study of these terms and correspondences will greatly enhance one's appreciation of its teachings.

KABBALISTIC SYMBOLS OF THE FEMININE

When there arose within the mind of the One and Only One a vision of two, gender emerged as a fact in the universe. The feminine archetype includes two primary constellations that are actually just sequential stages in a single life cycle. Nevertheless, they are depicted as two distinct personalities, called *woman* and *mother*. This book is primarily concerned with the "lower" feminine, or *woman*, and it is her associated symbols that will be elaborated in this section. Nevertheless, it is always good to define the larger landscape before concentrating on a single detail.

The primary source of gender correlations is the Tetragrammaton, or four-letter essential name of God. Its system of correspondence is as follows:

י = higher masculine, called *father*
ה = higher feminine, called *mother*
ו = lower masculine, called *man*
ה = lower feminine, called *woman*

It becomes clear that the final ה' of God's name is the most concise symbol of the *Shekhinah* and the primary subject of this entire book. Kabbalah, then, employs a variety of secondary symbols to highlight the different facets of her nature.

Concise Table of Kabbalistic Terms and Correspondences

#	Sefirah (Hebrew)	Sefirah (transliterated)	Sefirah (translation)	Body Correspondence	Attribute	Unification (an exclusive feature of sefirot that fall along the central pillar)	Partzuf (hebrew)	Partzuf (transliterated)	Partzuf (translation)
1a	כתר	keter	crown	crown of head	superconscious faith and pleasure	God with man; superconscious root of awareness with conscious mind	עתיק יומין	atik yomin	ancient of days (most ancient one) (great-grandfather)
					superconscious will		אריך אנפין	arikh anpin	long countenance (grandfather)
2	חכמה	chokhmah	wisdom	right brain	intuitive insight	—	אבא	aba	father
3	בינה	binah	understanding	left brain	discriminating intelligence	—	אמא	ima	mother
1b	דעת	daat	(internalized) knowing	corpus collosum, neck	pure and fully integrated awareness, capacity to bear paradox	right brain with left brain; mind with heart	—		
4	חסד	chesed	loving-kindness	right arm	expansive generosity, selfless giving	—			
5	גבורה	gevurah	might	left arm	justice, severity, restraint, and self-preserving limits	selfless generosity with self-preserving boundaries			
6	תפארת	tiferet	beauty	heart	graceful beauty, compassion	—	זעיר אנפין ז"א	zeir anpin	small-countenance, man (son)
7	נצח	netzach	victory, eternity	right kidney, right leg	decisiveness, conception of truth as absolute	—			
8	הוד	hod	splendor, gratitude	left kidney, left leg	whole-hearted commitment, relative truth, peacemaker	—			
9	יסוד	yesod	foundation	genitals	transmission to an "other" outside oneself	self with other			
10	מלכות	malchut	kingdom	feet, genital crowns	embodiment, consummation, circle-consciousness	soul with body; spirit with matter	נוקבא	nukva	woman, wife of man, daughter

Shekhinah (as opposed to her male counterpart, the Blessed Holy One). This is the generic term for the feminine expression of Divinity. It means, literally, Presence, and emphasizes the immanence of God, the indwelling Light that fills all things. The Shekhinah is that aspect of HaShem that fits inside the universe, and that actually comprises the "stuff" of the universe,

The Ten *Sefirot*
As *Partzufim*

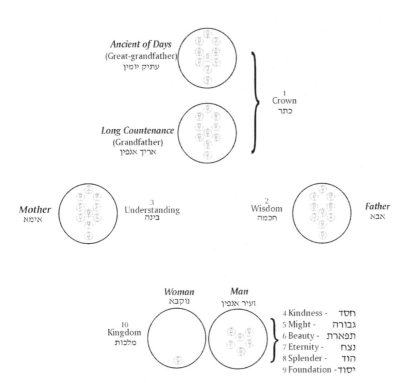

Ancient of Days
(Great-grandfather)
עתיק יומין

Long Countenance
(Grandfather)
אריך אנפין

1
Crown
כתר

Mother
אימא

3
Understanding
בינה

2
Wisdom
חכמה

Father
אבא

Woman
נוקבא

Man
זעיר אנפין

10
Kingdom
מלכות

4 Kindness - חסד
5 Might - גבורה
6 Beauty - תפארת
7 Eternity - נצח
8 Splender - הוד
9 Foundation - יסוד

for all of physical reality is nothing but Divinity in a state of concealment and contraction. The holy *Shekhinah* is filled with unconditional compassion, which She expresses by her willingness to adapt Herself to the capacity of each creature so as not to overwhelm it with more light (or love) than it can hold. When texts refer to a higher and lower *Shekhinah*, the higher is *mother*, the lower is *woman*. The Blessed Holy One is the transcendent expression of God.

Moon (as opposed to Sun). The most commonly employed symbol of the *Shekhinah* is the moon, which follows a monthly cycle of waxing and waning. The moon associates with change and transformation, in contrast to the sun with its constancy of shine. The Talmud recounts a tale (explicated in the next chapter) about the earliest moments of gender when the sun and moon were of equal stature. The moon expressed dissatisfaction with the power dynamics of that arrangement and the Blessed Holy One commanded her to step down from her throne. At that point the moon shrank in size, her light dimmed, and she became a reflector instead of a generator of light. She lost her stability and spiraled into a fluctuating cycle of waning and waxing, defined by her proximity to the sun.

Receiver and Vessel (as opposed to bestower and the light contained inside the vessel). The conventions of gender in kabbalah echo the physical differences between men and women. Bestowing is a masculine role; receiving is a feminine one. Consequently, since a vessel receives the lights of bounty and influence, it serves a feminine function. This is the most primary definition of the feminine in kabbalah: *she* receives and contains, *he* bestows and fills.

Below (as opposed to above). This is a direct result of the *Shekhinah*'s correspondence to *vessel*. Since gravity causes materials to flow downward, the giver (masculine) is depicted *above* the receiver (feminine). In kabbalistic writings there is no inherent superiority associated with the higher position (in fact, sometimes the opposite).[27]

Malchut (as opposed to *tiferet-yesod*). The lowest of the ten *sefirot* is called *malchut*, which means, literally, "royalty" and "kingship." It corresponds to the physical plane and thereby represents the final stage in the congealing of light into matter.[28] A vision arises (in the first *sefirah*, called *crown*) and a will formulates

---

27. *Leshem*, SHK, *Klal* 18:6:4 and 18:7:1.
28. It is perhaps more correct to associate *malchut* with embodiment. In the universe as we now experience it, where bodies are physical, so embodiment

to materialize that dream. Slowly, it descends level after level, world after world, until it contacts the physical plane, *malchut*, and becomes a work in progress. At that point it looks drastically different and deficient compared to its original plan. Yet, eventually, it becomes a final product that perfectly reproduces the vision that conceived it.

Malchut is the most time-bound of all the *sefirot*. While thought and emotions can transform in an instant, matter is subject to inertia and requires a stepwise sequence of development to change its form. *Malchut* includes this whole extended period of unfolding from birth to full flower. Yet only at the end of the process does her association with royalty finally make sense. Until then, her kingdom remains a work in progress, and all the ragged edges and gross imperfections seem anything but regal. Yet, eventually, it will embody the perfect vision that conceived it. On that day, the physical plane will shine with dazzling beauty, as the kingdom of heaven completes its descent and dwells fully below.

Woman (as opposed to *man*). In later kabbalistic writings, *malchut* evolves into the personality (*partzuf*) called *woman*. She possesses all of the traits associated with *malchut*, but this new designation emphasizes her role as wife to *man*, her beloved soulmate. In the writings that follow, this is the term primarily employed to indicate the feminine polarity, or *Shekhinah*. The details of *woman*'s life cycle and feminine role, as conceived by *kabbalah*, are discussed at length in the third chapter entitled, "The Small Light to Rule by Night."

Gevurot or *Dinim* (as opposed to *chassadim*). These terms mean, literally, "severities" and refer to the dark knots of unrectified

---

occurs on the physical plane. In Edenic times, when bodies were made of thought, embodiment then occurred on the mental plane as thought forms.

potential that are the driving force behind our universe. These
dense flecks of intensely compressed light formed in the earliest
moments of creation, and their natural direction of movement
is to unravel and lighten by actualizing their potential. That is
the only way they can release the enormous pressure of their
intensely compacted state.

The *gevurot* are feminine for several reasons, most notably
because of their identification with *malchut* as follows: In a
primordial era of creation before the Torah's beginning, all the
malchiot (plural of *malchut*) burst forth in a chaotic fashion,
burned out, and collapsed into a spray of cinders that dropped
into the lower world and became known as *gevurot*.[29] Though
transfigured by their ordeal, these *gevurot* are still *malchut* lights
and retain a continuity of identity with their *sefirah* of origin
and its feminine associations.

Circle World or World of Points[30] (as opposed to the Linear
World).[31] It is known that creation passed through several
eras before settling into the stable and familiar form that is
our current world. The stage immediately preceding ours is
called the Circle Universe,[32] while ours is the Linear World of
straight lines and hierarchy.[33] These terms are both technical
and metaphorical. They describe their arrangement of *sefirot*
(the former as concentric circles, the latter as three parallel
lines),[34] and the divergent nature of their worldviews. In the
Linear World everything occupies a unique position along a

---

29. This is called the *World* (or *Era*) of *Points*. See Ari, *Etz Chaim, Shaar* 8, 9, 11.
30. *Leshem*, "Treatise Addressing Confusions Surrounding the Circle and
Linear Worlds," 3:6. This treatise appears as an appendix to HDYH. Leshem
here explains the equation between the Circle World, and the World of Points.
31. Ibid., *Shaar* 1.
32. A term that is sometimes synonymous with the World of Points. See *Etz
Chaim, Shaar* 8, *Drushei Hanekudot*, 1:1.
33. Ibid. A term that is synonymous with the *Rectified World*.
34. See diagram, p. 161.

continuum extending from above to below. Each value imposes a hierarchy that orders the world according to its preferences. In the Circle World, it is gloriously clear that every soul is equally precious and singularly beautiful in a way that cannot be ranked. Just as a circle has no beginning or end and every point is equidistant from its center, so is this true for souls.

Again here, the conventions of kabbalah echo the physical differences between men and women. A woman's sexual center is circular, man's is linear. Second, in the original world of points and circles, only the *sefirot* of *malchut* manifested, and their feminine character thus defines the nature of that period.

Each one of these feminine symbols contains all the others within it as subfeatures; consequently, they are often employed as synonymous terms. Though a text may focus on one or another of these symbols, the whole constellation of associations is always implied.

GENDER IS RELATIVE

The king, although supreme, is feminine and receptive to the Highest Point and Most Hidden One, yet, simultaneously, he is masculine and active toward the lower king.[35] This bi-gendered status...characterizes the whole supermundane world.[36]

---

35. This *Zohar* refers to masculine and feminine archetypes, and not to men and women, who always contain the attributes of both genders within themselves (as discussed in the next chapter). When a woman assumes the role of influencer to a man, she is masculine in relation to him. In most couples the role of influencer shifts back and forth from him to her, depending upon their respective strengths. Since, in the physical world, the rule of gravity prevails, the transfer of influence generally proceeds from above to below. Though cultures have projected superiority onto the masculine role, and inferiority onto the feminine, these superimposed values are not, as a rule, supported by the texts.

36. *Zohar* 2:4a.

Everything is feminine in relation to its above and masculine in relation to its below. There is no person who is absolutely and exclusively male or female, for there is no escaping this network of relations with its shifting hierarchies and gender roles that vary from one context to the next.

The feminine of each level receives from her male partner and births the next generation into the world. Though obviously female, both physiologically and in her role of receiving seed, a mother is still masculine in relation to her children, for she bestows the food and influence that they receive from her.[37]

The kabbalistic model differs from the physical world in one significant regard: the *partzuf mother* always births an androgynous child, which contains both male and female halves bound to each other like Siamese twins. Later, when they mature, she performs a kind of spiritual surgery and separates them into a pair of free-standing individuals called *man* and *woman*. Thus *mother's* fruit always includes a pair of male and female siblings.[38] This is how kabbalah interprets the story of Adam and Eve: "And God created Adam... in the image of God... male and female... And the Lord God made *Adam* fall into a deep sleep, and he slept; and He took one of his sides, and closed the flesh in its place. God built the side that he took from the *Adam* into a woman, and He brought her to Adam."

One half of this *Adam* became *man* and one half became *woman*. Tradition teaches that the conscious portions of Adam remained with *man* while its unconscious aspects segregated off

37. *Zohar* 177b (*Sifra d'Tsniuta*); *Etz Chaim, Shaar HaClalim, Perek* 11.
38. This is the deeper reason behind the halachic ruling that the mitzvah "to be fruitful and multiply" is fulfilled only with a son and a daughter. R.Y.Y. Safron of Kamarna, *Heichal HaBracha* (*The Chamber of Blessing*), *Otzer HaChaim, Mitzvah Pirya V'Rivya*, Genesis 1:28.

into *woman*.[39] This explains why *man* maintained a continuity of identity throughout the process. If one defines identity as a conscious sense of self, then the "I" of that bi-gendered being, because it was conscious, stayed with man, and therefore he retained the name Adam. The unconscious portions separated off into *woman*, and now, for the first time, assumed an identity of their own. Before, they were subsumed by Adam's conscious "I"; now they received a name unto themselves, called Eve.

This unfolding of levels within Divinity proceeds as illustrated in the following diagram. Each layer is a couple that contains a male and female who are both united and independent. Together, they are feminine in relation to the level above them and masculine in relation to the one below. Although each member of a couple has a name of its own, the couple itself, as a collective unit, is nearly always called by the male partner's name. This is not unlike the familiar custom of women taking the name of their husband when they marry.

THE MAP IS NOT THE TERRITORY

THE CRITICAL DIFFERENCE BETWEEN ARCHETYPES AND PEOPLE

Our present universe is the Rectified World,[42] whose distinguish-

---

39. See pp. 82–87, where R. Luria explains how the *chassadim* (conscious lights) stayed with man and the *gevurot* (unconscious lights) collected in woman.
40. The arrows here show *father* and *mother* both being emanated, independently and directly, from the Infinite One, a developmental sequence that is different from all the other levels below it. "*Father* and *mother* emanated as one and stand as one" (*Zohar, Idra Zuta* 290b).
41. It is clear that on the physical plane, boys and girls emerge independently from their mother's womb and not first as an androgynous unit.
42. See Map of the Unfolding of Worlds, p. 166.

Kabbalistic Unfolding of Gender

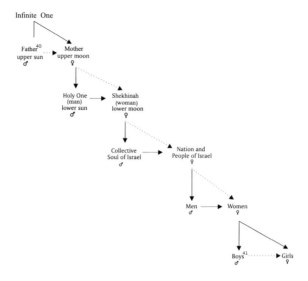

ing feature is its holographic structure – which means that every piece contains aspects of every other piece inside itself.[43] Every good contains a trace of evil and every evil a trace of good. Every Jew contains aspects of non-Jews, and every non-Jew contains a spark of Jew. And, what is relevant here, every man contains a shadow woman inside himself and every woman a shadow man. This is called the Principle of Interinclusion and each individual reflects the combination of traits that is his or her soul's unique truth.

Focusing on the gender scale, a whole continuum of possibilities exists for combining male and female elements. We find men and women who have all the stereotyped traits of their gender, and others who display many features that are more typical of the opposite sex. Wherever a person falls on this continuum, one fact remains: there is no man who does not include feminine elements inside himself, and vice versa for women.

---

43. See Glossary under Holographic Structure.

This is also true, but to a much lesser degree, with kabbalistic archetypes. Although a *partzuf*, by definition, contains both male and female aspects, its symbolic statement, in most cases, is purely one or the other. In the kabbalistic model the interincluded aspects of the opposite sex get projected outward as a separate individual and become a personality (*partzuf*) unto themselves. Then, in the kabbalistic odyssey, these two *partzufim* (that had originally been one) rediscover each other and unite in marital union.

Consequently, when kabbalah discusses the *partzuf woman*, its list of descriptors does not generalize to individual women, for the *partzuf* is a pure archetype and women are complex entities.[44] The kabbalistic portrait of *woman* refers equally to the feminine parts of real women and the feminine parts of men. This is an extremely important qualification, for many popular writings irresponsibly assert that women should think, feel, and behave in one way or another, based on kabbalistic "proofs."

In fact, *HaShem* intentionally designed each person with a unique combination of male and female attributes, and everyone must discover a place on the continuum of gender that integrates all the disparate parts of himself or herself in healthy and productive ways. A soulmate has the exact right combination of complementary attributes, which means that members of a couple only "fit" when expressing their true selves in this regard. If we try to mimic an archetypal ideal that is not the truth of our nature, we actually risk losing our soulmate, whose chemistry will not respond to this artificial scent.

---

44. The composite sum total of women is a kind of archetype unto itself (called Eve), and on this scale, meaningful parallels *do* hold.

2

TWO GREAT LIGHTS

A Cosmic Vision of Equality
(Babylonian Talmud, *Chullin* 60b)

BARE BONES LITERACY

SUMMARY

The Babylonian Talmud (*Chullin* 60b) presents a three-step sequence of relationship between male and female that appears whenever gender exists. It proceeds as follows:

- initial equality between masculine and feminine
- diminishment of the feminine
- re-attained equality (that is even more consummately equal than was possible before).

These three stages comprise a single moon cycle. They apply on all scales, from the span of an individual woman's life to the history of creation (for the entire period of existence from the beginning of time to its end is but a single circuit of the moon).

The moon symbol introduced by the Talmud refers to the feminine archetype and is synonymous with the kabbalistic term *woman.* These names are used interchangeably, and the proof of their equation appears in the following chapter.

VOCABULARY

HaShem – Literally, "The Name." It refers to God in general, though it specifically indicates the unutterable name (or Tetragrammaton) that emphasizes the transcendent, eternal, and compassionate attributes of God.

man and **woman** – Kabbalistic archetypes of male and female in their prime, as opposed to *father* and *mother,* which signify their later stages of life.

midrash – Third level of biblical interpretation in the model of PaRDeS, homiletical writings that explain the biblical text through the use of stories and sermons. The *midrash* often fills out a sparsely written biblical narrative, providing background, context, moral lessons, or legal implications.

Talmud – The main repository of the Oral Tradition, scribed in 499 C.E., which interprets and elaborates the Torah.

Torah – The first five books of the Bible revealed at Sinai. The word *Torah* often also includes the oral teachings and then denotes the entire body of knowledge generated from the Torah by the Jewish people through history.

tzaddik / tzaddikim – Literally, "righteous," "perfect." A person who has purged his or her entire being of all impurity and of every inclination (even subconscious) to act contrary to spiritual law.

TECHNICAL NOTES

The italicized terms: *man, woman, mother,* and *father* refer to kabbalistic archetypes (called *partzufim*) and, by extension, to the masculine and feminine attributes found in both men and women. The literal translation of the Hebrew text appears in bold print.

SYNOPSIS

TWO GREAT LIGHTS

The entire collection of translations that comprise this current work is but a sampling of a much vaster body of teachings that elucidate one particular verse in Genesis recounting the creation of sun and moon:

> "And God made the two great lights, the great light to rule by day and the small light to rule by night."[1]

This profusion of commentary on a single sentence is not unusual: each line of the Torah conceals a universe of wisdom. One finds tracts of mystical reverie sometimes explicating a single word.[2] Tradition teaches that all the commentaries on Torah, from its moment of revelation to present times, all the volumes of Jewish scholarship that proliferate with each generation, are but a trifle of the teachings that hide within the Torah's text and that will be fully elucidated in the end of days.[3]

The Talmud notes an inconsistency in the previous verse describing the genesis of sun and moon and relays a story from the Oral Torah that resolves its contradiction. The troubling discrepancy is as follows:

The verse begins by stating: "And God made the *two great* lights..." Here, the Torah ascribes equal *greatness* to both luminaries.[4]

It then proceeds to report a completely contrary reality: "...the *great* light to rule by day and the *small* light to rule by night." Now

---

1. Genesis 1:16.

2. For example, *Tikunei Zohar* is a three-volume work on the first word of the Torah, *"Bereshit..."*

3. *Midrash Rabbah, Kohellet* 11.

4. R. Boruch Epstein, *Torah Temima*, Genesis 1:17, note 51.

only one luminary is called great, while the other has become small.

A change in relative positioning has clearly transpired between the first phrase and the second. The verse presents a sequence in the relationship of sun and moon but offers no explanation of what prompted that shift. The two luminaries, originally identical in stature, have lapsed into inequality. The Talmud relates a tale that explains why and how this regression occurred. That story is the translated text of this chapter. In summary:

Originally, the sun and moon were of equal stature. The moon complained about the difficulty of maintaining a shared balance of power in that arrangement. The Blessed Holy One agreed with her assessment and proposed a solution: she should step down from the throne and leave the sun to rule on his own. The moon challenged the justice of that proposal and the Holy One accepted her complaint. He then tried to enlist her willful cooperation by enumerating the hidden benefits accruing to her apparently diminished role. They wrangled back and forth, as *HaShem* attempted to prove that her gains would outweigh the costs. The moon was not appeased until the Holy One admitted that by engineering her diminishment, He was committing a kind of transgression that would require millenniums to atone, and thereby accepted full accountability for all the negative consequences resulting from His decree. Thus the Torah specifies that a monthly sin-offering be presented on the New Moon "for *HaShem*," meaning, to atone for the Holy One's wrongdoing (so to speak) in diminishing the moon.

The Talmud's story defines a two-stage sequence in the power dynamics of sun and moon. To those versed in biblical exegesis and metaphysical laws, a third phase is obliquely implied.

PHASE 1: In their first phase of existence the sun and moon were equal in size and stature.

PHASE 2: At the Holy One's urging (and insistence) the moon
    assumed a diminished form, her light dimmed, she became
    a reflector instead of a generator of light, and her dark side
    became a breeding ground for impure forces. The sun remained
    in its full and pristine brilliance.

PHASE 3: This third stage is not explicit in the *midrash* but is
    explicated by commentators, based on prophetic verses and
    well-known metaphysical principles, as will be seen. In a pas-
    sage listing the promised blessings of the messianic time, Isaiah
    prophesies,

> "The light of the moon will become like the light of the
> sun...."[5]

Tradition interprets this as an explicit promise that the
moon will return to her greatness and reclaim her equality.
The idea is as follows:

> Kabbalah identifies a spiritual law that it formulates thus:
> It is the final outcome that was the original thought.[6] This
> means that every accomplishment begins as a thought in
> the mind of its creator, a vision that prefigures the end and
> perfected attainment of the entire process. Yet that *first
> thought* cannot instantaneously reproduce itself as a physi-
> cal reality. Its first appearance on the physical plane is always
> profoundly lacking relative to the vision that engendered
> its existence. Natural law requires that it start deficient in
> size, maturity, or refinement and develop over time; a seed
> or babe or blueprint that only eventually grows into full

---

5. Isaiah 30:26.
6. Standard Liturgy, Shabbat, Friday night.

flower. At journey's end the work-in-progress becomes a
final product. The last frame in its developmental sequence
then perfectly matches the vision of perfection that inspired
its creation.

The principle called "The final outcome was the original
thought" thus comprises three stages that exactly parallel
the previously mentioned phases of lunar development:

STAGE 1: The first thought and vision of attained perfection
that exists in the mind of the Creator and that initiates the
creative sequence.

STAGE 2: The developmental process on the physical plane that
starts in immaturity and refines over time.

STAGE 3: The final perfection and last frame in the developmental sequence where the physical reality now perfectly
matches the original vision of stage 1.

Based on this principle, since *HaShem's first thought* cast the
sun and moon as co-sovereigns, this original vision defines
the ideal and destined end of their shared journey through
history. And since *HaShem's* will *will* be done, it also guarantees the eventual realization of that vision as a physical fact.
The moon will again be great and, as Isaiah prophesied, she
will reattain her position of equality with sun.

This three-stage model of relationship between sun and moon
is neither controversial nor obscure and receives unanimous con-
firmation in the standard liturgy. Jews throughout the world affirm
its truth each month in their prayer for sanctifying the moon:

May it be Your will, God … to fill the flaw of the moon that
there be no more diminution in it. May the light of the moon
be like the light of the sun and like the light of the seven days

of creation, as it was before it diminished,[7] as it is said: "And God made two great lights…"[8]

The encounter between *HaShem* and the moon relayed in this *midrash* transpires on archetypal realms. The sun and the moon speak from the primordial depths of creation's inception, when there first arose within the mind of the Holy One the concept of *two*. The *midrash* personifies that first pair as sun and moon. And yet, like all archetypal symbols, they have real and profound implications for this world as well. For example:

1. The actual physical luminaries called sun and moon are the most direct representatives of these archetypes in the material world. This *midrash* teaches that the original design of our solar system, as it first arose in the mind of its Creator, contained the sun and moon as lights of equal stature. When that *first thought* began its descent into physical reality (for reasons explained earlier and others yet to be discussed) *HaShem* modified their relative configuration and introduced a disparity of stature by reducing the moon's radiance.

2. The sun, in a more general sense, represents the masculine polarity in the universe with all of its associated symbols and physical representations; the moon likewise symbolizes the feminine.[9] Some of the correspondences that will occur in the writings that follow are:

---

7. Although the decree for the moon to diminish occurred on the fourth day, its effect was suspended until after that first Shabbat. See Rashi, Genesis 1:14 (first words, *l'havdil*).
8. Standard Liturgy, *Kiddush HaLevannah* (Sanctification of the Moon).
9. *Zohar* 2:178a *(Sifra d'Tsniuta)*.

This *midrash* uses the symbols of sun and moon to depict the dynamic interrelationship of masculine and feminine at the most primary level of reality. Its paradigm underlies every other expression of gender in the universe, from the beginning of time to its end. Whenever there is *two* there is gender, and wherever there is gender there is a three-stage cycle of development:

- equality of masculine and feminine,
- feminine diminishment,
- reattained equality that is even more consummately "equal" than was possible at the beginning.

This midrashic tale is the primary source for all other commentaries included in this collection and, more generally, for nearly all source-based explorations of gender in Judaism's sacred literature.

Sun	Moon
males	females
man	woman
intellect	emotions
teacher	student
active and outward extending expression	passive and receptive expression
Written Torah	Oral Torah
study	prayer
Tree of Life	Tree of Knowledge
stable, unchanging	cyclical motion and transformation
perfection	perfecting

ANNOTATED TRANSLATION

TWO GREAT LIGHTS

Gemara, Chullin 60b

רבי שמעון בן פזי רמי וכתיב: ויעש אלקים את שני המאורות הגדולים וכתיב:
את המאור הגדול ואת המאור הקטן!

R. Shimon ben Pazzi pointed out a contradiction between two halves of the verse in Genesis describing the formation of the sun and moon on the fourth day of creation. It begins by **stating, "And God made the two great lights,"**[10] **and** continues with the phrase that **reads, "The great light** to rule by day **and the small light** to rule by night."

The first part of this verse ("And God made two great lights…") denotes that the luminaries were originally identical in their strength of illumination.[11] Then, in the second phrase a distinction suddenly develops between them. Only one still remains great, while the other is now called small (הקטן). R. Shimon ben Pazzi explains what happened between the lines; what constituted the chain of events resulting in the diminishment of the luminary known as the moon?

אמרה ירח לפני הקב"ה: רבש"ע, אפשר לשני מלכים שישתמשו בכתר אחד?

The moon said to the Holy One, "Master of the universe, is it really **possible for two kings to share one crown?"**

Is it really possible for two sovereigns to overcome their natural rivalry and rule under a single crown, reigning as equals in power and domain?

---

10. Genesis 1:16.
11. R. Boruch Epstein, ibid.

אמר לה: לכי ומעטי את עצמך!

The Holy One **responds by saying, "Go, and diminish yourself."**
Your assessment is correct. Equal partnership is not working. It is
simply not possible for two kings to rule under a single crown, at
least at this point in history. One of the heirs
must forfeit his throne. I am assigning this role
to you. Go! Make yourself small.

אמרה לפניו: רבש"ע, הואיל ואמרתי לפניך דבר הגון,
אמעיט את עצמי?

She answers Him, "Sovereign of the universe, because I spoke rightly must I diminish myself?" Why should I be penalized for
speaking truth? I simply articulated the obvious discrepancy between the real and the ideal.
I broke the silence of denial, which is the necessary first step in fixing the problem. Why is
Your solution for *me* to forfeit position and
standing? Why must the entire burden of sacrifice fall upon me?

אמר לה: לכי ומשול ביום ובלילה.

He replied, "Go and rule by day and by night."
I will compensate you for your loss by giving
you an even greater range of sovereignty than
the sun. He only rules by day, and never by
night. Your ruling presence will shine both by
day and by night.

אמרה ליה: מאי רבותיה, דשרגא בטיהרא מאי אהני?

She replies, "What is so great about that? Of what benefit is a
lamp in broad daylight?" Although I may be physically present

I.
The Talmud notes a contradiction in the biblical verse that first
presents the sun and moon as
equal in size and then ascribes a
disparity of stature between them.

II.
Shimon ben Pazzi reveals the
sequence of events that caused
this change in design.

A. The moon complained that the
initial arrangement of equality
wasn't working.
B. *HaShem* directed her to solve
the problem by diminishing
herself and accepting an
apparently less than equal
status.
C. The moon protested her fate
and *HaShem* attempted to convince her with appeasements,
but she was not persuaded.
D. The conflict resolved when
HaShem admitted that His
insistence upon her diminishment was a kind of "transgression" that would require active
atonement on His part.

also in the day, my appearance is totally washed out by the greatness of the sun's shine. My light is completely insignificant by day. It makes no difference whether I am there or not. This does not appease me. This is not a meaningful compensation.

אמר לה: זיל, לימנו בך ישראל ימים ושנים.

He replies, "Go! Israel will reckon by you the days and the years." Here is another compensation for your martyrdom, another distinction that will compensate for your sacrifice. Israel will count their days and years based on your cycle. Their entire ceremonial calendar, its marking of holy days with feasts and ritual practices, will be governed by your monthly cycle. The whole aligning of spheres and unfolding of supernal influence that happens in the course of each month and year will be placed in your domain.

אמרה ליה: יומא נמי, אי אפשר דלא מנו ביה תקופותא, דכתיב והיו לאותות ולמועדים ולימים ושנים.

She replies: The most basic unit of time is the **day**, which **is impossible to measure except by the** sun's **cycle** of rising, setting, and rising again. Night is supposed to be my sovereign time and yet I am not even always present then. Even my year is constantly adjusted to his cycle of seasons.

And so it says, "Let *them* be for signs and seasons and for days and years."

This is still not a "room of my own." Since it is not something that I have that he doesn't, it does not work as compensation. It is still not a space where I can rule independently of him, and consequently it does not appease me. The enormous loss entailed by diminishment is not balanced by this small compensating gain. Any "space" that we share is ultimately under his rule, for "the property of a wife belongs to her husband."[12] When he asserts his rights,

---

12. TB, *Sanhedrin* 71a; *Gittin* 77b; *Nazir* 24b; *Kiddushin* 23b. The *Zohar* teaches,

either I can resist and enter into a power struggle, or concede and lose myself again to his assessment and its demands.

זיל, ליקרו צדיקי בשמיך: יעקב הקטן, שמואל הקטן, דוד הקטן ...

"Go. The righteous shall be named after you as we find, Jacob the Small,[13] Samuel the Small,[14] David the Small.[15]" In the second part of the verse in Genesis 1:16 cited earlier as the source for this entire *midrash*, the sun is called *the great light*, and the moon is called *the small light*. The Holy One explains that smallness will become the mark of righteousness. "You will become the archetype of true piety, teaching, by example, that humility is the only path to *spiritual greatness*."

The entire universe exists in the merit of those God-serving ones who are righteous, precisely because they are small, in the sense of ego-*less*. It is a fact, hidden but true, that they truly rule the world. Everyone, without exception, kings and presidents, billionaires

I.
The Talmud notes a contradiction in the biblical verse that first presents the sun and moon as equal in size and then ascribes a disparity of stature between them.

II.
Shimon ben Pazzi reveals the sequence of events that caused this change in design.

A. The moon complained that the initial arrangement of equality wasn't working.

B. *HaShem* directed her to solve the problem by diminishing herself and accepting an apparently less than equal status.

C. The moon protested her fate and *HaShem* attempted to convince her with appeasements, but she was not persuaded.

D. The conflict resolved when *HaShem* admitted that His insistence upon her diminishment was a kind of "transgression" that would require active atonement on His part.

"God looked into the Torah and created the world." This means that everything later codified in halacha existed as a spiritual truth from the universe's beginning. Consequently this law "that the property of a wife belongs to her husband" was embedded into the structure of the universe and accessible to a pondering soul (i.e., the moon) even then.

13. Amos 7:5. "Then I said O Lord God cease, I beseech thee, how shall Jacob stand? For he is *small*."

14. 1 Shmuel 17:13. "And David was *the youngest*. And the three eldest followed Saul. But David went back and forth from Saul to tend his father's sheep."

15. A renowned Sage of the mishnaic period, called "the small" because of his humility.

and superstars, all owe their life and existence to them, as the Talmud teaches, "in the merit of thirty-six *tzaddikim*, the world continues to exist.[16] You will become the archetype of this teaching that self-negation is the only path to real power – that is, the power that comes from being a transparent channel of Divine Presence.

חזייה דלא קא מיתבא דעתה,

On seeing that she was not appeased . . . Although all this potential good comes from my diminishment, all the evil, darkness, failure, sin, and stumbling in the universe also comes from my ordeal as well, and there is no guarantee which will prevail. Perhaps the latter will overcome the former and this world will deteriorate to the point of self-destruction like the seven universes that preceded it.[17]

I do not want the sins of man and the evil of the universe to be on my account; none of these benefits are worth that.[18]

אמר הקב"ה: הביאו כפרה עלי שמיעטתי את הירח. והיינו דאמר ר"ש בן
לקיש: מה נשתנה שעיר של ראש חדש שנאמר בו, לה'. אמר הקב"ה: שעיר
זה יהא כפרה על שמיעטתי את הירח

The Blessed Holy One said, "Bring an atonement for Me, for I caused the moon to forfeit her greatness, I made her grow small." This is what R. Shimon ben Lakish meant when he declared, **"Why** does *HaShem* change His language when He commands us to offer a he-goat on the new moon?" A perplexing phrase appears here that does not occur elsewhere. **Concerning the new moon offering, the Torah writes, "A he-goat on the new moon** *for the Lord?"*[19] R. Shimon ben Lakish answers his own question: The Blessed Holy One is saying by this phrase, **"Let this he-goat be an atonement** *for* **Me, for the 'offense' that I have committed in reducing the moon."**

---

16. Actually, a merging of *Chullin* 92a and *Sanhedrin* 97b.

17. See Chapter 5, footnote 12.

18. *Leshem*, MHY, 6–10.

19. Numbers 28:11, 15.

DEBRIEFING

TWO GREAT LIGHTS

What Do We Know (Both from the Talmud and Its Commentaries)?

1. The original vision, as it arose in the mind of the Creator, was for the sun and moon (masculine and feminine) to be of equal stature.

2. The moon critiqued the way this vision first materialized, complaining that it wasn't working for two kings to rule under one crown. The Holy One accepted her complaint and proposed that the problem be solved by her diminishment. No alternative solution ever appeared in their discussion.

3. The moon did not accept her fate without protest. She boldly (if not brazenly) complained about the unfairness of this arrangement and insisted on compensations that would make her sacrifice worth its while.

4. The relationship of sun and moon (masculine and feminine) follows a three-step sequence of development:
   a. initial equality
   b. lunar diminishment
   c. reattained equality that is even more consummately equal than before.

5. The moon's diminished state manifests in several ways:
   a. The moon's light is many magnitudes weaker than the sun's.[20]
   b. The moon cannot generate her own glow. She only reflects what she receives from the sun.[21]

---

20. R. Chanoch Zundel ben Yosef, *Etz Yosef* and *Anaf Yosef, Shavuot* 9b, c. 1850; R. Yehuda Loewe ben Bezalel (Maharal), *Chidushei Aggadot, Chullin* 60b.
21. *Ari, Etz Chaim,* MHY 1:1.

   c. Her presence is not stable. She constantly loses her radiance and has to regain it again, a condition created not by her own merit but by the behavior of her offspring,[22] which determine her state of proximity to the sun.[23]

   d. The dark side of the moon is the metaphysical breeding ground for all the impure forces in the universe. Shaded from the searing light of truth, these dark forces find their safe haven in the moon's backside.[24]

6. Whereas at first, "two kings could not rule under one crown," in the end of days, when the moon completes her cycle, these same two kings will successfully rule under one crown, an arrangement that epitomizes their perfection.

What Don't We Know?

1. We don't know what, specifically, wasn't working in the original arrangement between sun and moon. What caused the moon to voice her complaint? There are many speculations in the literature and this translation presents but one possible interpretation.

2. We don't know why the only option ever considered was for the moon to diminish herself. We don't know how her affliction produces the chain of transformations that culminate in the reattained equality of sun and moon.

3. We don't know why the Holy One considers His insistence on the moon's diminishment a "sin" that requires active and ongoing atonement.

---

22. All of creation and particularly mankind are considered the offspring of *woman*, the moon.

23. *Etz Yosef, Anaf Yosef,* ibid.; Maharal, ibid.; *Leshem, MHY.*

24. *Leshem,* ibid.; R. Moshe Chaim Luzzato (Ramchal), *Adir BaMarom* (AB) 1.

3

THE SMALL LIGHT TO RULE BY NIGHT[1]

The Seven Stages of Feminine Development

Excerpt from *The Diminished Moon*
by R. Isaac Luria (*HaAri*) (1534–1572)

BARE BONES LITERACY

SUMMARY

This excerpt from *The Diminished Moon* by R. Isaac Luria identifies seven (really eight) stages in the feminine life cycle of waning and waxing. He describes *woman's* recovery from diminishment and her path of attaining full-statured equality. In the end, *woman* stands equal and opposite to *man* and they meet for the first time as spiritual, intellectual, and emotional mates. Until then, *woman* needs *man* to pull down her transcendent lights, for she cannot

---

1. *Ari, Etz Chaim (Tree of Life), Heichal Nukva, Shaar Miut Hayareach,* Chapter 1.

reach them on her own. In the final and seventh stage she becomes self-sufficient in that regard. Only when perfectly equal in stature, intellect, and access to resources can *man* and *woman* unite in consummate union. When they meet on every level, from the crown of their heads to the soles of their feet, every part of each finds its match in the other.

This is the Jewish vision of how *man* and *woman* should and will relate when they have healed themselves and fixed the world. The joy of their consummate union underlies all the anticipated pleasure of messianic times.

VOCABULARY

chassadim / chesed lights (generosities) – Lights of conscious awareness. The *chassadim*, when integrated, always inspire a generosity of spirit.

dinim (also called *gevurot*) – These terms mean, literally, "severities" and refer to the dark knots of unrectified potential that are the driving force behind our universe. *Dinim* and *gevurot* are generally associated with unconscious lights.

lights – *Lights* are always equivalent to consciousness in kabbalistic writings. Each *sefirah*, or spark, is a *light* that transmits a particular insight or capacity for awareness.

malchut – The lowest of the ten *sefirot* is called *malchut*, which means literally "royalty" and "kingship." It corresponds to the physical plane and represents the final stage in light's congealing into matter.

man and **woman** – Kabbalistic archetypes of male and female in their prime, as opposed to *father* and *mother*, which signify their later stages of life.

messianic era – The messianic era is a transitional time between *this* world and the next. It begins somewhere toward the end of the sixth millennium (we are now within the period of its likely beginnings) and will take us to the threshold of the world to come. It is the joyous stage of actualized perfection. Love of God, love of neighbor, and love of Torah reign.

nesira (surgical uncoupling) – Tradition teaches that Adam and Eve were originally created as a single bi-gendered creature with male and female halves fused together like Siamese twins. God then severed this bond, releasing them to meet face-to-face as freestanding individuals for the first time. This is how Jewish tradition interprets the biblical story of Eve's formation.

partzuf / partzufim – The set of six kabbalistic archetypes that coalesce into a family system, with each filling a unique role, for example: *father, mother, man, woman*. Equally frequently, these *partzufim* function as different "voices" or sub-personalities within a single individual.

Principle of Interinclusion – A distinguishing feature of our present universe is its holographic structure. Every piece contains something of every other piece inside itself. This is always true. No matter how small the fragment, no matter how many subdivisions one executes, the resulting particles always contain a complete set of the whole.

sefirah / sefirot – The ten channels of Divine flow and emanation that link the Transcendent Light with Its evolving and apparently finite creation.

TECHNICAL NOTES

The italicized terms *Man, Woman, Mother,* and *Father* refer to kabbalistic archetypes (called *partzufim*) and, by extension, to the masculine and feminine attributes found in both men and women. The literal translation of the Hebrew text appears in bold print.

SYNOPSIS

THE SMALL LIGHT TO RULE BY DAY

R. Isaac Luria, called the *Ari* (meaning *lion*), is the unrivaled grand master of modern kabbalah. He integrated the profuse body of Jewish mystical teachings that preceded him into a coherent metaphysical system that carries the full authority of Oral Torah.[2] His comprehensive revelations are the foundation truths upon which all subsequent kabbalistic writings build.

R. Luria's treatise on the diminishment of the moon is part of a much larger section on the *partzuf* called *woman*, which examines in minute detail the metaphysical underpinnings of the feminine archetype. In this present excerpt he expands upon the midrashic tale of the previous chapter, exploring the mystical implications of the moon's ordeal.

R. Luria revealed the science of kabbalistic archetypes, called *partzufim*, which adds a whole new layer of sophistication to the ten *sefirot*.[3] In this model a single point on the Tree of Life becomes a complete personality, an entire human being with mind and emotions, with head, arms, torso, and legs. These *partzufim* then coalesce into a kinship system, with each filling a unique role that becomes its identity, for example, *father, mother, man (son),* and *woman (daughter).*

A lone *sefirah* is but a single attribute of personality,[4] whereas its

---

2. R. Yoel Sirkes, *Shealot u'Tehsuuat L'HaBach (yeshanot)* 5 (beginning with the words, *V'hinei chelkhi...*).

3. The language of *partzufim* appears in Zoharic writings (*Sifra d'Tsniuta, Idra Raba, Idra Zuta*), but the complex science of their interactions was transmitted by R. Luria and his writings are characterized by this emphasis.

4. This remains true, even though it, too, contains all ten *sefirot* as interincluded elements. See diagram, p. 27.

associated *partzuf* blossoms into a whole person. The correspondences between the ten *sefirot* and six *partzufim* are as follows:

#	sefirah	partzuf	#
1	keter (crown)	great-grandfather[5]	1
		grandfather	2
2	chokhmah (wisdom)	father	3
3	binah (understanding)	mother	4
4	chesed (loving-kindness)		
5	gevurah (might)		
6	tiferet (beauty)	man (son)	5
7	netzach (victory)		
8	hod (splendor)		
9	yesod (foundation)		
10	malchut (kingdom)	woman (daughter)	6

The primary advantage of *partzufim* over *sefirot* is their greater resemblance to human beings. Real people are complex and multifaceted creatures containing a myriad of contradictory impulses inside themselves. And even more, they are active and willful participants in life. The gap between a simple *sefirah* (which defines a single, passive attribute of personality) and the complexity of a human being is so great that one cannot extrapolate meaningful teachings between one and the other. The distortion arising from their mismatch renders conclusions unreliable.

This troubling discrepancy between theory and reality shrinks dramatically when one substitutes *partzufim* for *sefirot*. The former

5. The source for using these familiar associations is *Leshem, Sefer Hakdamot v' Shearim* (HVS) 7:7:1.

are complex and human-like, with active wills and dynamic life cycles. In this way they mirror the realities of the physical world with greater accuracy.

This is especially true for the lowest two *partzufim*, called *man* and *woman*. Their whole point is to represent in some real and accessible way the patterns of life in the physical realms. The higher the *partzuf*, the more abstract its representation, and the link between it and the lower world grows thin. Not so for *man* and *woman*. They gestate for nine months in the womb of *mother*, nurse for two years, and then begin a multi-phased sequence of growth. *Man* reaches his first stage of maturity at thirteen and *woman* at twelve.[6] The parallels between them and real men and women are obvious and intentionally so.[7]

R. Luria frequently makes statements such as "because *woman* is in such and such a configuration, so women (below) do or do not do a particular activity."[8] It is clear from these statements that he conceives a fairly straightforward link between the *partzufim* of *man* and *woman* and human beings below.

The creation story of Adam and Eve serves as their primary point of interface. Both the human and the archetypal find their story told in this enigmatic tale about the origin of humanity and the roots of gender.

> God created *Adam* in His own image, in the image of God
> He created him; male and female He created them.[9]...And
> the Lord God formed *Adam* of the dust of the ground, and

6. R. Shalom Ulman, *Daat Elokim* (Jerusalem: Dafus Tfutza, 1983), *Tikun Partzuf Zu'n*.

7. Ramchal, *Klach Pitchei Chokhmah* (KPC), 115.

8. *Ari, Pri Etz Chaim* 19; *Etz Chaim, Tikun Nukva* 34:4; *Etz Chaim, Tikun Nukva* 34:2.

9. Genesis 1:27.

breathed into his nostrils the breath of life; and *man* became a living soul.[10] ... And the Lord God said, It is not good that the *Adam* should be alone; I will make him a help to match him.... And the Lord God made *Adam* fall into a deep sleep, and he slept; and He took one from his sides, and closed up the flesh. And from the side, which the Lord God had taken from *Adam,* He made a woman, and brought her to Adam. And Adam said, This is now bone of my bones, and flesh of my flesh; she shall be called woman, because she was taken out of man.[11]

Tradition teaches that every story in the Torah is always literally true. In addition to the psychological and metaphysical teachings that are also present, the Bible's stories are actual historical occurrences. Kabbalah explains, however, that although the first chapters of Genesis did literally happen, and as real events, they transpired on an entirely different plane of reality than what we experience as the physical world today.[12] Until Adam and Eve ate from the Tree of Knowledge of Good and Evil, the lowest level of the universe was the mental plane, which means that the bodies and objects of that era were actually thought forms.

When Adam and Eve ate from the Tree of Knowledge, they caused an intermingling of good and evil for the first time in history, and reality transformed completely. It turned inside out, upside down, and tumbled level after level before collapsing into the configuration that we now experience as the physical plane.[13] The six-day creation period thus serves a transitional function between the era of pure archetypes and the coarse materiality of our physical world.

---

10. Genesis 2:7.
11. Genesis 2:20–23.
12. *Zohar* 3, *Kedoshim* 83a; *Leshem,* HDYH, 2, pp. 16, 79.
13. *Zohar* 3, 83a.

The previous passage contains an inconsistency. Its first verse describes *Adam* as both male and female: "God created *Adam* in His own image, in the image of God created He him; male and female He created them."

This treats the word *Adam* as a generic term, like *human being*, that includes both genders. Translated thus, the verse reads, "God created human beings in His image, with male and female genders He created them."

And yet, shortly thereafter the Bible comments that Adam is alone and seeks a mate, for there are no other human beings around, and none of the animals feels like a soul partner: "And the Lord God said, "It is not good that *Adam* should be alone; I will make him a help to match him.... And God formed every beast of the field...and brought them to man.... And Adam gave names... to every beast of the field; but for man there was not found a help to match him."

This passage clearly suggests a contrary interpretation, that "Adam" is a single creature and not a species comprised of two (or more) individual members. Otherwise, he would not be alone. But if Adam is a single entity, what does the first verse mean when it states, "male and female He created them"?

Reconciling this discrepancy, Tradition teaches that the first human being was an androgynous creature like a Siamese twin, with male and female halves joined at the back. *HaShem* then caused an anesthetic sleep to descend upon this bi-gendered Adam and surgically severed its halves, creating two separate and freestanding entities called Adam and Eve.[14] Although this literal reading may seem farfetched relative to the physical laws of our world, it is perfectly credible when understood to transpire on the equivalent of our mental plane.

––––––––––––––

14. TB, *Eruvin* 18a, *Bereshit Rabbah* 8:1.

A three-stage sequence emerges that describes the origin of human gender:

- androgynous unity of male and female
- surgical uncoupling of the genders
- man and woman now standing as separate and independent entities

Kabbalah explains that the talmudic story of sun and moon and the Bible's story of Adam and Eve are the same sequence of events played out in different realms. The former relays the creation of *man* and *woman*, the latter the odyssey of men and women.[15] Two layers of correspondence emerge that follow this same three-stage pattern of unfolding:

	Masculine	Feminine
Archetypal Level	MAN (Sun)	WOMAN (Moon)
Collective Level	Adam (composite sum-total of all men)	Eve (composite sum-total of all women)
Individual Level	Individual Men	Individual Women

Because of their status as synonymous events, the *Ari* extrapolates freely from one to the other. Details that appear in either story apply to both, even when not mentioned explicitly as such. For example, the bisecting of Adam and Eve into two separate individuals also happened to *man* and *woman*,[16] while the moon's dissatisfaction with her supposed equality also occurred with Adam and Eve.[17] Similarly, individual men and women also follow this three-stage pattern to some metaphorical degree, depending

15. See also *Zohar, Kedoshim* 3:83a, which establishes this equation.
16. *Heichal HaBracha,* Genesis 1:14 (p. 15), first word, *V'lemoadim.*
17. *Zohar* 1:34b–35a; *Alef-Bet d'ben Sira.*

upon the distribution of gender traits in their souls and in their partnerships.

In this essay, R. Luria expands upon the talmudic *midrash* from the previous chapter that outlined its own three-stage cycle of relationship between sun and moon:

- (apparent) equality
- lunar diminishment
- re-attained equality

The entire span of earthly history, from the first day of creation to its messianic end, constitutes one lunar cycle. R. Luria identifies seven (really eight) sub-stages in this cosmic course of development. The criteria that determine whether a stage is higher or lower, more evolved or less so, are twofold:

QUANTITATIVE SCALE: The ten *sefirot* are here pictured as a yardstick extending from below to above, from one to ten, from feet to crown. As the feminine grows in height, she incorporates the upper and more exalted attributes into herself. "Height" is the metaphor that represents her emotional-intellectual maturity. Starting with the lowest *sefirah* (*malchut*), her consciousness develops up through the instinctive emotions (*netzach, hod, yesod*), conscious emotions (*chesed, gevurah, tiferet*), intellect (*chokhmah, binah, daat*), and finally to the deepest root of her soul (*keter*). At full length she is ten *sefirot* high and stands equal and opposite to *man*. As a perfect couple, they are identical in stature and matched from the crown of their heads to the soles of their feet.

The *Ari* focuses on a particular by-product of *woman's* quantitative development, which is her degree of dependency upon man, a condition that varies inversely with her height. The "shorter" she is, the more she depends upon him to fill the functions that she lacks. The "taller" she grows, the more capabilities she incorporates into herself and, consequently, the more self-sufficient she becomes. Her perfected state of development, according to R. Luria, is to be free of need for him. This does not dampen their union, but rather the opposite. For the first time they can build a truly mutual bond, free of the personal agendas and self-interests that inevitably contaminate relationships of dependency. Now, finally, their love is pure.

QUALITATIVE SCALE: R. Luria identifies two general categories of relationship that he labels back-to-back and front-to-front. The first is an immature and self-absorbed mode of relating where neither partner ever really "sees" the other, except as an object whose sole purpose is to satisfy his or her own narcissistic needs. The second mode, called front-to-front, describes a relationship of true and healthy love. The couple bonds from mutual desire and shared vision. Each sees the other as an "other" and honors the difference.

The promised goal and messianic ideal is for *woman* to integrate the perfection of both scales – to achieve a non-dependent, front-to-front relationship of absolute equality with *man*. Her step-wise journey from abject diminishment to self-realization is the subject of R. Luria's study. He identifies seven milestones along the way that organize into three primary phases of development:

back-to-back relating (stages 1, 2, 3) – This phase corresponds to the Bible's description of Adam as an androgynous creature with male and female elements joined at the back: "God created *Adam* in His own image, in the image of God created He him; male and female He created them."

surgical uncoupling (*nesira*) – This corresponds to the biblical description of Adam's separation into two free-standing entities called Adam and Eve: "And the Lord God made *Adam* fall into a deep sleep, and he slept; and He took one from his sides, and closed up the flesh. And from the side, which the Lord God had taken from *Adam*, He made a woman, and brought her to the man."

front-to-front relating (stages 4a, 4b, 5, 6, 7) – This corresponds to the cosmic dance of *man* and *woman* striving and struggling through history to consummate their relationship in full and joyous union.

The first three stages describe a sequence of developing equality between *man* and *woman*, but one that is never consummate or mutually satisfying because it all transpires within the narcissistic orientation of back-to-back. In her most diminished state *woman* shrinks to a single point occupying the lowest position possible, metaphorically below *man*'s feet, oriented with her back to his. On both the quantitative and qualitative scales this is the lowest rung. From there she extends in length step by step (stages 2, 3) until she attains a height equivalent to his. Their backs become essentially equal, but their insides still do not meet.

HaShem severs their backsided bond, releasing them to turn and meet face-to-face. *Woman*, however, immediately regresses to a single point, but this time oriented front-to-front, a qualitative improvement that makes worlds of difference. The soul satisfaction of now facing her spouse easily compensates for her quantitative loss of stature. Once again she proceeds to develop step by step (stages 4–7), building herself emotionally and intellectually, until she attains full maturity and independence.

Woman's relationship with *man* consummates (at stage 7) in the passionate meeting of two perfectly equal, mutually independent, intellectually matched, front-facing individuals whose love is pure and free from the manipulations of personal insecurity and external coercion. This is the Jewish vision of how men and women should and will relate when they have healed themselves and fixed the world. Its perfected ideal has not yet ever been in the history of the universe. From their holy and newly consummated marriage will flow all the promised sweetness of messianic times.

A SINGLE MOON CYCLE

Woman's Journey Through History

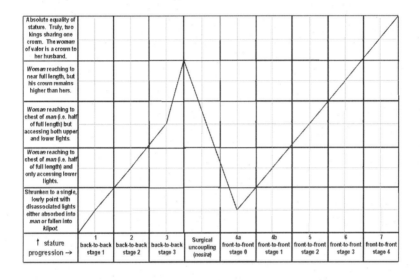

	1 back-to-back stage 1	2 back-to-back stage 2	3 back-to-back stage 3	Surgical uncoupling (*nesira*)	4a front-to-front stage 0	4b front-to-front stage 1	5 front-to-front stage 2	6 front-to-front stage 3	7 front-to-front stage 4
Absolute equality of stature. Truly, two kings sharing one crown. The *woman* of valor is a crown to her husband.									
Woman reaching to near full length, but his crown remains higher than hers.									
Woman reaching to chest of *man* (i.e. half of full length) but accessing both upper and lower lights.									
Woman reaching to chest of *man* (i.e. half of full length) and only accessing lower lights.									
Shrunken to a single, lowly point with disassociated lights either absorbed into *man* or fallen into *klipot*.									
↑ stature progression →									

ANNOTATED TRANSLATION

An Excerpt from *The Diminished Moon* by R. Isaac Luria

מיעוט הירח מאי ניהו, דאמר לה לכי ומעטי את עצמך, היינו דכולהו מלכיות
דידה, דהוי בכל הט"ס [העליונות] כולהו הפילו ונחתו לתתא בהדה. מה
דליתא הכי בכל ספיראן,

The diminishment of the moon, What is it? *HaShem* **said to
the moon, "Go and reduce yourself."**[18] **As a result she and the
feminine components of the entire universe**[19]disintegrated: A
part of their light was reabsorbed back up into the higher realms
and a part descended below. Only a bare remnant remained in its
original place.

This experience of exile and self-collapse **is unique** to *woman*
and **distinguishes her from all other** *sefirot*.

דכולהו איתך להו חולקייהו בספיראן דלעילא [בר] מנייהו, דהא כתר כלול
מכולהו, וכן חכמה, וכן כולם ...

Each[20] *partzuf and sefirah* **includes an entire set of** ten *sefirot within
it* (*i.e., each* **keter contains ten, and similarly each** *chokhmah, etc.*).[21]

---

19. Literally, in Hebrew, the "nine upper *sefirot*." There are many interpretations
as to what these "nine *sefirot*" refer to. The interpretation adopted here is from
Leshem, HDYH, 2:5:1:3; *Chelekh HaBiurim* (CH), *Shaar HaAkudim* 5:12 (first
word, *Ve'ha'inyan*).

20. For clarity's sake, the translation of this phrase follows a different order of
ideas than the original Hebrew.

21. See p. 27 for an illustration of *partzufim* with their interincluded parts.

The kabbalistic universe is holographic; every piece contains something of every other piece inside itself. This is always true. No matter how small the fragment, no matter how many subdivisions one executes, the resulting particles always contain a complete set of the whole. Consequently, **one always finds** *malchut* as the bottom point with nine other *sefirot* above it.

אבל מלכות אתנטלית מכולהו, וכולהו הוי ט' בלבד.
דכל מה דהוי מינה לעילא בהדייהו, נחית לתתא בהדה.
ואיהי שלימו דכולהו, דבר מינה הוי כלהו ט"ס, וכולא
דילה נחית לתתא... ומשו"ה בעינן לסלקה לה לעילא,
דלהדרו לאתרייהו כולהו מלכיות דידה, ואיהו בהדייהו.

The only exception is *man* in relation to *woman*, where she is his tenth *sefirah*. Unlike every other *partzuf*, whose *malchut* is exactly like its other nine *sefirot* (as pictured earlier), *man* is different. His tenth is not like his other nine; rather, it is a full *partzuf* unto itself. His *malchut* is on the same level as he. **Consequently,** man **has only nine secondary sefirot, and his tenth** is external to him, a personality unto itself, **the *partzuf* woman.** This is true at every level of his being.[22]

---

22. Each of *man's* secondary *sefirot* also only contains nine subunits, and their tenth also appears in *woman*, upgraded a notch, to a level equivalent to themselves. And so on, ad infinitum. This section is very difficult and not critical to an understanding of the ideas that follow. Don't get stuck here. Keep moving.

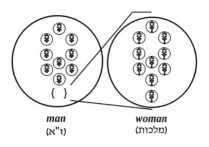

man
(ז"א)

woman
(מלכות)

Consequently, *woman* is built from the feminine components that had originally been included in *man*. Similarly, in the larger extended family of *partzufim* including *mother, father, grandfather,* and *great-grandfather,* each contains a piece of *woman* inside itself (which it can hold in trust or transfer directly to her). ALL OF THESE FEMININE ELEMENTS COMBINED TOGETHER FORM THE MOON. Though her visible base of operations is the actual *partzuf woman,* and that is what we point to and call the moon, in fact, the bulk of her lights are dispersed throughout the universe. Such is her condition since the fourth day of creation, when she consented to her fateful decree.[23]

When *HaShem* diminished the moon, **the feminine in** all its forms and **all its habitations plunged** into exile. *Woman* was most drastically affected, for *all* of her pertains to the moon. In contrast, her *husband's* nine *sefirot* were only affected in their lowest interincluded spheres; the bulk of him remained immune to the moon's ordeal.

No corner of the universe escaped unscathed. Since the world is holographic every piece contains its share of moondust.

---

23. One is struck by the parallel to the "cold, dark matter" that physicists postulate to be scattered throughout the universe but with properties that make it undetectable by visual or heat-sensitive instruments. See Michio Kaku, *Hyperspace* (New York: Anchor Books – Doubleday, 1994).

Consequently, no sliver of the universe can achieve perfection[24] until the moon recoups her losses and recovers her light. **As long as the feminine presence within each creature remains diminished, the entire organism lacks completion. Thus, the primal drive of the universe is to restore *woman* (and all her shattered pieces) back to her place on high. There is no other way to fix the world except by inviting her back up and in.**

The repercussions of this primordial trauma still reverberate through the cosmos, for every female soul recapitulates these events in the course of its life journey. In this sense woman's maturational process is different from *man's*, though they pass through the same milestones of development.

... עניין עיבור זו"ן, דע כי בעת עיבור זו"ן באמא עלאה, אז היה ז"א בבחי' ו"ק לבד. ונקבה בבחי' נקודה א', כלולה מי', שהוא בחי' מלכות שבה בלבד. ואז ע"י העיבור ויניקה ומוחין, נתגדל בחי' ז"א, עד שנשלם לי"ס כנודע. ואמנם גידול המלכות אינה אלא ע"ש אמצעית ז"א עצמו, כי אמא עלאה כשאר גדלה אותו, נתנה בו כח עוד גידול להמלכות. ואח"כ יצאה בחי' גידול זה של המלכות ... גם כן, עד תכלית הגידול שבה, שהוא עד שתשלם גם היא לי"ס שלימות שבה.

Man's and *woman's* life cycles parallel the stages of human development. Their sequence divides

---

24. Perfection means to possess ten fully integrated, actualized, and manifesting *sefirot*.

into three primary intervals called gestation, nursing, and intellectual maturity.

**Concerning the pregnancy of *man* and *woman*, know that
they gestate together in the womb of *mother*,** beginning their fetal
period as incomplete *partzufim*. **Man has only six *sefirot*** (instead of
ten) **and *woman* has only one, *malchut* (though it contains a full
set of ten lower-level *sefirot* within it). Man passes through** these
three developmental stages (**gestation, nursing, and intellectual
maturity**) **and attains completion, becoming a full *partzuf* often**
(counting woman as his tenth). Mother's provisions of milk and
nurturing supply the materials from which he fashions the three
upper *sefirot* that he was previously missing.

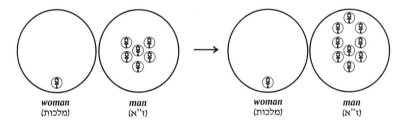

woman   *man*   *woman*   *man*
(מלכות)   (ז"א)   (מלכות)   (ז"א)

**Woman's path of development is different from *man's* and
she needs him to facilitate her passage. When *mother* raised
man, she** gave him his inheritance of resources and **designated a
special energy fund earmarked for *woman's* growth. This, too,
she transferred into *man's* possession** and he became its trustee.
He serves as an intermediary between *mother* and *woman* and
**passes these special resources on to *woman*, thereby enabling
her development.** With his help **she, too, evolves into a full**
partzuf of ten *sefirot.*

וא"כ מוכרח הוא, שכל זמן שעדיין לא נתגדל המלכות, שאותן הט"ס
עליונים, שחסרים מנוקבא, יהיו כלולין בז"א בט"ס שבו, כנודע שאין בו
רק עד היסוד, ונוקבא משלימתו לי'. ואז הם י"ט ספירות, ט' שלו, וי' שלה,

ונקרא עשירית, כיון שהיא עשירית אליו, ונשלם הוא בי"ס עמה. וגם היא
יש בה י"ס. ואמנם טרם התגלות בה ט"ס העליונות
שלה, היו כולן נכללין בט"ס שלו. נמצא, כי בכל ספירה
וספירה מן הט"ס דז"א, בה בחי' ספירה א' של נוקבא. אך
היא אינה רק חלק העשירית שבה בלבד, שהוא ספירות
המלכות שבה.

Until *woman* **attains maturity** and absorbs the lights she was previously missing, which will become **her upper nine *sefirot*,** these lights **are held** in trust **by man, temporarily absorbed into his upper spheres.** In truth, man **really has only nine *sefirot*, for** his *malchut* is a personality unto itself, that is, **the *partzuf woman*.**[25] **Consequently,** at maturity, **between the two of them, they have only nineteen *sefirot*, his nine and her ten. She is called his "tenth" since** she has two distinct roles; she is a personality unto herself, yet **she is** also *his malchut,* **and he only becomes complete by joining with her as his tenth. She,** in her maturity, **comprises a full set of ten.**

Before her legacy from mother is transferred to her, it resides with man, absorbed into his upper sefirot (i.e., the lights that will become her *crown* [כתר], are integrated into his *crown,* her *wisdom* [חכמה] into his *wisdom,* etc.), yet they are not randomly dispersed there. Rather, **the interincluded *malchut* of each of his nine *sefirot* actually belongs to *woman*, even while it resides with *man*** and fills an

---

I. PRELIMINARIES

A. The source for these teachings is the talmudic story of sun and moon.
B. Holographic structure of the universe; every piece contains aspects of every other piece inside itself.
C. Unique relationship of *man* and *woman*, that together they comprise a single whole *partzuf*.
D. Defines moon.

II.
Summary of *man's* and *woman's* growth processes and interdependencies.

III.
Detailed examination of *woman's* path of development.

A. The two extremes of *woman's* cycle – the lowest she falls and the highest she rises.
B. Definition of front-to-front and back-to-back types of relationship that divide *woman's* growth process into two distinct phases of development.
C. Three stages of back-to-back progression, with man and woman bound together at their backside.
D. Surgical uncoupling, which releases *man* and *woman* to now meet face-to-face as free-standing individuals.
E. Four stages of front-to-front relationship.

---

25. See Tree of Life, diagram p. 20.

absence in him. It is not that while he holds *woman*'s inheritance from *mother* he has certain lights in duplicate. Rather **the *malchut* included within each of his secondary *sefirot* belongs to *woman*** and when that transfer gets made, he is left with nine.

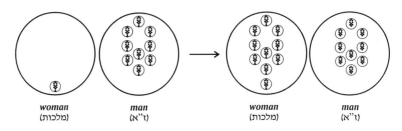

woman
(מלכות)

man
(ז"א)

woman
(מלכות)

man
(ז"א)

והנה גידול המלכות, אינה בפעם א', רק בזמנים הרבה, נתקנת, ונתגדלת מעט מעט כנ"ל. ונבאר עתה באורך כללותן, אע"פ שיש פרטים הרבה.

***Woman*'s development** into full intellectual **maturity does not happen in one smooth stretch,** but **rather in spurts and starts** and numerous regressions. **Yet, slowly but surely, she** blossoms into a full *partzuf.*

Here follows a general outline of *woman*'s development, **though each step contains a myriad of details** and qualifications that a full and complete understanding must incorporate. It is especially important to note that while each stage displays certain features that situate it at a specific point along *woman*'s life path, in truth, it spans a whole range of development from its lowest point (which is its definition) to its highest point (which is just before the next stage begins). Consequently, it is more accurate to think of these seven steps as dynamic chapters of growth rather than static points along a timeline.

הנה תכלית המיעוט אשר בה, אינה פחות מנקודה א' כלולה מי', שהיא נקודה מלכות האחרונה שבה כנ"ל.

The most diminished state of *woman* **is as a single *sefirah*** with

its interincluded ten (as opposed to full a *partzuf* of ten complete *sefirot* each with its interincluded ten). Not only is she one-tenth of full stature, but the lone *sefirah* that she possesses is also **the lowest one possible, that is, her** *malchut.* **Nevertheless,** as with all *sefirot,* **it contains its full** holographic **set of ten** subunits.

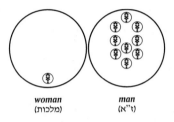

woman
(מלכות)

man
(ז"א)

ותכלית גידול שלה, הוא שיהיה בה כל הי"ס שלה, ותהיה עם ז"א פב"פ
שווה לגמרי, וישתמשו ב' מלכים בכתר א', שהוא מה שקטרגה הירח כנודע.

The highest that she attains is after she incorporates the lights **of all ten** *sefirot* **back into herself and achieves a stature equal to** *man.* **They meet in consummate union,** each part of one finding its match in the other, attaining a level of mutuality that kabbalah describes as **"two kings sharing one crown."** She achieves **exactly that which she doubted** when, on the fourth day, she complained, "Master of the Universe, is it really possible for two kings to rule under one crown?"

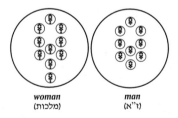

woman
(מלכות)

man
(ז"א)

והענין הוא, כי נודע, כי מת"ת של אמא, נעשה כתר לז"א, וכאשר גם היא
תעלה עד שם, ויהיה כתרה בת"ת של אמא כמוהו, יהיה כתריהן שוין, ויהיו

שניהן א', כי שניהן יהיו בחי' ת"ת דאמא, שהוא ספירה א', ואז לא תצטרך
היא לקבל הארתה ע"י ז"א, אלא יהיו שניהן מקבלין הארתן מאמא, כל אחד
ע"י עצמו, ולא יצטרכו זה לזה. ויהיו זו"ן שוין במציאותן, כדמיון או"א. כנזכר
באדרא, או"א כחדא נפקין, וכחדא שריין. וזהו תכלית הגידול שלה, ואז כל
העולמות בתכלית התיקון.

What exactly is this crown that *man* has been wearing for millennia and that he and *woman* will finally share in the messianic end of days? Kabbalah explains that **the heart center (תפארת)[26] of mother functions as man's crown.** What does this mean? The *partzuf mother,* which corresponds to the *sefirah* of *binah (understanding),* rules the mental plane. The traits associated with this sphere are discriminating intelligence, vision building, analysis, and synthesis. The heart of *mother* becomes the place that holds a loving vision of the highest potential of her children and thus serves as their crown. Just as a crown sits above the head and surrounds it, so does *mother's* vision hover above her children and guide their steps. Eventually, at full maturity, they will incorporate her aspirations into their lives, thus realizing *mother's* dreams for them. Until that point, their vessels of consciousness are too small to contain the full expanse of her prayerful vision and its lights get displaced into a surrounding position like a crown, exerting their influence upon the child's life from there.[27]

When woman develops to full stature and reaches a height

---

26. Each of the ten *sefirot* corresponds to a part of the human body. *Crown (keter)* to the crown of the head, *wisdom (chokhmah)* to the right brain, *understanding (binah)* to the left brain, *loving-kindness (chesed)* to the right arm, and *justice (gevurah)* to the left arm, *beauty (tiferet)* to the heart, *victory (netzach)* to the right leg, *splendor (hod)* to the left leg, *foundation (yesod)* to the genitals, *kingdom (malchut)* to the feet. See Concise Table of Kabbalistic Correspondence on page 24.

27. The lights of *mother (binah)* flow down to her children. Consequently, their first point of contact is with the head of the child, and whatever portion cannot enter spreads into a crown-like halo of lights above the head.

equal to *man*, **the crown of her head will also contact the heart**
(תפארת) **of** *mother,* and then she will receive
her flow of lights and bounty directly from
there, and no longer via *man*'s intermediary.

In this seventh and highest stage of development, **the statures of** *man* **and** *woman* **become
completely equal and their crowns the same.**
They will, for the first time, experience a truly
consummate union, for as long as woman is
diminished they never quite match; there are
always parts of one that don't meet the other.
Here they will unite in perfect complementarity,
**embodying the singular vision of perfection
in the heart of** *mother. Woman* **will no longer need to receive her flow of transcendent
bounty via the intermediary of** *man.* **Instead
they will both draw their lights and blessings
directly from** *mother,* **without need of each
other**'s emissarial services. *Man* **and** *woman*
**will have become completely equal in their
manifest realities, similar to the relationship
between** *mother* **and** *father* **described by the
Zohar: "Father** and *mother* emanated as one,
and stand as one.*[28]* **This is the culminating
stage of** *woman*'**s development, and** when
she attains her completion every piece of the
universe will realize its own perfection, for
the moon, in all her far-flung places, will finally
wax full.

I. PRELIMINARIES

A. The source for these teachings
is the talmudic story of sun and
moon.
B. Holographic structure of the
universe; every piece contains
aspects of every other piece
inside itself.
C. Unique relationship of *man*
and *woman*, that together
they comprise a single whole
partzuf.
D. Defines moon.

II.
Summary of *man*'s and *woman*'s
growth processes and interdependencies.

III.
Detailed examination of *woman*'s
path of development.

A. The two extremes of *woman*'s
cycle – the lowest she falls and
the highest she rises.
B. Definition of front-to-front
and back-to-back types of relationship that divide *woman*'s
growth process into two distinct phases of development.
C. Three stages of back-to-back
progression, with man and
woman bound together at
their backside.
D. Surgical uncoupling, which
releases *man* and *woman* to
now meet face-to-face as freestanding individuals.
E. Four stages of front-to-front
relationship.

---

28. *Zohar* 3, *Idra Zuta* 290b.

ואמנם בין זה לזה, יש בחי' רבות, ובין כולם הם ד' בחי', וזה סדרן ממטה
למעלה:

And yet, between these two extremes of low and high **there are many intermediate stages** that naturally divide into two primary modes of relationship, figuratively termed: back-to-back and front-to-front.

Each *partzuf* (like each person) has a front and back. And just as the front of a person includes the face with its eyes and sense organs that define its field of awareness, so is this true for a *partzuf.* The front associates with conscious will, cognition, rectified behavior, actualized potential, and personalized expression; the back with all that is unconscious, instinctive, compulsive, unrectified, and transpersonal.

In a back-to-back relationship the glue that binds the couple is primarily from unconscious forces that may even oppose each other's stated conscious intent. In contrast, a front-to-front relationship is one where the couple shares common goals and a mutuality of desire, at least to some extent.

In back-to-back relationship:[29]

  a. The couple's primary bond of attraction (and shared traits) derives from unconscious forces and unrectified layers of personality (projections, obsessions, addictions, narcissistic cravings, etc.). Whenever either one looks out into the world, the other is never visible.
  b. Even when attaining an equality of stature, they have opposite-facing wills, interests, and pleasures.
  c. They are like two people speaking *at* each other, both talking at the same time.
  d. Each partner has his or her own set of priorities and expects

---

29. These lists come primarily from the Ramchal, KPC, 135.

the other to drop everything and serve him or her instead. Each demands to be the center of the other's universe.

e. Lack of mutuality in goals, priorities, and pleasures.

f. The bond of relationship only engages the external layers of the individuals. It does not also embrace their inwardness. Each relates primarily to the role category of the other and not to his or her unique individuality.

g. Love (to the extent that it is present) comes from being served and serviced by the other, not from seeing his or her unique beauty and being inspired by that.

h. Their attachment is sustained by fear-based inducements: fear of being alone, fear of not being worthy of someone else's love, fear of not being able to provide for oneself, fear of the other partner being happy with someone else.

In a front-to-front relationship:

a. Wherever one looks, an "other" is there as a freestanding entity. Consequently, each partner's worldview includes this *other* as an independent agent, with his or her own wills, desires, and priorities. Each one's expectation, then, is to meet, discover, and come to know this other, as an *other*, and not as an extension of him- or herself.

I. PRELIMINARIES

A. The source for these teachings is the talmudic story of sun and moon.

B. Holographic structure of the universe; every piece contains aspects of every other piece inside itself.

C. Unique relationship of *man* and *woman*, that together they comprise a single whole *partzuf*.

D. Defines moon.

II.

Summary of *man's* and *woman's* growth processes and interdependencies.

III.

Detailed examination of *woman's* path of development.

A. The two extremes of *woman's* cycle – the lowest she falls and the highest she rises.

B. Definition of front-to-front and back-to-back types of relationship that divide *woman's* growth process into two distinct phases of development.

C. Three stages of back-to-back progression, with man and woman bound together at their backside.

D. Surgical uncoupling, which releases *man* and *woman* to now meet face-to-face as freestanding individuals.

E. Four stages of front-to-front relationship.

b. The couple bonds from mutual desire and shared vision.

c. Each takes genuine pleasure in giving the other pleasure.

d. The partners in a couple construct a shared vision of their life together, based on the elements they naturally have in common and negotiating the elements they don't.

e. True dialogue exists where each has a voice and listens to the other and accommodates his or her requests wherever possible.

f. Because each sees the other not as an extension of him- or herself, but as an independent entity, neither expects the other to give up his or her own goals and live only for his or her partner. And yet there is a generous flow of mutual giving inspired by love's desire to please its beloved.

g. Each relates to the other as a unique, beautiful, and complex individual and only secondarily to his or her role category.

h. The attachment endures from a place of free choice and love-based inducements.

Each of these two orientations of relationship theoretically **includes a four-step sequence of development,** though in practice one only finds a total of seven. *Woman* moves through three steps of back-to-back relationship with *man,* then turns and progresses through four stages of front-to-front.

BACK-TO-BACK

STAGE 1

א, תכלית המיעוט הנ"ל, שתהיה היא נקודה כלולה מי', והיא בחי' המלכות שבה, ואז אין לה פרצוף, ואז היא עומדת למטה מהיסוד שלו.

In this first and lowest stage (which was described previously), *woman* **is reduced to a single point,** her consciousness confined to **her lowest** *sefirah, malchut* **(with its ten levels).** She is shrunken to one-tenth of full stature, a solitary *sefirah*, **not even a full *partzuf*. And this** single point **sits** at the lowest position possible, **completely beneath man.** There is no area of overlap or equivalence between them.[30]

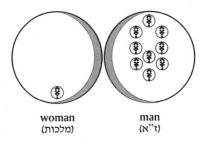

woman
(מלכות)

man
(ז"א)

STAGE 2

ב', היותה פרצוף גמור בי"ס, אלא שששיעור קומתה הוא באחור ז"א, מחזה ולמטה, אבל עדיין האורות שלה שיש בה' ראשונות של ז"א, כח"ב ח"ג, לא האירו בד"ת שבו, לכן לא נמשכו בה, ולא האירו בה...

Woman absorbs her first increment of *sefirotic* lights that *man* has been holding for her and **transforms into a full *partzuf* of ten. Nevertheless,** she remains shrunken and **stands behind man, her height extending from his chest downward.** Her entire stature overlaps his lowest five *sefirot*, which means that she is half his size.

---

30. Actually, stage 1 spans a four-step sequence of development, in which her single point gradually extends to enclothe *man* until his *keter*, attaining an equivalency of stature, though hers is an expanded single *sefirah* and his is a full *partzuf*.

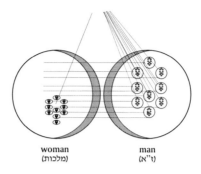

woman
(מלכות)
man
(ז"א)

She receives the lights that he holds of hers that are within their area of overlap, that is, from the heart down. However, **the lights** belonging to *woman* **that are held in *man's* upper five *sefirot*** (*crown* [כתר], *wisdom* [חכמה], *understanding* [בינה], *loving-kindness* [חסד], and *might* [גבורה]) **do not reach her;** they pass above her head. This is because *man* **has not integrated them into his heart and lower body.** He has not pulled them down into the levels of himself that are actively in relationship with *woman*, **and consequently they do not pass to her.**

STAGE 3

ג', בהיותה מקבלת אורות שלה מן ה"ר של ז"א, ואז נגדלת כמוהו, אלא
שעדיין כל זה בחי' אורות אב"א. והרי הם ג' בחי' בבחי' אחור.

Here *woman* receives the lights that are held for her **in *man's* upper five *sefirot*. She** becomes filled with them and **grows in stature until she reaches a height** nearly **equal to his. In all of these three stages, *man* and *woman* stand back-to-back.**[31]

───────────

31. As explained, each stage includes a whole range of expression. In stage 3 *woman* (*malchut*) grows from half height to full height in her back-to-back relationship with *man* (*zeir anpin*).

והטעם שאין ד' בחי' באחור, הוא ג"כ, מפני שאין הכתר ניכר, כ"א בפנים,
ולזה ג' בחי' באחור.

The developmental sequence of back-to-back only includes three stages instead of four, as would have been expected. The fourth stage should theoretically be when *man* and *woman* attain an equality of stature from the crown of their heads to the soles of their feet. **The backside,** however, by definition, **has no crown.** This is true both for *man* and for *woman*. Since *crown* corresponds to *will*, and backsided activity, by definition, lacks *will*, the back has no *crown*.

The transition from back-to-back relationship into front-to-front happens via a surgical-like procedure called *nesira*, severing. In order to present *woman*'s sequence of development in its proper chronology, it is necessary to insert here a short text from another chapter that describes the details of *nesira*.[32]

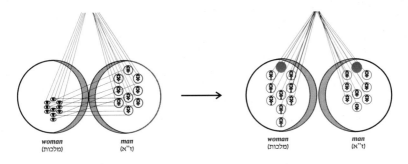

SURGICAL UNCOUPLING (*NESIRA*)

והנה אחר שנגלה אב"א מן החזה שלו ולמטה, והיתה אז מקבלת הארותיה
על ידי מחיצותיו, וטפילה אליו, וגרועה ממנו.

At stage 3 of *woman*'s **back-to-back relationship** with *man*, the crown of **her head reached to his chest** and their backs fused into

---

32. *Ari, Etz Chaim, Heichal Zeir Anpin, Shaar Nesira, 1.*

a common wall extending along the entire length of their contact, that is, from his chest to his feet.[33] Throughout this back-to-back arrangement **woman received all of her lights from man via this common wall.** In a back-to-back relationship, the stronger of the pair defines the front or forward direction, and the other, by default, becomes the tail or backside. When the disparity of strength is great, the "other" has no independent voice that can impact upon the decisions made and directions taken. This was the situation then, and, consequently *woman's* **identity was completely subordinate to** *man's* **will and authority.** Her only function was to serve his needs. For all these reasons **her stature was inferior to his.**

וכדי שתתתקן יותר לגמרי, שלא על ידו, צריך [לחתוך אותם והמעשה הראשונה היתח] שיסתלקו המוחין ממנו, וסילוק זה נקרא זה נקרא שינה, והבן זה.

In order for *woman* **to improve her condition and to develop herself completely and independently from** *man,* she needed to sever her backsided bond to him. The procedure by which their fused backsides were surgically uncoupled is called *nesira* (severing).

Man and *woman* are archetypes that exist in the highest spiritual world (*atzilut*),[34] whereas the Torah describes the unfolding of spirit onto the lowest physical plane. Nevertheless, the two are parallel and the biblical source for *nesira* appears in the story of Adam and Eve.[35]

---

33. Stage 3 begins with woman reaching to man's chest and ends with them equivalent, for although she still does not reach to his crown, his backside also does not manifest a crown.

34. See diagram called "Map of the Unfolding of Worlds," page 167.

35. Kabbalah explains that the first chapters of the Torah, until Adam and Eve's eating of the Tree of Knowledge, are actually not happening on the physical plane as we now experience it. Our level of materiality only came into being after their eating from the Tree of Knowledge of Good and Evil. Until then, the lowest level of reality (i.e., their physical plane) was the world of *briyah*, that is, the mental plane, or world of thought forms. See footnote 12 and its connected text.

The *midrash* teaches that the first human being was a kind of androgynous Siamese twin, with its male and female halves joined along their backs. Its interpretation derives from the verse: "And God created Adam in His own image, in the image of God He created him; male and female He created them."[36]

This back-to-back arrangement did not satisfy Adam's longing for a relationship of true encounter, and so *HaShem* severed their backsided bond, freeing them to meet face-to-face: "And God caused a deep sleep to fall upon the man, and he slept, and he took one of his sides and closed up the flesh in its place, and of the side which the Lord God had taken from the man, He made a woman, and brought her to the man."[37]

In this surgical-like procedure, the first step was to anesthetize the "patient": "And he caused a deep sleep to fall upon Adam."

This anesthetized state is called "deep sleep" because it is similar to what happens to the soul in sleep. **Man's faculties of conscious awareness (his "brains") withdrew,** and resituated themselves *above* his head, *beyond* his mind's grasp. **Consequently, *man* lapsed into an unconscious state similar to sleep.**

I. PRELIMINARIES

A. The source for these teachings is the talmudic story of sun and moon.
B. Holographic structure of the universe; every piece contains aspects of every other piece inside itself.
C. Unique relationship of *man* and *woman*, that together they comprise a single whole *partzuf*.
D. Defines moon.

II.
Summary of *man's* and *woman's* growth processes and interdependencies.

III.
Detailed examination of *woman's* path of development.

A. The two extremes of *woman's* cycle – the lowest she falls and the highest she rises.
B. Definition of front-to-front and back-to-back types of relationship that divide *woman's* growth process into two distinct phases of development.
C. Three stages of back-to-back progression, with man and woman bound together at their backside.
D. Surgical uncoupling, which releases *man* and *woman* to now meet face-to-face as free-standing individuals.
E. Four stages of front-to-front relationship.

36. Genesis 1:27.
37. Genesis 2:21–22.

כי קודם לכן היו אהוריים של שניהן כולם דינים, ולהיותן דינים, היו דבוקים
יחד, כי כולם כותל אחד להם.

Before the severing of their backsided union, **all the dark knots
of unactualized and unrectified potential in each of their souls
had collected at their rear quarters.** Consequently, the backs of
both *man* and *woman* became filled with the dense flecks of chaos
that Kabbalah calls *dinim*.

In the physical world, closeness means sharing neighborly
points in time and space. When two people are at the same address
at the same time, they are physically close. On the spiritual plane
closeness means affinity and similarity. Two people are close if they
are feeling the same emotion or thinking the same thought.

Similarly, ideas are "close" to each other when they are alike.
Since both *man's* and *woman's* **backsides were filled with these
dark knots of unactualized potential (*dinim*),** this became their
point of commonality, the place where they matched and even
overlapped. **Consequently, their backs, now effectively indis-
tinguishable, fused into a single wall of *dinim* that both joined
and divided them.**

ולכן הפיל עליו דורמיטא, ונסתלקו ממנו המוחין כנ"ל הנקרא שינה, ואז
נשמתו שהם המוחין שנסתלקו ממנו, היו מושכין לו חסד וחיות, אל ההוא
קיסטא דחיותא, שנשאר בתוכו בגוף בעת השינה, מן חסד דבינה, והיה
מתפשט בו בתוכו, ואז הדינין ואחוריים היו מסתלקין ונאחזין באחור
דנוקבא, ונפרדין זה מזה.

HaShem **caused a deep sleep to fall** upon *man*. This means **that
man's "brains," that is, his capacity for conscious self-awareness,
withdrew, and he entered** an unconscious, anesthetized **state
equivalent to sleep. His higher soul, though withdrawn,** maintained a thread of contact with him and **continued to provide
a flow of *chesed*-lights** (the opposite of *dinim*) **and general life
support to the residual traces of life and breath that remained in**

man's **unconscious body** (as is the case whenever the soul's light withdraws in sleep). **This flow** of life support **originated in *mother's chesed*** (חסד), her *sefirah* of expansive generosity, and consequently carried its energetic signature. These *chesed*-lights steadily accumulated in man, **spreading through his body** and building concentration. Soon they **entered his backside and displaced the *dinim* that were there, pushing them off to woman's** side of their shared wall. Eventually, his backside became filled with the *chesed*-lights that he received from *mother*, while *woman* now contained a double dose of *dinim*, those that were originally hers and those that were originally his.

Their backs now ceased to be alike: *man's* was filled with *chesed* and *woman's* with *dinim*. The law of affinity no longer bound them and **they fell apart,** re-emerging as separate and freestanding entities. Now they were free to reorient and, more important, to reunite on a whole other level of relationship where they could finally meet face-to-face.

...וְדַע כִּי אוֹתָן הַב׳ מוֹחִין, בִּינָה וּגְבוּרָה דז"א, שֶׁנִּסְתַּלְּקוּ
בִּנָה "י דְּבִינָה, הֵם שֶׁנִּכְנְסוּ בְּרֵישָׁא דְּנוּקְבָא מַמָּשׁ. כִּי
הַחָכְמָה וְהַהֲחָסָדִים, נִשְׁאֲרוּ בְּסוֹד מַקִּיף לז"א.

Before lapsing into anesthetic sleep, *man* contained all four *brains* (i.e., faculties of consciousness): intuitive insight (*chokhmah*), discriminating intelligence (*binah*), and the two subcomponents of knowing (*daat*), which are tenacity (*chesed*) and verbal skills (*gevurah*).[38] *Discriminating intelligence* and *verbal skills*, which associate with the left pillar of the Tree of Life,[39] are called feminine in expression; *intuitive insight* and *tenacity*, which lie along the right pillar, are masculine modes of intelligence.

The two feminine brains, **binah** (discriminating intelligence) **and** *gevurah* (verbal skills), **that withdrew from** *man*, **reabsorbed back into the womb area of** *mother*. **Now they were transferred directly to** *woman* by *mother* herself, and not via the intermediary of *man*, as was the mechanism when they were back-to-back. The two masculine brains, **chokhmah** (intuitive insight) **and** *chesed* (tenacity), remained connected to man but did not yet reintegrate into him. Rather, **they remained in a displaced and surrounding position** until *man* would awaken from his sleep.

This ends the passage on *nesira* (surgical uncoupling) and the text now continues with its discussion of the second half of the seven-stage sequence of *woman*'s development.

עוד יש ד' בחי' פב"פ, והם אלו:

Following the three stages of back-to-back relationship, *HaShem* severs *man* and *woman*'s bond of instinct, releasing them to find a more conscious, loving, mutual, and front-facing mode of rapport. **In** this new category of association called **front-to-front bonding,** *man* and *woman* evolve through **four stages of development** (which are really five).

---

38. These descriptive terms for the *sefirot* come from: R. Dov Ber of Lubovitch, *Shaar HaYichud* 1–4. *Daat* is the dynamic integration of the higher (mental plane) expressions of *chesed* (expansion) and *gevurah* (contraction). In *daat, chesed* expresses as tenacity and *gevurah* as verbal skills.
39. See diagram, page 20.

FRONT-TO-FRONT

STAGE 1A (4A)

והנה, בח' ראשונה שהוא תהיה ג"כ בח' נקודה א' כלולה
מי' כנגד היסוד פב"פ אין כאן מקום ביאורו ונתבאר
במ"א.

The first stage of front-to-front, paralleling stage 1 of back-to-back, is **where *woman* again collapses into a single point (containing ten), which sits at the lowest position possible, completely beneath man, yet this time front-to-front. This stage is not elaborated here but is discussed elsewhere.** Consequently, it is not presently counted as an official "stage" of the front-to-front sequence. If it were, there would be five.

It is appropriate to insert here an excerpt from that later chapter, which details *woman's* first front-to-front position:[40]

...שאחר שנגדלת אב"א אז חוזרת להיות נקודה קטנה
בפגים, פירוש הוא על אותו נקודה מבח' פנים שעדיין
בבח' פנים שלה אין לה רק נקודה...

After *woman* reaches her full stature of back-to-back, she separates from *man* (via the surgical procedure of *nesira*) and **reduces again to a shrunken point that is now facing toward man** instead of away from him. **Although she has entered** the more rectified mode of **front-to-front relationship, she herself has**

---

40. Ari, *Etz Chaim, Shaar Tikun Nukva* 1:2:8.

collapsed completely. From the full-length stature she attained in back-to-back development, **she reverts again to a single lowly point.** The only distinction between this and her diminished state is that now, **although but a point, she stands front-to-front.**

STAGE 1B (4B)

א' שתהיה היא פרצוף שלם פב"פ, אלא ששיעור קומתה הוא מחזה ולמטה דז"א, ועדיין אורות שלה דבחי' פנים שיש בה"ר של ז"א, לא נמשכו להאיר בה.

Woman is now a complete *partzuf* standing in front-to-front relationship with man. **However,** she is only half of full stature, **the crown of her head reaching to his chest.** She **receives the lights that** *man* **holds for her, that are within their area of overlap, that is, from the heart down.** However, the lights belonging to *woman* that are held in man's upper five *sefirot* (***crown*** [כתר], ***wisdom*** [חכמה], ***understanding*** [בינה], ***loving-kindness*** [חסד], **and** ***might*** [גבורה]) do not reach her, **but rather pass above her head. This is because he has not integrated them into his heart and lower body. He has not brought them down into the levels of himself that are actively in relationship with** *woman***, and consequently they do not pass to her.**

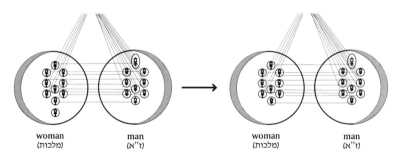

woman (מלכות)	man (ז"א)
woman (מלכות)	man (ז"א)

STAGE 2 (5)

הב', הוא הח"ר של ז"א, האירו בה מלמעלה, אבל עדיין היא מהחזה ולמטה
ואז הוא יורד בנצח שלו...

Here *woman* receives the lights that are held for her in *man*'s
upper five *sefirot*. He draws them down and they shine to her
from above. Nevertheless, she is still only half of full stature,
reaching to his chest. Man has thus succeeded in integrating them
into his lower *sefirot*.

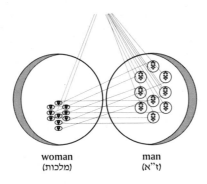

woman
(מלכות)

man
(ז"א)

STAGE 3 (6)

הג', שתהיה גדולה כמוהו, שיעור קומתו, פב"פ, ותקבל האורות של ה"ר
שם, בהיותה היא למעלה עמהם. ואמנם עדיין היא אינה מקבלת אורותיה,
אלא באמצעית ז"א, והכתר שלו יהיה גדול מכתרה, כי הוא יותר גדול וגבוה
למעלה מכתרה. נמצא שהמלכות שבה, אין לה בן זוג כנגדה בזכר, כי היא
למטה מן היסוד שלו, לכן היא צריכה לו, שהמלכות שבה היא למטה מכל
שיעור קומתו, ואז צריכה היא לקבל ע"י, ואז המלכות שלה אין לה בן זוג,
ונתעלה עד היסוד שבה עצמה, ונכללין יחד שם בסוד הכללות, כנודע
אצלינו, ואז תוכל לקבל מן היסוד של ז"א. ונמצא כי בבחי' זו, יש בה פרצוף
ט"ס שבה עליונות לבד, כי העשירית שבה, נכללת ביסוד שבה, ואז ג"כ
הכתר שלו גבוה מכתרה.

Here *woman* has attained her full stature. She is as tall as *man*
and they meet face-to-face. She now receives all of her lights

in their original form. *Man* no longer needs to bring them down to her reduced in quantity and quality, for her capacity to hold consciousness now equals his.

Nevertheless, she continues to need him as her intermediary. She still cannot draw lights directly from their source in *mother* **on her own. His crown continues to be larger than** (and consequently extends beyond) **hers. This means that her crown is still lower** than his.[41]

Woman's **lowest** *sefirah* (*malchut*) **extends below the bottom-most point of** *man's* **stature, which means that he does not "match" her there. Since she is completely dependent upon him as her intermediary, she must adapt herself** to the boundaries of his visual field and spiritual anatomy. Any parts of her extending beyond the perimeter of his stature would wither away from drought, for they have no alternative source of sustenance. Consequently, *woman* **withdraws her lowest** *sefirah,* **her** *malchut,* **up into her** *yesod,* like a telescope. **Now both her** *malchut* **and** *yesod* **stand opposite** *man's* **lowest** *sefirah,* **his** *yesod* **(for he has no** *malchut* **of his own) and receive their lights from there. At this stage, his crown is still greater than hers.**

---

41. Kabbalah distinguishes between two types of intermediaries: (1) the intermediary here acts as a simple channel that transfers lights from one place to another but does not alter them in any way. There is neither a qualitative or quantitative alteration; and (2) the intermediary can act as a transformer, actually integrating the original lights and reformulating them in a totally new and tempered expression that suits the capacity of the receiver. This can entail both quantitative and/or qualitative alterations.

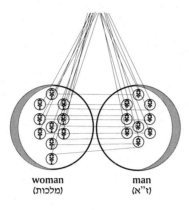

woman
(מלכות)   man
(ז"א)

STAGE 4 (7)

הד', שתהיה גם היא משמשת בכתר א' כמותו, ומקבלת אורותיה מאמא
עצמה, שלא ע"י ז"א דמיון או"א. ותהיה שלימה בכל י"ס. וזהו תכלית
הגידול שלה.

Man and *woman* now share a single crown. She receives her lights directly from *mother*, **not via *man*'s intermediary. Their relationship is like the model of *father and mother*** who are equal in stature, deeply bonded, yet independent. **She is complete in all her ten** *sefirot*. **This is the culminating stage of her development.**

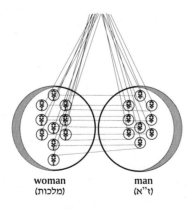

woman
(מלכות)   man
(ז"א)

DEBRIEFING

THE *DIMINISHED* MOON

What Do We Know?

1. *Woman* matures through a seven-step process of development that extends from the fourth day of creation through messianic times. Step by step, gradually through history, the feminine archetype builds into full stature. This same sequence transpires on a micro scale and its model serves as a rough sketch of the developmental course of each individual woman's life (depending upon where she stands along the continuum of gender).[42]

2. Each step not only marks a shift in *woman's self*-development but also (and perhaps primarily) a change in her relationship to *man.*

3. The fact that this seven-step process extends through history means that the feminine archetype is in constant flux. Consequently, gender expressions (and expectations) that applied at one period of history might not be appropriate for later points in the process, when *woman* has evolved to a whole different level of stature.

4. The primary distinguishing feature of each forward step in *woman's* development is an expansion and integration of intellect. The *sefirot* from below to above represent a continuum of consciousness from: instinctive emotions (*netzach, hod, yesod*), conscious emotions (*chesed, gevurah, tiferet*), intellect (*chokhmah, binah, daat*), and will (*keter*). When woman reaches to man's chest, the *sefirot* she is missing are those associated with intellect and conscious

---

42. See section called Gender Is Relative, p. 31.

emotion. The disparity between *man* and *woman* in these areas is constantly decreasing, and this, according to the *Ari*, is a predicted and positive development.

5. *Man's* work is to actively facilitate *woman's* development by providing her with the resources that she needs to build herself up in stature and intellect. *Man* must remember that many of the lights that seem to be part of his own stature are actually only temporary loans, which really belong to *woman*, and he must be willing to part with them when she comes of age and asserts her rightful claim.[43]

6. The situation today is more difficult than the odyssey of the moon's diminishment described herein. Its general pattern applies, but with one additional complication. The *Ari* teaches that the moon actually recovered nearly completely from her fall, only to collapse again, and this time more drastically, when Adam and Eve ate from the Tree of Knowledge of Good and Evil. Many of the lights that had previously been held in trust for her by *man* now tumbled into the *klipah* (the impure realms). This means that *woman's* recovery process now requires her to retrieve lights from two places:

   a. from *man*, who absorbed many of them back into himself when she fell this second time; and

   b. from the *klipot*, for every evil entraps a holy spark which provides it with life juice. The implications of this second category of fallen lights are not explored in this work.

7. *Woman's* seven-stage odyssey in relation to *man* is a mutually beneficial progression. *Man* wants to build *woman* up.

---

43. See section beginning on p. 70.

It is in his interests to do so, for he seeks to consummate his relationship with her, an act that only happens when they meet as equals.

8. Each step is defined as a positive development based on four criteria:

   a. Front-to-front relationship is preferred over back-to-back.

   b. *Woman* grows in height at each step, and the closer she comes to an equality of stature with *man*, the more perfected their relationship.

   c. Her forward progress is most essentially measured by an expansion of her intellectual capabilities.

   d. At each step *woman* becomes more self-reliant, moving toward the culminating point of her development, where she becomes completely independent of man's mediating assistance.

9. While the constant changes and adjustments entailed in *woman*'s evolutionary development may place stresses on social stability, the process itself is positive, it is part of the messianic vision, and its benefits will outweigh its costs. True and full encounter between *man* and *woman* is only possible when they meet as equals in stature and intellect. The satisfaction of consummate union will be worth the discomfort of its process.

10. The entire universe was affected by the moon's ordeal, for every sliver of the cosmos contains a piece of her inside itself. As long as the moon remains diminished, no single individual can achieve perfection. Consequently, a win-win situation prevails: Helping the *moon* build herself up will always feed back to benefit oneself.

11. *Man* and *woman* are enmeshed to a greater degree than

mother and *father*, for each literally holds pieces of the other inside itself:

- *Woman* is *man's malchut* and this entanglement is a permanent condition.
- *Man* holds the lights of *woman's* abstract intellect while she is still too diminished to contain them herself. This is not a permanent arrangement. Slowly, over time, he transfers them to her, and eventually she absorbs them completely.

12. The kabbalistic vision of the perfected relationship between *man* and *woman* is one that is:
- completely equal in stature
- face-to-face (i.e., deeply bonded union)
- with each drawing its own independent flow of light, bounty, and consciousness from above; neither being dependent upon the other to mediate between themselves and their transcendent flow of resources.

13. The surgical procedure called *nesira* (surgical uncoupling), which affects the transition from back-to-back into front-to-front, happens while *man* is asleep (i.e., lapsed into an unconscious state). This would seem to suggest that it is something that happens *to man*, and not necessarily something that he consciously participates in.

What Don't We Know?

1. We still don't know what is accomplished by the moon's diminishment. How does it serve the purpose of creation? If they are just going to come back around to "two kings ruling under one crown," why did the moon have to bear this ordeal of waning to arrive at the same place that she started?

2. What does "equality of stature" mean? How is it different

from being identical to each other? What will distinguish them?

3. What will *man*'s mature and idealized masculinity look like when he has passed *woman*'s lights back on to her? And similarly mature femininity, when she receives them and comes in to her fullness?

4. What do *woman*'s intellectual lights look like? How are they different from *man*'s intellect? How are they similar?

5. We don't know what stage we are in at the present, although we have some tools and principles from which to speculate.

6. We don't know how this translates into real life.

7. We don't have a rule of thumb to identify, on a practical level, which of the lights that *man* is holding actually belong to *woman* and which are fully his.

Logical Implications and Speculations

1. It is possible that many of the gender-associated traits that one considers typically male or female are only reflections of our transitional situation, in which *man* has been holding women's lights and, in the meantime, making use of them. It might be that many of the intellectual functions that *man* has been fulfilling (particularly the *binah*-associated ones, e.g., discriminating intelligence) will be transferred to *woman,* and the distribution of gender traits will then look very different from the way they appear in the present.

2. The effort of *tikun olam* is synonymous with repairing the moon, rectifying the feminine, and enabling *woman* to attain her perfection. Just as the former effort is continuous and ongoing, so is the latter.

3. What will keep *man* and *woman* bonded when she no longer needs his assistance to draw down her lights from above? What will keep her around and devoted? Until the seventh

stage, much of *man* and *woman*'s motivation to maintain a relationship comes from need: *man*'s need to be needed and *woman*'s need to be provided for. When these factors no longer apply, what will bind the couple together? This question, and its fear, no doubt underlies much resistance to the concrete changes in feminine expression observed today (and anticipated by the *Ari*). A not-irrational fear looms, that *woman*'s independence will result in a total breakdown of gender relations, for one very powerful incentive to marriage has been *woman*'s "need" to be married.

Similarly, *man*'s sense of worth and purpose is now often associated with his being "needed" to draw down the lights that *woman* cannot access on her own. Who will he become, what will his purpose be when she no longer needs him to perform this task? Triggered by all these transformations in *woman*'s stature is *man*'s fear of becoming obsolete.

R. Luria explains that *woman*'s ascension will not undermine gender relations but rather the opposite. For the first time *man* and *woman* will experience a consummate and pure union, motivated by love of the other alone, free of the self-interests that always slightly contaminate relationships of need. The couple's years of mutual devotion will have forged a bond that transcends need. In particular *man*'s generous commitment to building up *woman* by providing her with the resources she needs to grow into full stature binds her to him in love and trust and gratitude. If, instead, he begrudges her lights, refusing to assist her development, and hoards the resources for which he was only a temporary trustee … an adversarial relationship will develop between them, and her independence might, then, very well happen at the relationship's expense. *Man*'s challenge is to overcome his fear of not being needed, trust that *HaShem* has even greater blessings in store for him, and get on with his *chesed* work, which is to generously provide *woman* with the resources she needs to develop into full stature.

4

CONSTRICTION PRECEDES EXPANSE

The Woodgatherer Was Tslofchad

R. Yehuda Ashlag's Commentary on *Zohar* 3:157a

BARE BONES LITERACY

SUMMARY

The Woodgatherer Was Tslofchad explores one fascinating implication of R. Luria's seven-stage cycle of feminine development.
Each step does not proceed smoothly from the one before. Rather,
woman first develops a kind of false equality, collapses again quite
suddenly, and starts a new push toward growth and full stature,
which she eventually attains at the end of her effort. R. Ashlag
explores the difference between the false equality of her first phase
of development and the true equality that prevails in the end. His
teachings have intriguing implications for feminism today.

VOCABULARY

back-to-back relationship – An immature and self-absorbed mode of relating, in which neither partner ever really "sees" the other, except as an object whose sole purpose is to satisfy his or her own narcissistic needs. Adam and Eve's relationship before their *nesira* was back-to-back.

drash / midrash – Third level of biblical interpretation in the model of PaRDeS. Homiletical writings that explain the biblical text through the use of stories and sermons. The *midrash* often fills out a sparsely written biblical narrative providing background, context, moral lessons, or legal implications.

front-to-front relationship – A relationship of true and healthy love. The couple bonds from mutual desire and shared vision. This possibility of relationship only arises after *nesira*.

man and *woman* – Kabbalistic archetypes of male and female in their prime, as opposed to *father* and *mother*, which signify their later stages of life.

nesira (surgical uncoupling) – Tradition teaches that Adam and Eve were originally created as a single bi-gendered creature, with male and female halves fused together like Siamese twins. God then severed this bond, releasing them to meet face-to-face as freestanding individuals for the first time. This is how Jewish tradition interprets the biblical story of Eve's formation.

partzuf / partzufim – The set of six kabbalistic archetypes that coalesce into a family system, with each filling a unique role, for example: *father, mother, man, woman*. Equally frequently, these *partzufim* function as different "voices" or sub-personalities within a single individual.

pshat – The literal interpretation of scripture.

remez (hint) – References to less obvious teachings that are based on idiosyncrasies in syntax or language.

sod (secret) – Kabbalah. The mystical teachings embedded within scriptural text.

The *Ari* – R. Isaac Luria (1534–1572). Master kabbalist who wrote the previous essay that presents the seven stages of woman's life cycle upon which this (and all subsequent pieces) are based.

Tree of Knowledge of Good and Evil – The forbidden tree in Eden that represents a fallen state of consciousness, in which truth is twisted by emotional attachments and narcissistic needs.

Tree of Life – One of two trees at Eden's center and mentioned in Genesis 2:9. To eat from the Tree of Life is to extract the spark of eternal spirit from each moment by acting according to God's will. One who ate only from the Tree of Life would not die.

SYNOPSIS

THE WOODGATHERER WAS TSLOFCHAD

In this essay R. Yehuda Ashlag, called the *Sulam* (meaning "ladder," after his annotated translation of the *Zohar* by that name), explores a fascinating implication of the *Ari*'s seven-stage model of feminine development. He examines the pros and cons of one type of *woman*'s liberation by comparing the dignified independence that *woman* attains at the end of her back-to-back sojourn versus her reduced and dependent status after turning front-to-front. He focuses particularly on the most dramatic interval of *woman*'s development – the period immediately preceding and immediately following her surgical uncoupling from *man* (stages 3–4a).

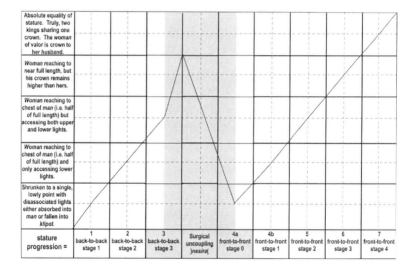

What persuades *woman* to take the plunge (literally) and trade in her self-sufficient equality for abject diminishment? The losses are obvious, but what are her gains? There must be some hidden incentive that motivates her cooperation.

The excerpt here translated is extremely complex, for it builds on several layers of teachings that are not obviously related except via their connection to R. Ashlag's line of thought. A *midrash* fuses two previously distinct biblical stories, the *Zohar* adds a mystical interpretation, and R. Ashlag elaborates with kabbalistic commentary. Both R. Ashlag and the *Zohar* (upon which he comments) assume a conversancy with sources such that a single word suffices to conjure a whole bouquet of associated ideas that are critical to the full and seasoned understanding of the text. A brief review of the following sources aims to accomplish a similar end:

- First, is the original story of the daughters of Tslofchad (Numbers 27:1–8), which, on the surface, is but a tangential source, but whose woman-centered theme permeates the entire discussion and sets its tone.
- Next is the story of the woodgatherer (Numbers 15:32–36), which is the explicit passage upon which the *Zohar* comments.
- A *midrash* (TB, *Shabbat* 96b) then joins these two stories by identifying the woodgatherer as Tslofchad, the father whose daughters appear in the first passage in the original story. The *midrash* bases itself on a hint in the text.
- The *Zohar* (3:157a) interprets that same hint to indicate that the woodgatherer's sin entailed some kind of insult to the *partzuf man* and to Shabbat. It does not elaborate.
- R. Ashlag then brings the *Ari*'s teachings on the diminished moon to elucidate the metaphysical underpinnings of the *Zohar*'s comments.

Let us examine these five threads in more detail, clarifying their respective contributions to the thematic structure of the piece and to the ladder of PaRDeS.

Pshat (Sod) – Daughters of Tslofchad

The story of the daughters of Tslofchad, along with its midrashic explications, presents an extraordinary example of women as active, intelligent, and welcomed participants in a legal discussion affecting their lives.[1] Its uncontroversial status in the tradition is especially noteworthy, given the unusual expression of femininity it depicts.

The story is as follows: When the Jews approached their promised land, they began to plot out the distribution of territory based on tribal claims and family divisions. Each of the 600,000 heads-of-household who left Egypt were to receive a portion of real estate in the land of Israel, which would become their family's legacy. The laws of inheritance limited the transfer of property to males, but a man named Tslofchad died leaving only daughters. What should be done with his plot? All assumed that it would pass to his closest male relatives, that is, his brothers, and be absorbed into their respective legacies. Yet Tslofchad's daughters did not want their father to lose his rightful portion in the land as a bequeathal to his own direct lineage. They petitioned Moshe, asking to possess their father's portion themselves, despite the law's apparent preclusion of female inheritors.

They received unqualified praise for their action and prevailed in their claim:

> God spoke to Moshe saying, "The daughters of Tslofchad have a just claim. Give them a hereditary portion of land alongside their father's brothers. Let their father's hereditary property thus pass over to them. Speak to the Israelites and tell them that if a man dies and has no sons, his hereditary property shall pass over to his daughter."[2,3]

---

1. See Susan Schneider, "The Daughters of Tslofchad, toward a Methodology of Attitude around Women's Issues," in Ora Wiskind-Alper and Susan Handelman (eds.), *The Torah of the Mothers* (Jerusalem: Urim Publications, 2000).
2. Translation by Aryeh Kaplan, *The Living Torah*.
3. Numbers 27:1–8.

Every commentary, without exception, compliments the daughters on their wisdom, righteousness, and learned intelligence. When *HaShem* informed Moshe that the law followed their petition, He let it be known that their insight reached to the heavenly throne and revealed a truth that Moshe, himself, did not see.[4,5]

The implications of their story go very deep. Besides its positive example of women having profound impact on the inner workings of Jewish law, and besides the unparalleled distinction of their revealing an actual mitzvah of the Torah that Jews have practiced from that time on, the actual content of their issue and its practical resolution bursts with metaphysical significance.

In the *Ari*'s seven-stage sequence of feminine development, he identifies a dramatic shift that occurs when *woman* passes into her last phase of growth (stage 7). At all other levels (except for a moment at the end of her back-to-back sequence, stage 3),[6] *woman* is not able to draw her own light, bounty, and consciousness from above. This inability makes her dependent upon *man*. She needs him to pull down the resources that belong to her but that she cannot access directly on her own. She is "shorter" than he and cannot reach them by herself. This dependency is a temporary condition. It decreases from stage to stage and eventually ceases entirely. A distinguishing feature of *woman*'s culminating maturity (stage 7) is her total self-sufficiency in this regard. Until *woman* attains this

---

4. Rashi on Numbers 27:7; *Targum Yonatan* 27:7; *Yalkut Shimoni, Pinchas* 27; *Sifri*, Numbers 27:7.

5. There are various opinions about whether Moshe, in fact, knew the judgment but chose to consult God directly on the matter for other reasons (*Midrash Rabbah, Bereshit* 21:14, *Targum Yonatan* 27:5, *Torah Temima* 27:5). But regardless of whether Moshe knew the judgment already, God wanted the ruling to come down in the daughters' merit, and so the matter was held suspended until they initiated its discussion.

6. See pp. 81–83.

perfection, she has not realized God's highest will for her (or for them as a couple).

This promised ideal, says *Heichal HaBracha*,[7] is symbolically achieved by the daughters of Tslofchad when they acquire a portion of the Holy Land directly, as their own personal possession, and not via the agency of spouse or father, as is usually the case.

The story of the daughters of Tslofchad, with all its layers of metaphysical resonance, is the latent content of the entire discussion. Its looming implications exert their subliminal influence on all that follows.

Pshat – Woodgatherer

The woodgatherer appears in the Bible as an unidentified man who desecrates Shabbat by performing one of its prohibited activities in public.[8] The last of the thirty-nine categories of restricted "work" on Shabbat forbids the carrying of objects from place to place in a public domain.

Perhaps because the spiritual survival of the Jewish people depends so essentially upon their observance of Shabbat, the desecration of its sanctity, according to Kabbalah, corrupts the soul at its deepest levels.[9] And when the violation is public, the souls of all who witness the act are also injured in some subtle way. The punishments prescribed by the Torah are not arbitrary. Rather, each is perfectly sculpted to mend the damage of its initiating transgression. Consequently, the public desecration of Shabbat carries a sentence of death, for no other penalty can reach the insidious decay that is its particular mark.

In this instance, however, several ameliorating factors confounded the judgment. According to one opinion, the woodgath-

---

7. *Heichal HaBracha* (*The Chamber of Blessing*), Numbers 27:5.
8. Numbers 15:32–36.
9. R. Chaim Vital, *Shaari Kedusha* (*The Gates of Holiness*), 2:6.

erer was a zealot who purposely broke the law in order that others should see him stoned to death and be shocked into taking their own religious commitments more seriously.[10] For various reasons, the people of his generation had started to question whether the full weight of obligation still applied to them. The woodgatherer wanted to convey the truth, in no uncertain terms, that as long as they lived they were fully beholden to the Torah and to all of its dictates.

For this and other reasons, Moshe was unsure of what penalty applied and sought heavenly guidance. *HaShem* sentenced the woodgatherer to death by stoning, and so it was.

Remez – Drash

The *midrash* exposes the identity of this anonymous woodgatherer who desecrated Shabbat, although the Bible makes no mention of his name. R. Akiva derives it from a hint that appears in a later chapter when Tslofchad's daughters petition Moshe to inherit their father's land. They begin with the words: "Our father died ... in his *own* sin," thereby distinguishing his death from other occasions where people died from transgression. Throughout their desert wanderings, many plagues befell the Israelites, each instigated by a collective trespass, lapse of faith, or gross ingratitude. The daughters were communicating to Moshe that their father did not die in any of those plagues: his sin was not of their coarse variety. Rather, the daughters explain, "he died ... from his *own* transgression."

By a process of elimination, R. Akiva proves that he was the woodgatherer and divulges his name.[11] An explicit link is thus forged between the man whose female progeny set the precedent of "inheriting daughters," with the man who gathered wood on Shabbat and was penalized with death.

---

10. *Moshav Zekanim, Bava Batra* 119b.
11. TB, *Shabbat* 96b.

Sod – Zohar

The *Zohar* is a mystical commentary on the Torah. It follows the
Bible's order of books and chapters, yet reveals a reservoir of won-
drous teachings that are not usually visible to uninitiated readers.
The *Zohar* elaborates upon the previous *midrash*, which identifies
the woodgatherer as Tslofchad. By reinterpreting several key words,
it exposes an entirely new landscape of metaphysical content.

The *Zohar* notes that the word for "gather" also means "to
compare," and the word for "wood" also means "trees." It concludes
that Tslofchad was not really "gathering wood" but actually "comparing trees." What could this possibly mean? It answers that he
was comparing the Tree of Life (which corresponds to *man*) with
the Tree of Knowledge (which corresponds to *woman*). He was
questioning the hierarchy of values, status, and moral judgments
that derive from these symbolic trees, that pose as absolutes when
perhaps, in fact, they are not.

The *Zohar* concludes, based on further analysis, that Tslofchad's
questioning was not benign. His inquiry unleashed profound
metaphysical consequences that shook *man* and *woman* to their
core and actually caused them harm.

Sod – R. Yehuda Ashlag

R. Ashlag further identifies the *Zohar*'s two "trees" with two modes
of feminine expression explicated by the *Ari*. He associates the Tree
of Knowledge with *woman* in her culminating state of back-to-back
relationship, where she stands at full stature, equal, opposite, and
independent of *man* (stage 3). R. Ashlag calls this *mode A*. When
HaShem dissolves their backsided bond, *woman* immediately collapses back into the shrunken point that is her maximally diminished state, yet now she is oriented front-to-front (stage 4a). R.
Ashlag associates this with the Tree of Life and what he calls *mode
B*. *Woman*'s universe turns upside down when she takes the step

from *A* to *B*. Quantitatively, she loses everything, yet qualitatively she gains the possibility of real relationship, an option that only arises when both partners can meet face-to-face.

Tslofchad's sin was that he seriously considered ascribing preference to *woman* in her back-to-back mode of expression when she is fully extended and self-contained, despite the fact that she faces away from *man* and lives her life without need of him. Perhaps *woman* should cleave to her equality of stature, for it is certainly more dignified to stand at full height than crumpled up into a shrunken point.

Tslofchad's reasoning was flawed because his cost-benefit equation failed to incorporate the qualitative factors that, though less tangible, are equally relevant. If equality of stature were the only virtue, his conclusions would be foregone. Yet other powerful strivings operate here that actually override these more obvious considerations.

This, explains R. Ashlag, was Tslofchad's blunder. He underestimated the superiority of front-to-front relationship over back-to-back. In stage 3 *woman* is completely self-sufficient – drawing her own independent flow of light, bounty, and consciousness direct from Above, she has no need of *man*. And yet, since she has no need, there is no chemistry between them. In these phases of relationship (i.e., until stage 7) her need is the glue that binds *man* and *woman* together with sufficient strength to overcome the repulsive forces always present when two egos attempt to merge.

Consequently, while this mode provides her with a full and equal stature, an active and expanded intellect, and the dignity that associates with all this, the hidden cost is that she remains barren. Without need, and its chemistry of attraction, *man* and *woman* do not join in generative union. For *woman*, the toll of not bearing children is an impossible price to pay.

This is the incentive that lures *woman* to endure another cycle of diminishment. And yet, from this shrunken point (stage 4a), she builds herself back up into a full stature that eventually even surpasses the peak of back-to-back attainment. At the end of her journey she reaps the best of both worlds. Her initial investment of self-sacrifice bears a richer and more satisfying equality than was possible in her back-facing orientation. Now she has children, a consummately satisfying marriage, *and* full equality; whereas before, the latter came at the expense of the former.

Tslofchad's problem was his limited horizons. His vision extended only to the sixth of *woman's* seven-stage process. As far as he could see, she would always remain dependent upon *man* and "less" than him. Without knowledge of *woman's* crowning achievement at stage 7, and without incorporating the critical factor of children, his aversion to diminishment makes sense.

But with these additional considerations his conclusions become dangerous. The cost-benefit picture he paints is liable to convince women to stick to their full-statured, stage 3 equality and resist inducements to diminish. From his myopic perspective, women have only to lose by accepting the constriction that inheres in their next step.

There is no doubt that Tslofchad's intentions were sincere and that he truly sought to honor women and to affirm their inherent dignity, equality, and self-sovereignty. And yet, it is women who lose by heeding his advice – by cleaving to back-to-back equality and fixating there. This brand of liberation comes at the expense of children and a love-based relationship, sacrifices that need not be made.

Diminishment is a temporary state, and yet, for some mysterious reason, a necessary one. Before diminishment, two kings could not share one crown; afterward they can (and will). For reasons discussed in later chapters, diminishment initiates a process that culminates in *woman's* full, relational, and generative equality (in

contrast to her ultimately unsatisfying achievements of stage 3).
Though it looks like *woman* loses (and she does in the short term),
the last scene (stage 7) will reframe all that preceded it and make
all her sacrifices worth their while. It will be perfectly clear that
the gains of consummated equality unquestionably outweigh the
costs of self-diminishment that enabled it.

ANNOTATED TRANSLATION
THE WOODGATHERER WAS TSLOFCHAD

R. Yehuda Ashlag's Commentary on *Zohar* 3:15 7a

While the Israelites were in the desert **they discovered a man
gathering sticks on the Sabbath.** The ones who found him
gathering sticks brought him to Moshe and Aaron and the
entire community. Since it was not specified what must be
done to him they placed him under guard.

And God said to Moshe, "That man must die. Let the entire
community pelt him with stones outside the camp." The entire
community took him outside the camp and they pelted him
to death with stones. It was done as God had commanded
Moshe.[12]

ZOHAR

אמר רבי חייא כתיב וימצאו איש מקושש עצים ביום השבת. מאן עצים הכא
ומאן הוא דא אלא דא צלפחד.

Rabbi Chiya asks two questions on the bolded verse from the
passage above: "**And they discovered a man gathering sticks
on the Sabbath.**" **What were those sticks, and who was that**

---

12. Numbers 15:32–36.

man? He answers that the woodgatherer was **Tslofchad**, the man whose daughters later approached Moshe and asked to inherit their father's portion of the Holy Land, despite the tradition that hereditary property only passes through sons.

> A petition was presented by the daughters of Tslofchad... saying, "Our father died in the desert. He was not among the members of Korach's party who protested against God, but he died of his own sin, without leaving any sons. Why should our father's name be disadvantaged in his family merely because he had no son? Give us a portion of land along with our father's brothers." Moshe brought their case before God.
>
> God spoke to Moshe saying, "The daughters of Tslofchad have a just claim. Give them a hereditary portion of land alongside their father's brothers. Let their father's hereditary property thus pass over to them. Speak to the Israelites and tell them that if a man dies and has no sons, his hereditary property shall pass over to his daughter.[13],[14]

[מקושש, פירושו היה מקיש ומשווה העצים][15]

Furthermore, the word for "sticks" also means "trees," **and the word for "gather"** derives from the verb *to compare* (להקיש). With these substitutions the original verse now reads, "And they found a man **comparing (and equating)** two **trees** on Shabbat." Rabbi Chiya's second question then becomes: "What were those trees that Tslofchad was analyzing, and what was he trying to figure out?"

---

13. Translation by Aryeh Kaplan, *The Living Torah.*
14. Numbers 27:1–8.
15. This line is pulled from later commentary but is inserted here for clarity's sake.

[עצים פירושו ב' העצים שהם עץ החיים שהוא ז"א ועץ הדעת שהוא
הנוקבא].[16]

Once the question is stated thus, the answer is obvious. The **"trees"** under scrutiny can be none other than the famous two that were mentioned in the second chapter of Genesis, **the Tree of Life** and **the Tree of Knowledge of Good and Evil.**

The former **is identified with** the Written Torah and corresponds to **the *partzuf man.*** Its associations are always good. To "eat" from the Tree of Life is to partake of the world in a way that serves God through self-nullification. At any moment one is willing to die for truth, to sacrifice one's ego on the altar of divine service.

The Tree of Knowledge has more complicated associations. It **corresponds to** the Oral Torah and the *partzuf woman.* The Oral Torah, in its broadest sense, includes all the wisdoms and insights pressed from the hearts of Jews who struggle to live lives of integrity on whatever level of halachic observance they may currently practice. "There is no truth except Torah."[17] A person who discovers a new insight, whether from the school of hard knocks or an interpretation of scripture, generates a new piece of the Oral Tradition, for if it is true, then it is Torah. This Tree is identified with

I.
Biblical story of the woodgatherer; who was he and what was he doing? The *Zohar* answers by . . .

A. redefining "gather" as "compare";
B. redefining "wood" as "trees";
C. reformulating his sin as an offense against *man* and Shabbat.

II.
R. Ashlag equates these two trees with two modes of feminine expression that correspond to stages 3 and 4a of the *Ari's* sequence.

III.
R. Ashlag explicates the woodgatherer's sin against *man* and Shabbat based on these two modes of feminine expression.

IV.
A. The sin's implications for *woman.* The woodgatherer's name (Tslofchad) hints to the secret of his error and his sin.
B. Where did Tslofchad go wrong? What was the flaw in his reasoning? He sought to elevate *woman* but damaged her instead.
C. The dangers inherent in his sin.
D. Woman's rectified path requires the diminishment that Tslofchad sought to avoid.

---

16. This line is pulled from later commentary but is inserted here for clarity's sake.
17. TY, *Rosh HaShana* 3:8.

Knowledge of Good and Evil because it includes wisdom acquired through wrong choices as well as right ones.

והוה דייק על אלין אילנין, הי מנייהו רב על אחרא.

Tslofchad was trying to determine which of these "trees" is the greater one. Party line says the Tree of Life is always greater than the Tree of Knowledge. A perfect record is certainly better than one riddled with errors. There is no option but to choose right, avoid failure, and evade sin.

Yet there are also teachings that hint to a more mysterious truth: that knowledge acquired through the clumsy process of stumbling, purgation, and repentance may penetrate more deeply into the soul than that acquired through more passive means. For example, the *Gemara* teaches: "In the place where a fully transformed sinner stands even a perfectly righteous *tzaddik* cannot reach,"[18] and "No person can fully integrate a teaching of Torah unless he has first stumbled over it."[19]

Suspending party line, Tslofchad proceeded to explore his question without moral preconditions: On the deepest, most mysterious level, which of these two paths is quantitatively superior? Which accomplishes the greatest *tikun*? Which mode of service ultimately furthers God's purpose the most? This is what it means that Tslofchad was "comparing trees."

ולא חשש ליקרא דמאריה ואחלף שבת לשבת.

His inquiry drew censure on two counts:

a. **He disrespected his Master,** that is, the *partzuf man.* Whether this insult derived from the way he conducted his inquiry, the conclusions he reached, or the mere fact of it, remains unclear.

---

18. TB, *Brachot* 24b.
19. TB, *Gittin* 43a.

b. **He substituted one Shabbat with another.**

Both points beg explanation.

הה"ד כי בחטאו מת בחטא ו' מת.

Rabbi Chiya derives Tslofchad's identity, and his heresy, by mid-rashic analysis. When Tslofchad's daughters approached Moshe with their petition, they said, concerning their father, "**He died in his sin.**" The Hebrew word for the phrase "in his sin" (בחטאו) can be broken down into three parts (ב חטא ו):

> ב – means *in, through, because of.*
>
> חטא – means *sin.*
>
> ו – means *his.*

Midrashic analysis permits one to translate these three elements less literally, in which case the word could also read "in his sin against the letter ו (בחטא ו')". In this translation the ו' at the end of the word no longer means "his" and instead becomes the object of his sin. The entire verse now reads, "**Because of his sin against the letter** ו [our father] died."

As clearly illustrated in the Tree of Life diagram (page 20), each of the *partzufim* corresponds to one of the letters of God's most holy name, called the Tetragammaton (ה/ו/ה/י):

> *father* corresponds to י',
>
> *mother* to the first ה',
>
> *man* to ו', and
>
> *woman* to the second ה'.

Consequently, a sin against the letter ו' is a sin against the *partzuf* man, which corresponds to the letter ו'.

בגין כך, הוה דיניה סתים, ולא אתפרש דיניה, כדינין אחרנין. בגין דמלה דא בעי בחשאי וסתים ולא גלייא, וע"ד לא אתמר באתגלייא וקב"ה עבד יקר ליקריה.

Because of the delicate **nature** of Tslofchad's sin (as will be explained) Moshe and Aaron were **unsure how to handle the case, as the passage itself states,** "Since it was not specified what must be done to him they placed him under guard."

Rabbi Chiya further explains that **the details** of Tslofchad's case, **and the calculations** behind his sentencing, **were** deliberately **concealed from the public. This** suppression of information **was** highly **irregular. In all other legal encounters, full disclosure** was always forthcoming. **In contrast, this incident was cloaked in secrecy; it was never discussed openly and explicitly.** Rabbi Chiya ends with the statement that "*HaShem* **attached honor to His honor,**" but does not specify who or what this refers to.

THE COMMENTARY OF
R. YEHUDA ASHLAG

פירוש. כי יש בנוקבא ב' מצבים, מצב א' כשהוא גדולה כמו ז"א, כלומר ששניהם במדרגה אחת, שז"א מלביש קו ימין דבינה והנוקבא מלבשת קו שמאל דבינה ואז אינה בזווג עם ז"א, כי מקבלת הכל מבינה,ואינה צריכה לז"א.

Binah is the *mother* that gestates and births both *man* and *woman.* And once they are born, she extends herself below by generating a whole new increment of *sefirot,* reduced in intensity, that emanate down into her children's more infantile world. In this way a part of her remains inside them, nurturing their emotional and intellectual growth.

The *partzuf woman* assumes two postures of relationship with *man,* called back-to-back and front-to-front,[20] and both span several stages of development. Rav Ashlag reduces each to its most exaggerated form and equates them to Tslofchad's trees. *Mode A*[21]

---

20. See Chapter 3, "The Small Light to Rule by Night."
21. *Mode A* corresponds to stage 3 of the *Ari's* back-to-back sequence of feminine development. See pp. 81–82.

is *woman* standing back-to-back with *man,* **at full height, equal, and opposite to him.** In this posture **he enclothes the right pillar of** *binah* **and she enclothes the left.**

In this arrangement, *man* and *woman* do not face each other and **no relationship of intimacy develops between them.** In *mode A* **woman is completely self-sufficient. Drawing her own independent flow of light, bounty, and consciousness direct from** *mother,* **she has no need of man.** And since she has no need, there is no chemistry between them. *Her* need is the glue that binds *man* and *woman* together with sufficient strength to overcome the repulsive forces always present when two egos attempt to merge. R. Ashlag identifies *mode A* with the Tree of Knowledge of Good and Evil.

ומצב ב', אחר המיעוט, שחזרה לבחינת נקודה תחת
היסוד דז"א, ונבנית משם לפרצוף שלם פב"פ עם ז"א
אומנם נחשבת כבר למדרגה תחתונה מז"א, ששורשה
בנקודת החזה דז"א.

Mode B of feminine expression **is post-diminishment** (stage 4a). After severing her back-to-back relationship with *man,* **woman collapses again to a single point,** occupying the lowest position possible, **completely beneath** *man.* Yet though her stature is profoundly diminished relative to the height it had attained by the end of her back-to-back sojourn, this point (though but a point) is now oriented front-to-front. The qualitative advantage of front-to-front relationship must be weighed against the quantitative loss of collapsing down

I.

Biblical story of the woodgatherer; who was he and what was he doing? The *Zohar* answers by . . .

A. redefining "gather" as "compare";

B. redefining "wood" as "trees";

C. reformulating his sin as an offense against *man* and Shabbat.

II.

R. Ashlag equates these two trees with two modes of feminine expression that correspond to stages 3 and 4a of the *Ari's* sequence.

III.

R. Ashlag explicates the woodgatherer's sin against *man* and Shabbat based on these two modes of feminine expression.

IV.

A. The sin's implications for *woman.* The woodgatherer's name (Tslofchad) hints to the secret of his error and his sin.

B. Where did Tslofchad go wrong? What was the flaw in his reasoning? He sought to elevate *woman* but damaged her instead.

C. The dangers inherent in his sin.

D. Woman's rectified path requires the diminishment that Tslofchad sought to avoid.

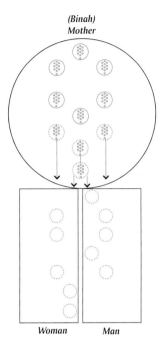

from a full-sized stature into a single point. R. Ashlag identifies the Tree of Life with *mode B* and the union with *man* enabled by her diminution.

From this extremely constricted **state**, with *woman* collapsed into a single lowly point beneath *man* yet oriented front-to-front, **she begins her journey of self-development.** The *Ari* identifies four ascending stages, **culminating in a full-statured union of equals.** Yet since stage 7 will not be realized until the messianic end of days, R. Ashlag presents stage 6 as *woman*'s highest attainment, since it does happen in this world, at least on Shabbat. And here, although she is but a hair's breadth from full equality, **because she derives from the midpoint of *man*'s *partzuf*,** even when she attains an equal stature, **she remains conceptually lower than he.**[22]

---

22. This is a complicated idea. For more information, see *Daat Elokim*, 93–137.

ומצב א', הנוקבא בפרודה מז"א והיא באחורים ומלאה דינים. ומצב הב' היא
מלאה בכל השלמות.

In *mode A* **woman** is connected to *man*, yet **separate from him.** They are bound along their fused backsides yet face away from each other. Consequently, in their conscious lives, they stand apart. **Woman occupies the back** of their joint stature, enclothing the left pillar of severity. **Consequently, the** dark knots of unactualized potential (*dinim*) **collect** on her side and **she becomes filled with them.** Conversely, in *mode B,* even while still incomplete, **she is filled** instead **with all manner of perfection.**

וביום השבת היא בזיווג עם ז"א פנים בפנים ומלבישים
לאו"א עלאין. והחטא של צלפחד היה,שביום השבת
שז"א ונוקבא הם בתכלית קומתם פנים בפנים היה הוא
מקושש עצים פירושו ב' העצים שהם עץ החיים שהוא
ז"א, והעץ הדעת שהוא הנוקבא. מקושש, פירושו היה
מקיש ומשווה העצים. שהם ז"א ונוקבא שיהיו שום
זה לזה, כמו שהיתה הנוקבא במצב הא'. ונמצא בזה
שהפריד הנוקבא מזיווג פב"פ עם ז"א שביום השבת
והחזירה לפירוד ואחורים כמו שהיתה במצב הא'. ולא
עוד אלא שהחשיב מצב הא' של הנוקבא על בחינת
הזיווג דפנים בפנים שביום השבת, כי דחה זיווג הזה
דפב"פ והחזיר הנוקבא לפירוד ואחורים ובזה עשה
פגם גדול במדרגת ז"א, ובכל מדרגת השבת, כי החשיב
האחורים דנוקבא יותר מפב"פ של ז"א ... שהיה רוצה
להחזיר הנוקבא למצב א', והתבונן לדעת אם מצב הא'
והפרודא של נוקבא אינה חשובה יותר מפב"פ של ז"א.

I.
Biblical story of the woodgatherer; who was he and what was he doing? The *Zohar* answers by . . .
A. redefining "gather" as "compare";
B. redefining "wood" as "trees";
C. reformulating his sin as an offense against *man* and Shabbat.

II.
R. Ashlag equates these two trees with two modes of feminine expression that correspond to stages 3 and 4a of the *Ari's* sequence.

III.
R. Ashlag explicates the woodgatherer's sin against *man* and Shabbat based on these two modes of feminine expression.

IV.
A. The sin's implications for *woman*. The woodgatherer's name (Tslofchad) hints to the secret of his error and his sin.
B. Where did Tslofchad go wrong? What was the flaw in his reasoning? He sought to elevate *woman* but damaged her instead.
C. The dangers inherent in his sin.
D. Woman's rectified path requires the diminishment that Tslofchad sought to avoid.

On Shabbat the cosmic spheres align, channels open, and a burst of holy light fills the world. Knowledge of God trickles down from souls into bodies and all life-forms raise to levels beyond themselves. The world, for these moments, leaves ordinary reality behind, glimpses perfection, and even touches it.

Similarly for *man* and *woman*. Whatever might be her current level of development, **on Shabbat *woman*** flowers into a full-statured (stage 6) *partzuf* and **enters a nearly consummate front-to-front union with *man*** (she enclothing *mother* and he enclothing *father*).

Tslofchad's sin was that on Shabbat itself, in the midst of this sweet and **nearly consummate union between *man* and *woman*, he obtusely proceeded to "compare trees"** (i.e., the Tree of Life and the Tree of Knowledge) and his jarring intrusion broke their mood. **Dispassionately, he examined** *mode A* and *mode B* of feminine expression, analyzing their respective attributes, **equating them,** contrasting them, trying to determine which was preferable from *woman*'s perspective. In *mode A woman* is equal and opposite to *man*, in *mode B* she is subordinate.

Tslofchad seriously considered the possibility of ascribing preference to *woman* in *mode A*, because of her equality of stature, despite the fact that she stands with her back to *man* and lives her life without need of him.

His analysis and its timing (apparently, independent of its conclusions) **poisoned the Shabbat union between man and woman,** splitting them apart. They reverted to *mode A*, she manifesting as a full *partzuf* facing away from man, and he from her. **Whatever his final conclusion, since the de facto effect of his analysis was to replace union with separation,** it is *as if* he gave **preference to the latter,** no matter what he was actually going to conclude. **His overvaluation of *woman* in her back-facing state of separation (*mode A*) injured *man* and marred the pristine sweetness of Shabbat.**

This is what the *Zohar* means when it says that Tslofchad was carefully analyzing these two *trees*, trying to determine which was greater. **Perhaps *woman* should cleave to her *mode A* position, separate but equal to man, for despite its back-to-back orientation it seems more** dignified for her to manifest as a full *partzuf* than as a shrunken point. **And even in the best of times, that is, Shabbat, she never attains full equality in *mode B*,** at least as far as he could see.

ולא חשש ליקרא דמאריה, פירושו ולא איכפת לו
שמבזה בזה כבוד ז"א, ואחלף שבת לשבת, כלומר
שהחליף חשיבות הגדול של זיווג פב"פ ביום השבת, על
בחינת שבת של חול שהיא הג"ר דאחורים של הנוקבא
שבמצב הא' שה"ס עצה"ד טוב ורע.

The *Zohar* criticizes Tslofchad in strong terms: "His tactless inquiry disrespected his Master (for he didn't consider the insulting implications it would have for *man*)[23] and he substituted Shabbat for Shabbat" (inverting their traditional hierarchy of correspondence).

A distinguishing feature of our universe is its holographic properties. Every piece contains aspects of every other piece inside itself. Every man contains aspects of woman, every woman contains aspects of man. Every evil contains at least a trace of good and every good contains a trace of evil. Similarly, embedded within each weekday is a spark of Shabbat and each Shabbat contains a spark of weekday light.

I.
Biblical story of the woodgatherer; who was he and what was he doing? The *Zohar* answers by . . .

A. redefining "gather" as "compare";
B. redefining "wood" as "trees";
C. reformulating his sin as an offense against *man* and Shabbat.

II.
R. Ashlag equates these two trees with two modes of feminine expression that correspond to stages 3 and 4a of the *Ari*'s sequence.

III.
R. Ashlag explicates the woodgatherer's sin against *man* and Shabbat based on these two modes of feminine expression.

IV.
A. The sin's implications for *woman*. The woodgatherer's name (Tslofchad) hints to the secret of his error and his sin.
B. Where did Tslofchad go wrong? What was the flaw in his reasoning? He sought to elevate *woman* but damaged her instead.
C. The dangers inherent in his sin.
D. Woman's rectified path requires the diminishment that Tslofchad sought to avoid.

23. The aspect of God that we primarily relate to as *HaShem* is the *partzuf man*, the source of *HaShem*'s providential flow of justice. Ramchal, *Daat Tevuna* (DT) 135–146; ibid., *Clalei Chokhmat HaEmet* (CCH), 34, p. 22a.

Rav Ashlag explains that *mode B of feminine expression cor-responds to Shabbat* in the weekday cycle: work stops, holy light suffuses creation, **and *man* and *woman* come together in sacred union. Conversely *mode A* corresponds to the Shabbat light that hides behind and within each moment of the week (and which derives from the light of *woman*'s backside when the higher three *sefirot* of intellect are fully integrated) and corresponds to the Tree of Knowledge of Good and Evil.**

Which is higher? A similar discussion occurs around Purim and the Book of Esther, which does not contain *HaShem*'s name (except as a hidden acrostic). Any text that has *HaShem*'s name written in full has an official status of sanctity. One must treat it with special respect: one may not bring it into a privy, or rest objects upon it, or place it on the ground, and so on. Many additional laws apply to the actual scribing of *HaShem*'s name, including the requirement of immersion in a *mikveh* before doing so.

When *HaShem*'s name is present, a hierarchy exists. His name is on one level, and all the other words that fill in the storyline are on a lower level. Similar to this is the discrepancy between Shabbat and the work week.

The special sanctity of *HaShem*'s name is a deep, holy, and relevant truth. Yet it also reinforces the illusion of duality, when the truest truth is that *God is one.* And since "There is nothing but God," it necessarily follows that *all is one.* The world is not divided into God and other-than-God. Rather, the deepest truth is that *there is only God.*

This teaching is conveyed through *Megillat Esther*, which is, paradoxically, the only book in the Bible where *HaShem*'s name does not appear. Its story demonstrates that *HaShem*'s guiding Presence infuses every detail of life, the natural as surely as the miraculous. In the Purim story, each event, in and of itself, was no wonder at all. The whole "miracle" of the story of Esther was that the underlying design, though absolutely hidden, became crystal clear. No one could deny that it was the hand-of-God inside the glove of nature that had brought redemption. The mundane level of existence become a miracle on Purim, for *HaShem* made His Presence visible through the ordinary.

The fact that there is "nothing but God" is conveyed through the *Megillah* precisely *because* His name does not appear. When *HaShem* is not confined to the space of His explicit name, His presence spreads out to fill everywhere equally.

Which is the higher truth? *HaShem* manifesting through His name, despite the unavoidable message of duality that contaminates that expression? Or, *HaShem* manifesting through the ordinary, forfeiting the special power of name but preserving the deepest truth that God is one and *equally* present in every point of time and place? Similarly, which is greater: the Shabbat of the seventh day as distinct from the previous six, or the dimension of Shabbat consciousness that infuses and sanctifies each moment of the week? This was Tslofchad's question.

Yet the fact that he engaged in this analysis on Shabbat, when he should have been basking in the bliss of Shabbat union, is considered a desecration and insult to the Shabbat groom. Shouldn't *woman's* attachment to *man* in near consummate union be a pleasure worth any cost? To even consider otherwise is a humiliation to *man*.

I.

Biblical story of the woodgatherer; who was he and what was he doing? The *Zohar* answers by . . .

A. redefining "gather" as "compare";

B. redefining "wood" as "trees";

C. reformulating his sin as an offense against *man* and Shabbat.

II.

R. Ashlag equates these two trees with two modes of feminine expression that correspond to stages 3 and 4a of the *Ari's* sequence.

III.

R. Ashlag explicates the woodgatherer's sin against *man* and Shabbat based on these two modes of feminine expression.

IV.

A. The sin's implications for *woman*. The woodgatherer's name (Tslofchad) hints to the secret of his error and his sin.

B. Where did Tslofchad go wrong? What was the flaw in his reasoning? He sought to elevate *woman* but damaged her instead.

C. The dangers inherent in his sin.

D. Woman's rectified path requires the diminishment that Tslofchad sought to avoid.

וז"ש בגין כך הוה דיניה סתים וכו' בגין דמלה דא בעי בחשאי וכו': כי ענין
חטא הזה שהיה מחשיב מדרגת הנוקבא על ז"א, אינו לכבוד לנוקבא, וקב"ה
עבד יקר ליקריה, שז"א עשה כבוד לכבודו. דהיינו שעשה כבוד למלכות
הנקרא כבוד, שלא לגלות ההקפדה והחטא על מי שמחשיב הנוקבא ביותר.
שזה אינו לכבוד הנוקבא.

Because of the complex and metaphysical **nature of** Tslofchad's **sin** and its complete lack of precedent, **Moshe was unsure of the appropriate response. Furthermore,** the case's details were so delicate and potentially heretical that **it seemed best to keep the whole subject under wraps. It would not serve** either party's interests, neither *man* nor **woman, to publicize** the details of Tslofchad's sin **and his mistaken over-valuation of *woman*** when she stands with her back **to man.** In this way *HaShem* **added honor to the level of Himself called honor or glory,** that is, His feminine Presence, the *Shekhinah*, who manifests the radiant glory of God.

To explain: the fact that God *is one* means that Divinity is now and always has been equally present in every point of time and space: equally present in a newspaper as in a Torah scroll, in a murderer as in a saint, in an outhouse as a holy site. Yet this is not how things appear. We experience a hierarchy of Presence. We pilgrimage to sacred sites and observe holy days because Divinity feels more accessible there. The explanation is this: Although God is equally present in every point of time and space, He is not equally revealed through them. When the everpresence of God is perceptible in a place, we say the *Shekhinah* dwells there and the place or moment becomes a Tabernacle in time or space that holds the manifest glory of God.

In what way did *HaShem* add honor to His feminine presence, that is, *woman*? Rav Ashlag explains that He did so **by not publicizing the seriousness** of the sin **and the penalty** of death **that comes to anyone who overvalues the feminine** in her self-contained and independent state, over her dependent yet bonded relationship with *man*. Though it may first seem that the former truly honors the feminine by affirming her equal and independent status, in fact, **it does not serve *woman* in the end.**

וסוד החטא הזה מרומז בשמו שנקרא צלפחד, שהוא אותיות צל פחד. כי מאחר שז"א ממעט הג"ר דשמאל ומשאיר רק הו"ק דג"ר, נבחן שעושה צל על הג"ר דשמאל אמנם על צל הזה נאמר, שהנוקבא אמרה בצלו חמדתי וישבתי, כי מקודם לכן במצב הא' אע"פ שלא היה לה אז צל על הג"ר, עכ"ז היתה סתומה ולא עשתה פירות. אבל עתה כשקבלה הצל מז"א, ופריו מתוק לחכי, כי עתה יש לה פירות ממנו. אומנם צלפחד, פחד מן הצל הזה, והיה רוצה לבחור מצב הא' שאז לא היה שום צל על הנוקבא. ובשביל זה מת.

The explanation is to be found in the secret of Tslofchad's name, which reveals the root of his sin. Tslofchad's name (צלפחד) divides in two, and each half becomes a word unto itself: צל (*tsal*) means "screen" or "shadow" and פחד (*pachad*) means "fear."

When *woman* and *man* are bound at their backsides, she is the left and he the right. **Woman's lapse into diminishment coincides with a withholding of her "brains" (i.e., the upper three *sefirot* of the left side). Her range of access constricts to the lower six *sefirot* that** comprise the emotional plane, and she loses touch with her higher intellectual functioning. **It is as if *man* spread a screen (צל) before these three *sefirot* of the left, or feminine brain,** rendering them unavailable to woman and necessitating her diminishment.

I.

Biblical story of the woodgatherer; who was he and what was he doing? The *Zohar* answers by . . .

A. redefining "gather" as "compare";
B. redefining "wood" as "trees";
C. reformulating his sin as an offense against *man* and Shabbat.

II.

R. Ashlag equates these two trees with two modes of feminine expression that correspond to stages 3 and 4a of the *Ari's* sequence.

III.

R. Ashlag explicates the woodgatherer's sin against *man* and Shabbat based on these two modes of feminine expression.

IV.

A. The sin's implications for *woman*. The woodgatherer's name (Tslofchad) hints to the secret of his error and his sin.
B. Where did Tslofchad go wrong? What was the flaw in his reasoning? He sought to elevate *woman* but damaged her instead.
C. The dangers inherent in his sin.
D. Woman's rectified path requires the diminishment that Tslofchad sought to avoid.

At first glance this seems like an oppressive act, that *woman* is being forced into submission. **And yet,** at least in the end, **she** herself welcomes the experience and even **sings** its praises. This is how Rav Ashlag interprets **the verse "In his shadow (צל) I sat with great delight,** and his fruit was sweet to my palate."[24]

The explanation of her seemingly illogical response is as follows. There are costs and benefits to *woman* in each of her two modes of expression. While *mode A* provides her with a full and equal stature, an active and expanded intellect, and the dignity that associates with all this, **the cost is that she remains barren.**

Even though she has no screen restricting access to her brain, her self-contained state of separation from *man* prevents her from bearing fruit. Because she has no need for him, there is no chemistry of attraction between them, and, consequently, she does not join herself to him in generative union. For *woman,* the cost of not bearing children is an impossible price to pay. **Conversely, in mode B,** *woman* is diminished and dependent, for **the screen blocks her from full intellectual expression** and the exquisite pleasure that comes through that channel. And yet, these lacks translate into needs and desires that she projects onto *man* (for he is holding her missing lights) and a chemistry of mutual attraction builds between them. They couple in marital union and **she bears fruit.** The joy and pain and satisfaction of bearing children is, apparently, worth the cost of her diminishment. **And so the verse attests, "And his fruit was sweet to my palate."**

And still, Tslofchad shrank from the task of imposing this screen that would necessitate *woman*'s diminishment. It seemed possible that *woman*'s more dignified option was *mode A*, where she remained equal to *man* and independent of him. **He questioned (פחד) the screen's merit (צל)** that compelled diminish-

---

24. Song of Songs 2:3.

ment, **and because of** the dangerous implications of **his error, he incurred death.**

ZOHAR

Biblical story of the woodgatherer; who was he and what was he doing? The *Zohar* answers by . . .

...ת"ח ב' אילנין אינון חד לעילא [שהוא עץ החיים,

ז"א] וחד לתתא [שהוא עץ הדעת, הנוקבא] בדא חיין

ובדא מותא מאן דאחלף לון גרים ליה מותא בהאי עלמא

ולית ליה חולקא בההוא עלמא. וע"ד אמר שלמה דבש

מצאת אכול דייך וגו'

A. redefining "gather" as "compare";

B. redefining "wood" as "trees";

C. reformulating his sin as an offense against *man* and Shabbat.

R. Ashlag equates these two trees with two modes of feminine expression that correspond to stages 3 and 4a of the *Ari's* sequence.

... **Come and see. Of these two trees, one is above** (i.e., the Tree of life, which corresponds to *man* joined to *woman* when she is manifesting as *mode B*) **and one is below (the Tree of Knowledge, which corresponds to *woman*** manifesting as *mode A*). **One brings life and one brings death** (for the path of ascent through the clumsy method of fall, purgation, and repentance associates with the Tree of Knowledge, and every fall is a mini-death. And furthermore, one who is barren [the end result of choosing the Tree of Knowledge] is considered *as if* dead).[25] **One who inverts the polarity** of these *trees* and ascribes superiority to the latter, **incurs death in this world and loses his portion in the next. Concerning this subject, King Solomon writes, "Have you found honey? Eat only as much as is sufficient for you,** lest you be oversatiated and vomit it up."[26]

R. Ashlag explicates the woodgatherer's sin against *man* and Shabbat based on these two modes of feminine expression.

A. The sin's implications for *woman*. The woodgatherer's name (Tslofchad) hints to the secret of his error and his sin.

B. Where did Tslofchad go wrong? What was the flaw in his reasoning? He sought to elevate *woman* but damaged her instead.

C. The dangers inherent in his sin.

D. Woman's rectified path requires the diminishment that Tslofchad sought to avoid.

---

25. TB, *Nedarim* 64b; *Midrash Rabbah, Bereshit* 71:6.
26. Proverbs 25:16.

RAV ASHLAG'S COMMENTARY

פירוש אע"פ שמצב הא' של הנוקבא היא בחינת פרוד ואחורים עכ"ז לולא
מצב הא' לא היתה הנוקבא יכולה לקבל חוכמה בעת שהיא במצב הב', בי
הכלים של מצב הא' נשארים בה במצב הב' שבהם היא מקבלת החוכמה.

Although *woman's* **separate and backsided expression as** *mode A*
was rejected, for it ultimately results in a barren condition, **nevertheless she must pass through that state** in her life cycle, for she
acquires something critical from that experience. As explained,[27]
woman proceeds through three stages of back-to-back relationship
with *man*, then turns, reduces again to a single point, and proceeds
through four stages of front-to-front development. At the end of
stage 7 she attains a stature equal to *man* in every respect. She is
completely independent from him in terms of need, and yet they
cleave in a profound and mutual bond of face-to-face union. However, this culminating stage has never been and will only come to
be in the messianic end of days. Until then, her stature remains (at
least apparently) subordinate to his. Each stage of front-to-front
relationship has a preceding back-to-back counterpart, which
engraves its pattern of experience and expectation onto the neural
network of *woman's* soul. In stage 3 (*mode A*) of *woman's* back-to-
back relationship with *man*, she incorporates all of her brain-lights
and stands equal and opposite to him. This primes her to seek
and enables her to contain these same lights again in her front-to-
front path of development. In this way it programs her direction
of growth and yearning. **If not for this initiating experience, she
would not be able to absorb the lights of consciousness in her
front-facing relationship with** *man*.

This early conditioning **experience of her full intellectual
stature,** and the permanent engraving that it leaves on her soul,

---

27. See Chapter 3, "The Small Light to Rule by Night."

remains with *woman* in all her subsequent stages of development. **It serves as a kind of vessel that enables her to receive the same brain-lights again in *mode B* at the second half of her journey.**

ולפיכך אחר שאדם זכה לקבל ממצב הא' דנוקבא, מחוייב להעלות מ"ן לצורך מצב הב' דנוקבא ואז יהיה לו כל השלמות חוכמה וחסדים יחדיו. אבל אם אינו עושה כן אלא בוחר במצב הא' דפרודא. עונשו מיתה. וז"ש דבש מצאת שה"ס מצב הא' דנוקבא, אכול דייך. ואח"כ תמשיך את מצב הב', שאל"כ, פן תשבענו והקאתו. דהיינו שיסתלקו ממנו אורת החיים.

The temptation is to stay in *mode A*, for consciousness is the sweetest pleasure. All the rational explanations of why it is worth the loss pale against the wrenching anticipation of estrangement from one's brains. Consequently, **once a *woman* experiences** the expanded consciousness that characterizes **stage 3 of *woman*'s back-to-back unfolding, she is compelled to** diminish and assume a position of lack and longing. This is what it means to *"raise feminine waters for the necessity of mode B."*[28]

When she **then** reclaims her brains, it will not be at the expense of relationship with *man* (as it was in *mode A*). Instead, **she attains a fully perfected and integrated state of both wisdom and loving-kindness together. One** who

I.
Biblical story of the woodgatherer; who was he and what was he doing? The *Zohar* answers by . . .

A. redefining "gather" as "compare";
B. redefining "wood" as "trees";
C. reformulating his sin as an offense against *man* and Shabbat.

II.
R. Ashlag equates these two trees with two modes of feminine expression that correspond to stages 3 and 4a of the *Ari*'s sequence.

III.
R. Ashlag explicates the woodgatherer's sin against *man* and Shabbat based on these two modes of feminine expression.

IV.
A. The sin's implications for *woman*. The woodgatherer's name (Tslofchad) hints to the secret of his error and his sin.
B. Where did Tslofchad go wrong? What was the flaw in his reasoning? He sought to elevate *woman* but damaged her instead.
C. The dangers inherent in his sin.
D. Woman's rectified path requires the diminishment that Tslofchad sought to avoid.

---

28. The term *feminine waters* refers to the "lower waters" of Genesis 1:6, 7. Because they are "lower," they long to unite with the upper waters from whom they are estranged, and this longing is the force that drives their transformation.

advocates that *woman* fixate in *mode A,* **preferring her separative mode of expression, is punished with death. Thus** King Solomon warns, "*Have you found honey*" (*referring to* the sweet pleasure of expanded consciousness in *mode A*), "**eat only so much as is sufficient**" (don't gorge, and don't get fixated). Take enough as is sufficient, **diminish yourself, and proceed to *mode B.*** Know that if you get stuck, the second half of the verse applies with all its unpleasant consequences: "**Lest you be oversatiated and vomit it up,**" **meaning that the lights of life will be withdrawn from you.**

DEBRIEFING
THE WOODGATHERER WAS TSLOFCHAD

What Do We Know?

1. The natural life course of *woman*'s soul spans three phases of growth:

   Mode A – A period of back-to-back development, where it attains a level of intellectual skill and confidence equal to (and independent of) its male counterpart. Because it feels no need for *man* at this stage of life, there is no chemistry of attraction between them.

   Mode B_1 (nesira) – Diminishment (and collapse) into a single shrunken point subordinate to man yet oriented face-to-face with him.

   Mode B_2 – Re-development through four sequential stages of maturity and augmentation until she attains full equality with *man,* yet this time within the context of a deeply bonded relationship with him.

2. In *mode A,* where *woman* stands with her back to *man,* full statured and self-reliant, she has no need of him. And

since she has no need, there is no chemistry between them. According to kabbalah, *her need* is the glue that binds *man* and *woman* together with sufficient strength to overcome the repulsive forces always present when two egos attempt to merge. Consequently, the cost of fixating at this pre-diminishment state of equality is barrenness. Because she does not bond with man, she does not conceive children, and does not bear fruit.

3. The diminishment that defines *woman's* role seems to deny her equality and cast her into second-class citizenship, which it *does* in the short term. However, by the end of the story, everything turns around, and she emerges the winner. Her initial investment of self-sacrifice actually bears a richer and more satisfying equality than was previously possible. Now she has children, a consummately satisfying marriage, *and* full equality, whereas before (in *mode A*) the latter came at the expense of the former.

4. *Mode A* (with all its unsatisfactory qualities) is critical to *woman's* developmental process. The fullness of her self-exploration and intellectual attainment (independent of *man*) enables her to realize the full potential of front-sided possibilities in the second half of life. *Woman* cannot attain the perfection that is her God-given mission without first experiencing the back-sided equality of *mode A*.

5. *Woman's* diminishment accomplishes two things that, apparently, could not happen otherwise:

   a. It enables fertility, most explicitly indicated by the production of children, though other creative endeavors also follow this model.

   b. It enables her to attain full equality without having to sacrifice a fruitful and consummately united relationship with *man*.

What Don't We Know?

1. We don't know how these stages actually translate into the real life of a human being. A possible correspondence is as follows:

Back-to-back: birth ———— marriage ·······································
Nesira[29]: ············ puberty———— child bearing/rearing ···············
Front-to-front: ···························· marriage ——————— death

2. What are the implications of these teachings for the education of women? What is her ideal time for marriage and childbearing? How does one identify the point where backsided individuation has proceeded enough that *woman* will be able to receive her full lights of consciousness in the second half of life, yet not so much that she bonds too deeply with that side of herself that it becomes too painful for her to bear the sacrifice of diminishment inherent in marriage and childrearing?

3. What is it about diminishment that enables women who pass through it to re-attain full equality, yet this time within deeply bonded relationship? What makes *man* and *woman* able to "share one crown" after diminishment, a feat that they could not do before?

4. What does it mean for the implications of this paradigm that technology now enables women to conceive children through artificial insemination, without having to first bond

---

29. The *Ari* explains that *nesira* is a gradual and sequential process that moves from above to below. In the yearly ceremonial cycle between Israel and *HaShem*, *nesira* begins on the first day of Rosh Hashanah and continues twenty-two days until Shemini Atzeret. Throughout that time woman exists in a hybrid state: the parts of her that are severed immediately reorient front-to-front, while the rest of her remains back-to-back.

with a man in marital commitment? There is no longer a direct equation between *mode A* and barrenness.

5. It is clear how *woman* benefits from her development toward equality, but what does *man* gain in this process? Why is it in *man's* self-interest to generously and whole-heartedly support the project of "raising the feminine"?

6. Those operating from a political paradigm generally blame the necessity of *woman's* diminishment on man's ego-need to dominate women. The kabbalistic model suggests that some deeper metaphysical law underlies this pattern, something built into the primordial structure of the universe that precedes human beings and even egos altogether. Why did *HaShem* design the world this way?

Logical Implications and Speculations

1. In every generation a tension exists between two conflicting patterns of growth:

   a. The entire 6,000 years of biblical history is a single moon cycle. Consequently, each generation embodies a particular stage in *woman's* seven-step sequence of development, and the "obvious truths" of that stage "rule" the generation and condition their understanding of the feminine role.

   b. Each individual woman of each generation must pass through all seven stages in the course of her life. A positive tension exists whenever she is moving toward the personal stage equivalent to her generation's developmental point. A negative tension exists whenever she is moving out of, or in an apparently opposite direction from, that point.

   Our generation is toward the end of the macrocosmic cycle, fast approaching the messianic end of days. That means that *woman* is moving through the latter stages of her life path. One could speculate that she is making the transition from stage 5 to stage 6, which means that she is "coming into her brains," and the concept of equality between *man* and *woman* now becomes imaginable and, for many, an ideal.

Consequently, a negative tension exists between the "necessity" of diminishment in the first half of life and the generational value of equality that pervades these times. The direction of diminishment is "downward" toward contraction and disparity of stature between man and *woman.* Conversely, the generation is actively engaged in upward striving, augmentation of stature, and equality between the genders.

2. Tslofchad (as the woodgatherer) was sentenced to death for his heretical questioning, which threatened to lock *woman* into *mode* A, splitting her apart from man, and blocking the generative flow of light from the universe. His unconditional insistence upon equality lacked the discrimination of timing. And yet, his daughters are the ones who successfully petitioned to inherit a portion of the Holy Land as a direct possession, not via the intermediary of father, husband, or brother, the only options available until then.

God spoke to Moshe saying, "The daughters of Tslofchad have a just claim. Give them a hereditary portion of land alongside their father's brothers. Let their father's hereditary property thus pass over to them.

"Speak to the Israelites and tell them that if a man dies and has no sons, his hereditary property shall pass over to his daughter."

How do these two paradoxical pieces fit together? Tslofchad received the death penalty, yet his daughters received unconditional praise and positive regard for their legal action. And yet, they were unmarried women when presenting their petition and so, apparently, in *mode A*. Without the slightest hint of rebuke, each is granted a portion of the Holy Land as a direct and personal possession, a decision that seemingly validates (and even reinforces) their independent and unbonded state. Generally, a woman's access to the inherited land of Israel is only vicarious; she lives on her father's or husband's property and makes use of it while she is there.

It is as if Tslofchad is (at least partially) vindicated through *HaShem*'s endorsement of his daughters' legal claim.

3. The *Zohar* teaches: "Everything is feminine in relation to that which is above it, and masculine in relation to that which is below."[30]

Consequently, each person participates in relationships in which he or she is the "masculine" player and others in which he or she is the "feminine." This means that *everyone* is challenged, in some aspect of his or her life, to diminish in relation to a "masculine partner" for the sake of uniting in fertile union (even if only before *HaShem*). Consequently, while Rav Ashlag's paradigm describes a literal man and woman uniting to produce physical children, its principles extend to all fruitful and creative endeavors.

4. *Mode A* and *mode B* of feminine expression are not only stages in *woman*'s life cycle; they are also archetypes that have permanent standing in the universe. Both exist,

---

30. *Zohar* 2:4a.

simultaneously, and will until the end of time. Because of their archetypal status, they are always embodied by some real people with real lives in every generation. R. Ashlag explains that *mode A* serves *mode B*, for the feminine, even in her most diminished state, always remains linked to *mode A*, and this bond enables and inspires her subsequent expansion of front-sided consciousness.

In kabbalah these two archetypes are often associated with Lea and Rachel, though Lea is a complex symbol that sometimes corresponds to Rav Ashlag's *mode A* and sometimes to the *Ari*'s final and consummating stage of front-to-front development. The connection between them is obvious (for at both of these points, *woman* stands at full stature).

There are souls, in each generation, whose role is to hold the light of a particular archetype and to serve as its point of contact with the physical plane. Consequently, there are women whose role is to embody the archetype of *mode A*, and their living presence in each generation holds the place in woman's collective psyche for the reawakening of independent and full-statured consummation that is *HaShem*'s highest vision and blessing for them.

5

DISPARITIES OF GENDER ARE THE CAUSE OF EVIL

Excerpt from
The Diminished Moon[1]

by R. Shlomo Elyashev (The *Leshem*)

BARE BONES LITERACY

SUMMARY

The Diminished Moon by R. Shlomo Elyashev (*Leshem*) cracks the whole subject open and proves that gender disparities are the ultimate cause of evil in the universe. The question of why God would design a world with gender inequalities is the same question as why he purposely incorporated evil into creation. R. Elyashev addresses these questions in profoundly satisfying ways. It becomes manifestly clear that the elimination of evil requires the elimination of all disparities between *man* and *woman*.

---

1. *Leshem*, HDYH, *Miut HaYareach* (MHY), end of section 3, 4.

VOCABULARY

atzilut – The highest of the four planes of existence (physical, emotional, mental, spiritual)[2] is called *atzilut*. It is the realm of pure archetypes, and means, literally, the "world of emanation." In *atzilut* created things are merged with the light of God's Presence.

chassadim / chesed lights (**generosities**) – Lights of conscious awareness. The *chassadim*, when integrated, always inspire a generosity of spirit.

dinim (**also called** *gevurot*) – These terms mean, literally, "severities" and refer to the dark knots of unrectified potential that are the driving force behind our universe. *Dinim* and *gevurot* are generally associated with unconscious lights.

lights – *Lights* are always equivalent to consciousness in kabbalistic writings. Each *sefirah*, or spark, is a *light* that transmits a particular insight or capacity for awareness.

man **and** *woman* – Kabbalistic archetypes of male and female in their prime, as opposed to *father* and *mother*, which depict their later stages of life.

vessel – Kabbalah groups the world into lights and vessels, roughly paralleling energy and matter. Souls are lights and bodies are vessels. The earliest vessels formed from the outer layers of emanated light that congealed into sac-like forms, which remained even after their light withdrew. Vessels are feminine and always associate with the *sefirah* of *malchut*. See "Kabbalistic Symbols of the Feminine."

---

2. This definition of the four worlds is based on the levels of soul associated with each plane of reality. See *Leshem*, HVS 2:3:1, and 4:3 (first words, *Gilui shlishi*). "Spiritual" here refers to the state of union between created and Creator.

TECHNICAL NOTES

The italicized terms *man, woman, mother,* and *father* refer to kabbalistic archetypes (called *partzufim*) and, by extension, to the masculine and feminine attributes found in both men and women. The literal translation of the Hebrew text appears in bold print.

SYNOPSIS

THE DIMINISHED MOON

R. Shlomo Elyashev (The *Leshem*)[3]

In his extraordinary treatise on the diminished moon, R. Shlomo Elyashev explores the question of why *HaShem* designed the universe in a way that would require the moon's affliction. Why did He build this inequality and injustice into the very structure of creation? The question goes deeper still, for R. Elyashev identifies the moon's diminution with the origin of evil and suffering altogether. When *HaShem* directed the moon to relinquish her crown, she stepped down from her throne and at once reduced to a bare cinder of her original glory. Dimmed and shadowed, the dark side of the cosmic moon became the very root of evil and the font of its continued nurture from that point on.

R. Elyashev thus reframes the whole subject of the diminished moon. He identifies *woman*'s collapse and descent with the

---

3. *Leshem* is the Hebrew translation of jacinth, the first precious stone in the third row of the breastplate of the High Priest, after which R. Shlomo Elyashev's books are titled. Greek sources translate this as ligure, a bright orange stone often likened to the carbuncle or amber (Pliny 8:57). Many other sources have it resembling the topaz in color (Ibn Janach; Radak, Schneerson; cf. Bachya; MeAm Loez). Other sources, however, see it as a blue stone (*Bamidbar Rabbah* 2:7; *Shemot Rabbah* 38:8). Thus some sources identify it with turquoise (*Shiltey Gibborim*) or beryl (*Lekach Tov; Targum* on Song of Songs 5:15). From R. Aryeh Kaplan, *The Living Torah*.

single-most overwhelming question of the universe: "If God is all powerful, and only good, and He created a world of creatures for the sole purpose of bestowing upon them His good,[4] then why has evil and suffering become as much a part of their lives as the 'good' that is (presumably) His intention to impart?" According to Rav Elyashev, this is exactly the same as asking, "Why did *HaShem* reduce the moon?"

This question, restated in one of its many forms, has baffled theologians, threatened believers, broken the faith of many, justified the sins of many, and continues to wreak havoc on the hearts of mankind. Its paradox is so deep that its solution lies outside the universe as we know it. The "lights" required to fully answer its challenge simply cannot fit into our world, given its current state of immaturity.[5]

And yet, it is impossible not to seek answers. The question is too compelling to be neatly set aside, despite the wisdom of such a move. Efforts with no hope of success only leave frustration in their wake. Yet with faith in the process as an end unto itself, the tenacious pursuit of explanation will eventually lead its inquisitor to the innermost frontiers of mystical contemplation.

As explained, kabbalah is the science of correspondences. By creating an equation between the origin of evil and the disparity of *man* and *woman* (arising from the diminished moon), R. Elyashev creates a set of associations that is ripe for kabbalistic meditation. Each half illuminates the other and as the mind shuffles between them, a vibration builds, and a path opens, in the form of a ladder, that leads to the heart of darkness (which is light). All the teachings about the mysterious purpose of evil in the universe, the strategies against it, and the inevitability of its demise now also apply to the

4. Ramchal, *Derekh HaShem* (*The Way of God*) 1:1–2.
5. R. Nachman of Breslov, *Likutei Mohoran* 1:65.

disparity of *man* and *woman* and the reduced moon. Similarly, all that is known about the mystery of gender, the reason for *woman's* diminution, and the generative transformations that emerge from her ordeal – all these apply as well to the subject of evil.

Suddenly, the study of gender takes center stage, for *it* holds the key to unraveling the origin, purpose, and elimination of evil. Anyone committed to the holy work of turning darkness into light must also labor for the moon's *tikun*. The rising of the feminine and the conquest of evil are inextricably linked – neither can happen without the other.

In those earliest moments when the moon diminished, a primordial flaw entered the universe, which R. Elyashev identifies as the disparity of stature between *man* and *woman*. Every layer of unfolding from that point onward reproduced that defect but in a progressively coarser form. The lower the world and the denser its substance, the more pronounced the disparity between *man* and *woman*.[6]

The problem, explains he, is not the political incorrectness of the condition but the impossibility of consummate union between *man* and *woman* when their "anatomies" do not match. Their asymmetry has two effects most relevant here.

First, as explained, God created the universe to dispense good and holy pleasure upon His creatures. The mechanism by which this bestowal occurs is via the cosmic union of *man* and *woman*

---

6. *Leshem* explains that the original disparity between masculine and feminine occurred in the Bound World. That subtle flaw then expresses itself in a progressively coarser form at each subsequent level of unfolding. The shattering of the vessels in the World of Points/*tohu*; the moon's complaint in the world of *atzilut*; the eating from the Tree of Knowledge in the world of *briyah*; and the sins of our lives in the world of *assiya* are all expressions of the same flaw (Ramchal, KPC 131). The "diminishment of the moon" is both a specific stage in this sequence and the generic term for all these expressions of disparity between masculine and feminine.

(*HaShem* and creation).[7] The more fully they match, the more pleasurable their union.[8] The joy of their coming together is, itself, the flow of reward and bounty that God seeks to bestow.[9] Anything that disrupts their bond retards the speedy realization of creation's purpose.

Second, wherever *woman* is not matched by *man*, those parts of her stick out of their relationship, exposed, because he does not meet her there.[10] These vulnerable places become the sites that nurture evil. They are notorious for their energy leaks, which, cultivated by the forces of no-good, become the mainstay of evil's diet.

R. Elyashev thus shows that the elimination of evil requires the elimination of disparities between *man* and *woman*. As long as the moon is diminished and *woman's* stature remains less than *man's*, evil will continue to prosper. As long as it has "food," it will survive.

The original question remains: Why does *HaShem* tolerate evil? And even worse: Why did he deliberately engineer its entry into the system by diminishing the moon?

All hinges upon the sublime mystery of free choice, says R. Elyashev. The idea is as follows:

- By definition, before creation, *HaShem* was lacking nothing except, in some mysterious sense, the experience of actualized relationship, because there was no "other" with whom to relate. *HaShem* had no intrinsic need for this experience and yet for reasons unknown (and essentially unknowable) chose to create it. And so *HaShem* brought forth a universe

---

7. Ramchal, KPC 73, 80.

8. Ramchal, KPC, 59.

9. *Zohar* 1:162a, b.

10. When *woman* shrinks in stature, it is as if she stands lower than *man*. Her legs and lower torso stick out below him, exposed, and extend down into the lower worlds (*briyah, yetzira, assiya,* and *klippot*), vulnerable to the impurities unique to those worlds.

that could serve as this *other* and with whom He could experience all the myriad possibilities of relationship. Every creature is a spark of this *other* and actualizes, through its life, some unique expression of relationship with God.

- This cosmic goal cannot be realized without free will, for it is the necessary and sufficient criteria of otherness. One who cannot choose freely is not a true *other* but a narcissistic extension of one's master. Consequently, an essential prerequisite to relationship is that there be creatures capable of making decisions based on autonomous considerations, who are not governed by inner or outer compulsions.

- A second prerequisite to free will is that there be options. Without at least two equally plausible alternatives, by definition, there is no choice. And yet, the truest truth is that there is only God, and God is one, and the only real option is to choose Him. All other paths net zero, for their gains turn to dust and their hidden costs mushroom to overwhelming proportions.

- Consequently, if *HaShem* wants free choice to exist in His universe, He must conceal the truth of His one-and-only-ness and present an array of alternatives that seem truly plausible. The option of other-than-God must appear as attractive (and reasonable) as the option of choosing God.

- This, precisely, is the function of evil, literally defined as "the illusion of separation and independence from God." The word *illusion* is significant, since nothing can actually be separate from God for God is one. To the extent that something presents the appearance of self-containment, self-sovereignty, and multiplicity, to that extent it partakes of the quality of evil. (Conversely, to the extent that it communicates through itself the truth of God's goodness, oneness, compassion, and generosity, to that extent it partakes of the quality of holiness.) *HaShem* concealed His one-and-only-ness by creating the illusions of multiplicity and autonomy, whereby the universe appears to run on its own without a Master that one need serve. These deceptions are the subtle stuff of evil.

- R. Elyashev demonstrates that the mechanism *HaShem* employed to create the illusion of other-than-God (i.e., evil) was to diminish the feminine, thereby introducing gender disparities into the universe.
- R. Elyashev enumerates three inequalities between *man* and *woman*, which he identifies as the primordial flaws that are the first expressions of evil and the roots of all its secondary manifestations.
- Like a multiple-choice test, the goal is for this *other* to eventually see right through the illusions conjured by evil, and to choose truth and God consistently, despite temptations to the contrary. Whenever illusion prevails and a person chooses *it* instead of God, evil diverts a bit of spoil into its coffers. When, finally, no one is duped by its ruse, evil will starve into non-existence for it will have no booty upon which to feed.

R. Elyashev's equation of evil with the asymmetry of *man* and *woman* has profound implications. It means that it is impossible to be rid of evil's scourge without eliminating the gender inequalities that are its root and primary expression.

ANNOTATED TRANSLATION

AN EXCERPT FROM THE
DIMINISHED MOON[11]

by R. Shlomo Elyashev (The *Leshem*)

In the previous (untranslated) chapters of his essay, Rav Elyashev presents a detailed and technical description of creation's unfolding. He begins with the seven universes that were created and destroyed before the Torah's opening line ("In the beginning...") that inaugurates the history of *our*, eighth, world.[12] He proceeds step by step, from above to below, from the point of pure thought that arose in the mind of God, to the coarse and material universe that is our present habitation.

Rav Elyashev concludes that the disparity between *man* and *woman* derives from three defects in the fabric of creation. A foundation premise that permeates his writings is that per-

I.
Three primordial inequalities between *man* and *woman* produce the diminished moon and are the very source of evil.

II.
Why did God design the universe with these three defects?

A. Defect is a relative assessment.
B. Defect itself can accomplish things that perfection cannot.
C. The purpose of creation, for some mysterious reason, cannot be realized except via the agency of defect and evil.

III.
How does evil serve the purpose of creation?

A. Transformation requires a movement from flaw to perfection.
B. Purpose of creation is that there be an "other" with whom divinity can relate.
C. A true "other" must be a free agent with free choice.
D. Free choice, by definition, requires that options exist that are not God's will (i.e., evil).

IV.
How does God create evil?

A. The three disparities between *man* and *woman* cause the production of gevurot. the seeds of concealment and evil.

V.
The elimination of gender disparities.

---

11. *Leshem*, HDYH, MHY, end of 3, 4.

12. Genesis 36:31–39 describes eight kings who "ruled in Edom before there reigned any king over the children of Israel." Kabbalah teaches that the seven who "ruled and died" hint to seven shattered universes that preceded our own in the World of Points. The eighth, called Hadar, who didn't die and who is the only one whose wife is mentioned (and even by name, Mehitavel) is the primordial root of our own universe, called the Rectified World. This teaching originates in the *Zohar* (2:176b; 3:128a, 135a–b, 142a–b) and is ubiquitous in kabbalistic and chasidic writings. See diagram entitled "The Map of the Unfolding of Worlds."

fection requires the absolute equality of *man* and *woman*, for only as equals can they unite in consummate union.

והרי ישנם עתה באצילות ג' חסרונות כלליים. מה שהם חסר עתה ולא יתוקנו אלא רק לעתיד. והיינו. א'. עיקר הגלוי דהמ"ה וב"ן כי לעתיד יוכללו בהס"ג כנז'. ב'. מה שלא נשתוו בחלוקת המ"ה וב"ן כנ"ל סי' ב'. ולא יתוקנו בזה אלא רק לעתיד. ג'. מה שהוזכר הוא לעולם גבוה מהנוק'. ולא נמצא עתה בשום פנים שיהיו שניהם שוה בשוה משתמשים בכתר אחד עד לעתיד לבוא. והרי הם ג' חסרונות כלליים באצילות. והם נמשכים זה מזה והם כולם משורש החסרון האחד. אשר הוא מעוקודים ג"כ וכנז': אמנם הוא כי הנה כ"ז הוא בסוד קטרוג ומיעוט הירח הנודע בדברי רז"ל.

There exist even now, in the world of *emanation*,[13] **three flaws** that prefigure *woman*'s secondary status in relation to *man*. Though each moment leaves them more repaired, **their final fixing will only culminate in the** messianic **future.**

These three imperfections are summarized as follows:[14]

> a. The fact that *man* and *woman* exist at all is a kind of flaw.[15] *Father* and *mother* are the higher expression of masculine and feminine in the universe. *Father* and *mother* share a common root, which makes them essentially equal, as the *Zohar* states, "*Father* and *mother* emanated as one, and stand

---

13. The world of *emanation* (*atzilut*) is the plane and realm of Divine archetypes. See "The Map of the Unfolding of Worlds," p. 167.

14. In the earlier part of this chapter, and in the earlier chapters of the original essay, R. Elyashev elaborates on these ideas in great detail. Here he simply enumerates them in brief.

15. There are four ways of spelling *HaShem*'s essential name in its fully expanded form, and each has a different *gematria* (numerical value). One adds to 72 (ע"ב) and corresponds to *father*; one adds to 63 (ס"ג) and corresponds to *mother*; one adds to 45 (מ"ה) and corresponds to *man*; and finally one adds to 52 (ב"ן) and corresponds to *woman*. For simplicity's sake, when these terms appear, the translation will substitute their corresponding *partzufim*, which are now familiar terms to the reader. The subtle difference in emphasis between the two notations is not significant at our level of discussion.

as one."[16] In contrast, since *man* and *woman* derive from hierarchically separate roots,[17] the disparity between them widens dramatically. **In the messianic future** (whether toward its beginning or end is not specified) *man* **and** *woman* **will both be absorbed back up into** *mother,* at which point their lower and unequal expression of gender will cease altogether. Only *father* and *mother* will remain to complete the final uniting of masculine and feminine.

b. **The second flaw is their lack of symmetry.** The raw materials used to construct *man* and *woman* were imported from higher-level *sefirot,* and they were not distributed symmetrically between them. Consequently, *man* and *woman* do not match each other in the one-to-one correspondence that is their ideal. Their spiritual anatomies clash at numerous points, which makes a full meeting between them impossible. **This, too, will be remedied but** again, **not until the future.**

c. **Their final deficiency is that** wherever a disparity exists between *man* and *woman,* he **is always higher. There is**

I.
Three primordial inequalities between *man* and *woman* produce the diminished moon and are the very source of evil.

II.
Why did God design the universe with these three defects?

A. Defect is a relative assessment.
B. Defect itself can accomplish things that perfection cannot.
C. The purpose of creation, for some mysterious reason, cannot be realized except via the agency of defect and evil.

III.
How does evil serve the purpose of creation?

A. Transformation requires a movement from flaw to perfection.
B. Purpose of creation is that there be an "other" with whom divinity can relate.
C. A true "other" must be a free agent with free choice.
D. Free choice, by definition, requires that options exist that are not God's will (i.e., evil).

IV.
How does God create evil?

A. The three disparities between *man* and *woman* cause the production of gevurot. the seeds of concealment and evil.

V.
The elimination of gender disparities.

---

16. *Zohar* 290b (*Idra Zuta*).

17. This is a technical point discussed earlier, in the portions of the essay that precede the translated paragraphs.

no area of the universe where *man* **and** *woman* **have achieved** the **equality** that is their perfection. They will not attain this idyllic state called "the sharing of a single crown"[18] until the messianic end of days.

These flaws in the very fabric of creation continue to disrupt the relationship between *man* and *woman* **in the world of** *emanation,* which is their home. **Each** imperfection **devolves from the one before it (and all three derive from** an even more primordial lack, the subtle disparity of origin between masculine and feminine in the very first era of creation called the **"Bound World"**[19]**). All this relates to the secret of the moon's complaint and her diminishment,** for that is the metaphor kabbalah employs to describe *woman*'s ordeal (even on planes technically higher than the moon itself).[20]

והענין הוא כי הרי פשוט הדבר שכל מה שאנו קוראין אותן בשם חסרונות הנה הוא רק בערך התיקון העתיד אבל כל משך זמן דהעוה"ז אשר עד ביאת המשיח הנה היה כל חסרונות הללו לצורך ובכוונה מהמאציל ית"ש. כי עי"ז יצא ונעשה מציאת העולמות על מדרגתם שהם עתה ובכל ההנהגה שבהם אשר עתה. שכל זה הוא מגזרת מחשבתו הנעלמה ית"ש ובסוד מה שאמר למשרבע"ה שתוק כן עלה במחשבה לפני.

The question becomes: Why would a perfect God create a universe riddled with defects? A paradoxical fact helps to clarify this matter: **Any assessment of lack comes from comparing a moment or object to some perfected ideal** and noting a disparity between them. The critical variable becomes the "ideal." What criterion does one apply as the standard of reference? Is it an abstract concept of ultimate perfection? Is it a previous experience? Is it a

---

18. TB, *Chullin* 60b.
19. See diagram below, p. 167, called "The Map of the Unfolding of Worlds."
20. See footnote 6 in this chapter.

more sober prospect tempered by realistic expectations? The same objective phenomenon might evoke radically different assessments in each case.

Extending this principle to its cosmic scale: On one hand, each present moment is pitifully lacking when compared to its messianic ideal. Ignorance rules, suffering prevails, cruelty prospers, atheism is a plausible (and popular) philosophy. And yet, at the same time, each frame of history, from its chaotic inception to its messianic end, might still be perfectly fulfilling *HaShem*'s expectation for it as an intermediate step in the ongoing project of building a perfect world. In fact, says kabbalah, it is.

Two distinct standards of reference emerge:

a. One is to measure the present against its projected ideal, holding a picture of utopian perfection and comparing *this* to *that*.

b. Two is to measure the present against what can be reasonably expected from it as one step in our collective journey toward perfection. As a work in progress, does this moment (or person) accomplish its mission or not?

A building contractor with a strict deadline and a projected timetable for getting there provides a useful metaphor. At the end of each day he assesses the progress made. His primary concern is whether enough work got done and

I.
Three primordial inequalities between *man* and *woman* produce the diminished moon and are the very source of evil.

II.
Why did God design the universe with these three defects?

A. Defect is a relative assessment.
B. Defect itself can accomplish things that perfection cannot.
C. The purpose of creation, for some mysterious reason, cannot be realized except via the agency of defect and evil.

III.
How does evil serve the purpose of creation?

A. Transformation requires a movement from flaw to perfection.
B. Purpose of creation is that there be an "other" with whom divinity can relate.
C. A true "other" must be a free agent with free choice.
D. Free choice, by definition, requires that options exist that are not God's will (i.e., evil).

IV.
How does God create evil?

A. The three disparities between *man* and *woman* cause the production of gevurot. the seeds of concealment and evil.

V.
The elimination of gender disparities.

whether it was of satisfactory quality. The building's lack, when compared to its final completion, is not really relevant (except as a curiosity and to guide each day's work toward the right goal). No one expects it to look like that now.

Similarly, *HaShem*'s primary assessment relates to His expectation for each moment and the quota of work that needs to get done. Applying *this* standard, **each moment of history perfectly reflects HaShem's will for it** as an indispensable step in the process. This remains so, **despite its** obvious **deficiencies when compared to** the absolute standard **of messianic perfection. The whole configuration of worlds, with its hierarchy of levels and chains of cause and effect** that unravel through time, the agonies and the ecstasies, the glories and the profanities, **all these reflect *HaShem*'s explicit and mysterious will. It is precisely this subject that Moshe questioned and *HaShem* confirmed** in the disturbing story about Rebbe Akiva.[21]

> When Moshe ascended on high he found the Holy One adding tiny adornments (called crowns) to the Hebrew letters.
> Said Moshe, "Master of the Universe, who stays Your hand? [Is the Torah lacking anything? Does it need ornaments to make it beautiful?]"
> He answered, "There will arise a man, at the end of many generations, by the name of Akiva ben Yosef, who will expound mounds of laws on each embellishment."
> "Master of the Universe," said Moshe, "let me see such a man."
> He replied, "Turn back to the future."
> Moshe found himself in the Torah academy of R. Akiva and took a seat in the eighth row ... [He listened to R. Akiva give

---

21. TB, *Menachot* 29b.

discourse]... Thereupon he returned to the Holy One and said, "Lord of the Universe, if there is such a man, why do You give the Torah through me?"

He replied, "Silence. Thus the thought arose before Me."

Then said Moshe, "Lord of the Universe, a man who has attained the pinnacle of Torah, let me see his reward."

"Turn back to the future," said He. Moshe turned around and saw [R. Akiva being skinned alive with red-hot combs].[22]

"Master of the Universe," cried Moshe, "this is how You reward one who devotes himself to Your Torah?!"

He replied, "Silence. Thus the thought arose before Me."

Moshe is confronting *HaShem* with the timeless question, "How can You let the righteous suffer? How can You allow such flagrant injustice into Your universe? We are enjoined to believe that You are omnipotent, just, and only-good, yet righteous suffering belies those claims. What do I say to the weak-of-faith who see all this and conclude that either: You are good but powerless to stop it, or You are

I.
Three primordial inequalities between *man* and *woman* produce the diminished moon and are the very source of evil.

II.
Why did God design the universe with these three defects?

A. Defect is a relative assessment.
B. Defect itself can accomplish things that perfection cannot.
C. The purpose of creation, for some mysterious reason, cannot be realized except via the agency of defect and evil.

III.
How does evil serve the purpose of creation?

A. Transformation requires a movement from flaw to perfection.
B. Purpose of creation is that there be an "other" with whom divinity can relate.
C. A true "other" must be a free agent with free choice.
D. Free choice, by definition, requires that options exist that are not God's will (i.e., evil).

IV.
How does God create evil?

A. The three disparities between *man* and *woman* cause the production of gevurot. the seeds of concealment and evil.

V.
The elimination of gender disparities.

---

22. TB, *Brachot* 61b. The original passage quoted above is from *Menachot* 29b. It ends with Moshe seeing "them weighing out R. Akiva's flesh at the market stalls." This doesn't communicate that R. Akiva died a martyr's death at the hands of the Romans as clearly as the passage from *Brachot* 61b, which also describes R. Akiva's death.

omnipotent and have actually brought this 'bad' upon those who, by all counts, have earned 'good,' in which case You become, in their eyes, anything but just, anything but good?"

וא"כ הרי לפי האמת אינם חסרונות כלל אלא כולם הם תיקונים להוציא מחשבתו ית"ש לפועל. וכנודע שהתעלמות האור ומיעוטו הוא סיבת תיקונו. כי ע"י שנתמעט האור העליון והיה כל חסרונות הנז'. הנה עי"ז נעשה האפשרות למציאת העולמות בי"ע על מדרגתם שהם.

R. Elyashev uses this story of R. Akiva to illustrate two points:

a. *HaShem's* will for each moment is unfathomable. He **can will something for the present that** (apparently) **totally contradicts** the standards of justice, truth, and **perfection** that He *wills* to prevail in the end. **This is because what appears as defect or lack is a perfectly engineered tool to accomplish a critical task that fullness and perfection simply could not get done.**

b. Since evil is ever-present in the universe and will remain so until the messianic time, it must be that *HaShem* wants it here, for some strange reason, and that His "perfect" design for each moment includes the dark face of evil.

For some mysterious purpose, about to be explained, the world did not emerge from Divinity's womb in its fully perfected state. Rather, Adam and Eve (representing the entirety of creation) were assigned the task of *tikun olam,* of finishing the work of creation by managing its resources and directing its final stages of actualization. The *midrash* teaches that their command to "tend and keep the garden"[23] was a heavenly call for mitzvah practice, a most powerful agent of personal and global transformation.[24] In so doing, they would complete their own maturation and lead the world to its fully

---

23. Genesis 2:15.
24. *Midrash Tanchuma Bubar,* Genesis 25; *Zohar* 1:27a; *Tikunei Zohar,* end of *Tikun* 21.

realized state. *HaShem* could have created a faultless universe from the start. Instead He chose to birth one that would have to acquire its maturity by its own efforts.[25] More than *HaShem* willed perfection, He willed that this perfection be earned by the creatures themselves. It must be that perfection attained by the fruit of labor is superior to that bestowed as an unearned gift. Consequently, by design, the world moves from immaturity to enlightenment, flaw to perfection, darkness to light.

A principle emerges: **The concealment of light at the beginning of creation,** that "negative" state itself, **actually catalyzes its final attainment**. The eternally deepening ecstasy of perfecting that is creation's promised end, must, apparently, build from a previous state of lack. The difference between "perfec*tion*" and the bliss of "eternal perfec*ting*" is exactly this: The latter only emerges as the fruit of a prolonged chapter of hard work.

Lack and deficiency, the painful facts of life on planet earth, sprout like weeds in the cracks and dark spaces of Divine concealment. When there is light, there is bounty. When the light withdraws, lack appears. And yet, Divine concealment is an essential ingredient to the creating of worlds. The Hebrew language itself

I.
Three primordial inequalities between *man* and *woman* produce the diminished moon and are the very source of evil.

II.
Why did God design the universe with these three defects?

A. Defect is a relative assessment.
B. Defect itself can accomplish things that perfection cannot.
C. The purpose of creation, for some mysterious reason, cannot be realized except via the agency of defect and evil.

III.
How does evil serve the purpose of creation?

A. Transformation requires a movement from flaw to perfection.
B. Purpose of creation is that there be an "other" with whom divinity can relate.
C. A true "other" must be a free agent with free choice.
D. Free choice, by definition, requires that options exist that are not God's will (i.e., evil).

IV.
How does God create evil?

A. The three disparities between *man* and *woman* cause the production of gevurot. the seeds of concealment and evil.

V.
The elimination of gender disparities.

---

25. We earn this perfection both through our suffering and through our good deeds.

attests to this fact, for the word for world (עולם) can be literally
defined as "a place where God is hidden (נעלם)."

**Consequently, the creation of worlds and the creation of lack
are two faces of the same event. Both emerge from the darkness
that remains when *HaShem* withdraws His supernal light and
radiant perfection.**

ולכל ענין הבחירה אשר נתייסד בעולם הזה. והוא ע"י שהסתיר המאציל
ית"ש את פניו והמעיט את גילויו בכל החסרונות הנז'. עי"ז נעשה רצונו
וכוונתו ית"ש בכל מציאת העולמות בי"ע ויסוד הבחירה כחפצו ורצונו.
והיינו כי הרי יסוד הבחירה הנה הוא ע"י המציאת דטוב ורע ומציאת הרע
הנה הוא מגלוי הגבורות.

**The key to understanding why a perfect God chose to create
(an apparently) imperfect world is the mystery of free choice.**
HaShem seems willing to pay any price for the preservation of free
will among His creatures. Why is choice such an essential ingredient to the purpose of creation?

It can be said that, before creation, Divinity, by definition, was
lacking nothing except, in some mysterious sense, the experience
of actualized relationship, for there was no "other" with whom to
relate.[26] Divinity had no intrinsic need for this experience, and yet,
for reasons unknown and essentially unknowable, chose to do so.
The history and evolution of creation becomes the life cycle of this
"other," and his/her evolving relationship with his/her Creator as
infant, child, servant, consort, mother, and so on.

---

26. Most sources mention certain aspects of "relationship" as the purpose of
creation (for example, giving or self-revelation) but do not discuss "relationship" itself as the underlying intention that unifies them all. See Ramchal, *The
Way of God*, 1:2:1.
Also, "The term 'Father' indicates the Holy One, Blessed Be He, and 'Mother'
(or *Shekhinah*) is the Community of Israel" (TB, *Brachot* 35b). This statement
in the Talmud suggests the idea of God and Israel as a "couple."
Similarly, "For the sake of the unification [i.e., relationship] of the Holy One
and His *Shekhinah* [the community of Israel]..." (This is an affirmation
said before mitzvot. It expresses the intention of relationship as the essential
motivation for religious acts.) See: R. Tsadok HaKohen, *Dover Tsedek* 2a.

Free choice cuts to the very core of what it means to be an *other*. In fact, it is the necessary and sufficient definition of that term. One who cannot choose freely is not a true *other* but a narcissistic extension of his master. He may occupy a different body but, driven by remote control, he is not an independent agent.

The matter is complicated by layers of paradox. On one hand, *HaShem* absolutely wants us to be true *others*, but on the other hand, He also wants us to obey His commands and to use our free will to choose what *He* wants us to choose.

Yet *HaShem*'s commitment to free will overrides all. More than He wants to be obeyed, He wants His creatures to choose their path freely. Confident that love, wisdom, truth, and even the pleasure-principle itself will eventually lead them to see things His way, *HaShem* (so to speak) wants each individual to discover from the inside that the best choice and greatest pleasure, the biggest bargain in the universe, is to choose God.

The relationship between God and *man* consummates when a person's authentic and spontaneous desires exactly coincide with *HaShem*'s will. Intimacy then occurs at the most core level of being, called *crown (keter)*, the highest and innermost root of soul corresponding to *will*. This is as close as any *two* can get, and the pleasure of their union surpasses all earthly delights.[27]

I.

Three primordial inequalities between *man* and *woman* produce the diminished moon and are the very source of evil.

II.

Why did God design the universe with these three defects?

A. Defect is a relative assessment.
B. Defect itself can accomplish things that perfection cannot.
C. The purpose of creation, for some mysterious reason, cannot be realized except via the agency of defect and evil.

III.

How does evil serve the purpose of creation?

A. Transformation requires a movement from flaw to perfection.
B. Purpose of creation is that there be an "other" with whom divinity can relate.
C. A true "other" must be a free agent with free choice.
D. Free choice, by definition, requires that options exist that are not God's will (i.e., evil).

IV.

How does God create evil?

A. The three disparities between *man* and *woman* cause the production of gevurot. the seeds of concealment and evil.

V.

The elimination of gender disparities.

---

27. This idea is elaborated in "A Still Small Voice," Correspondence School, s.v. *Prayer and Destiny*, Lessons 8–10.

The six creation days culminate with the appearance of human-kind, a collection of individuals who fulfill the criterion of *other*. They are capable of making independent decisions about whether to obey their Creator, or whether to believe that there even *is* a Creator, or whether He really does communicate His will through scripture and revelation.

Each stage in the downward unfolding of creation and the congealing of light into matter springs from a prior veiling of Divine Presence. Yet what exactly disappears when *HaShem* with-draws?

There are six truths that comprise the very definition of Divinity:

a. The fact of His existence
b. His perfection
c. The necessity of His existence
d. His absolute independence
e. His simplicity
f. His unity[28]

Consequently, **when God hides,** these six truths hide with Him and their opposites appear instead. **Perfection displays** a mask of **lack and defect (particularly, the three flaws** of gender disparity **enumerated at the beginning of this piece).**

In this way, *HaShem* **materialized His will for the creation of worlds that would house creatures possessed of free choice.** *HaShem*'s mysterious purpose for creation required that *man* be free to oppose His will.

If free choice is the endpoint of the downward flow of creation, then once it appears, that phase of work is over, and the next leg of the journey can begin. Since *woman* was the last to emerge in

---

28. Ramchal, ibid. 1:6.

the six-day sequence of creation, the mystery of free choice must
be intricately linked to her.

The literal definition of "choice" is the opportunity to select options from multiple possibilities. Consequently, the implementation of free choice in the universe requires two complementary components.

a. There must be multiple options available from which to choose. On a cosmic scale this is no small task, for the cornerstone truth of the universe is that *God is one*, which means that *there is only God*. Consequently, there is only one real choice, and that is Him. How does *HaShem* create the appearance of plausible options if everyone can see that there is only one?

b. A creature must arise who possesses the psychic space and sophistication of consciousness to actualize free will. The criteria being twofold:

— it cannot be ruled by instinct, for one who is slave to his animal nature is not a free agent.

— it cannot be controlled by external forces, for one who is ruled by another, even invisibly by remote control, is also not a free agent. If someone puts a gun to your head and says, "Your money or your life," you may *choose* to empty your pock-

---

I.

Three primordial inequalities between *man* and *woman* produce the diminished moon and are the very source of evil.

II.

Why did God design the universe with these three defects?

A. Defect is a relative assessment.
B. Defect itself can accomplish things that perfection cannot.
C. The purpose of creation, for some mysterious reason, cannot be realized except via the agency of defect and evil.

III.

How does evil serve the purpose of creation?

A. Transformation requires a movement from flaw to perfection.
B. Purpose of creation is that there be an "other" with whom divinity can relate.
C. A true "other" must be a free agent with free choice.
D. Free choice, by definition, requires that options exist that are not God's will (i.e., evil).

IV.

How does God create evil?

A. The three disparities between *man* and *woman* cause the production of gevurot. the seeds of concealment and evil.

V.

The elimination of gender disparities.

ets, but you have not made a *free* choice about how to distribute your cash.

Free choice means that, based on a spread of alternatives, each with its built-in costs and benefits, one can choose any one of them based on the *belief* that its gains will be most worth its losses, that its cost-benefit ratio is the best one possible. Belief is the key here. Calculations such as these always contain "unknowns," and once one is dealing with "unknowns" one has entered the realm of belief.

With each choice a person accumulates the wisdom of retrospect, which enhances his judgment the next time around. Now he anticipates a whole other set of factors that were invisible to him before. His beliefs concerning the hidden costs and benefits of any given set of options correct themselves with each generation of data.

The greater the consistency between belief and reality,[29] the more one's decisions will consistently yield good and enduring results. The more one's beliefs clash with reality, the more one's decisions will fail to accomplish their intended goals and pull unintended consequences in their wake, and the good they *do* accrue will not endure.

Jews *believe* that the body of teachings, commands, rituals, and faith-principles that comprise the Torah are exquisitely consistent with the multidimensional landscape of reality and with all its varied layers of invisible truths. Consequently, choices based on *its* advice are trusted to reap positive results.

As explained, free choice requires options that are (at least apparently) real. Yet since God is one, the creation of options

---

29. Reality here means the physical and metaphysical laws of the universe that are built into the structure of reality: $\pi=3.14$; $e=mc^2$; murder damages the soul and brings purgating consequences in its wake, etc.

requires the concealment of God, along with all the attributes that devolve from His oneness. In their place appear multiplicity, imperfection, indifference, and so on. This means that free choice requires, as its prerequisite, the creation of evil, defined as the illusion of separation and independence from God. The word *illusion* is significant, since nothing can actually be separate from God for God is one. To the extent that something presents the appearance of self-containment, self-sovereignty, and multiplicity, to that extent it partakes of the quality of evil. To the extent that it communicates through itself the truth of God's goodness, oneness, compassion, and generosity, to that extent it partakes of the quality of holiness.

How does a radiant, consuming, and infinite Oneness create evil and make it plausible, when it is really a ridiculous hype that denies the most basic and obvious truth of reality? How can anything hide the telltale stamp of its Creator and not "spill the beans" that God is one? This is actually a complicated logistical problem.

The mechanism *HaShem* devised to conceal both Himself and the truth of His oneness is amazing indeed. It is called the mystery of the "breaking of the vessels."[30]

I.
Three primordial inequalities between *man* and *woman* produce the diminished moon and are the very source of evil.

II.
Why did God design the universe with these three defects?

A. Defect is a relative assessment.
B. Defect itself can accomplish things that perfection cannot.
C. The purpose of creation, for some mysterious reason, cannot be realized except via the agency of defect and evil.

III.
How does evil serve the purpose of creation?

A. Transformation requires a movement from flaw to perfection.
B. Purpose of creation is that there be an "other" with whom divinity can relate.
C. A true "other" must be a free agent with free choice.
D. Free choice, by definition, requires that options exist that are not God's will (i.e., evil).

IV.
How does God create evil?

A. The three disparities between *man* and *woman* cause the production of gevurot. the seeds of concealment and evil.

V.
The elimination of gender disparities.

30. For an expanded treatment of this subject in English, and a thorough bibliography of original sources, see: Rav Immanual Schochet, *Mystical Concepts in Chassidism*, which appears as an appendix to the Hebrew-English translation of the

Previous to the creative act that brought our present universe into being, God existed in a state of undifferentiated, infinitely potent Light that, figuratively speaking, was equally present at every point of time and space (though time and space, themselves creations, did not yet actually exist).

This Light was so powerful that it negated even the possibility of transitory existence. Form and physicality could not maintain their boundaries in the face of this infinitely powerful Light. They would be overwhelmed and annihilated by its strength of illumination, in the same way that the individual lights of stars are washed out by the more potent radiance of the sun, or a delicate crystal glass shatters and disintegrates from the impact of water rushing from a fire hose. In order to create the physical universe, God needed first, from our perspective, to conceal His Infinite Light from a particular area and to create a dark, womb-like vacuum wherein His Presence would not be readily felt. Then, into this apparently "empty space," He emanated a "thin" ray of light (from His infinite surroundings), the unfolding and dissipation of which is the history and progression of creation as we know it.

Tanya: R. Schneur Zalman of Liadi, *Likutei Amarim, Tanya* (Brooklyn, N.Y.: Kehot Publication Society, 5740), pp. 875–878.

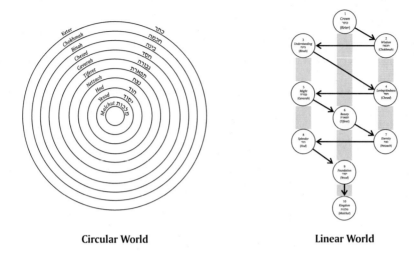

Circular World   **Linear World**

This transition from Infinite Light to present reality did not happen smoothly but rather in two trials.[31] The original beam of emanation first formed ten circular and concentric channels of flow (or *sefirot*) that were not, themselves, interconnected. Each functioned as an independent unit at a single frequency. These circular *sefirot* were pure "tones," which means they did not contain inter-included aspects of the other *sefirot* within themselves. Their narrow range of self-definition made them brittle. This flaw in their personal and collective gestalt brought a critical weakness into the system.[32] When the light entered, it moved in stages, from circle to

---

31. Actually three. See the "Map of the Unfolding of Worlds" (p. 167), which includes an earlier stage that precedes these two, called the Bound World. Thus the actual sequence of the creation of worlds passes through three epochs: the Bound World (which was reabsorbed back into the Infinite Light); the World of Points (which shattered); and the Rectified World (which is the universe within which we live). Since the Bound World is not directly relevant to our present discussion, it is not mentioned.

32. This "flaw" was deliberately introduced by *HaShem*, for the "shattering" that followed was His means of creating the "illusion" of separation from God, i.e., evil.

circle, from outer to inner. Each *sefirah* had to contain all the light that was ultimately destined for it, as well as, temporarily, all that was intended for those below it in the sequence of emanation. The *sefirot*, in this arrangement, were too inflexible to bear the stress of overload, and they shattered under the impact, one after the other. Some were immediately rectified and reconstituted into another arrangement. This newly established array was holographic (which meant that every "piece" contained something of all the others within it) and was organized along three pillars with interconnecting pathways linking each *sefirah* to the others. This is the Tree of Life, whose diagram appears on p. 20.

Most of the light from the original vessels (that spilled out when they shattered) was immediately reabsorbed back into its root on high. Nevertheless, some of it had actually penetrated into the walls of the vessels, so that the shattered pieces now carried a residual glow of trapped light within themselves. The shards fell from level to level through the new system of ten *sefirot* organized along three pillars. Like food passing through a digestive tract, at each stage in their descent the higher and more refined frequencies of light were absorbed by the newly established pattern of *sefirot*. At the end of this process, only the lower and denser frequencies remained within the fragments themselves. The lights trapped within the fallen shards of circular *sefirot* are called *gevurot*, defined as dark knots of unactualized potential.

Since there can never be *actual* discontinuity within the spiritual realms, for this would create a fundamental duality, everything must (and does) exist as a continuum, as part of an unbroken chain of connection with the Source. Therefore, these shattered fragments could not fall below a certain point – the point of commonality and overlap between their highest and the new system's lowest band of radiation. They were hanging on by their fingernails (so to speak) at the last possible point of contact, at the lowest edge of the lowest *sefirah* (*malchut*). They remained connected with their Source, but only indirectly now, via the newly emanated hierarchy of *sefirot*, to which they clung. Since their higher frequency light had been extracted from them, there was an *apparent* discontinuity between themselves and their Creator – a breach between their vibratory level and His. As such, it *appeared* as if their light arose independently, from within the fragments themselves, and not from a higher source.

This is the origin of evil defined as the illusion of separation and independence from God. We are built from the debris of these shattered vessels and its wasteland is our reality. Our physical plane is the band of interpenetration between the shards of the World of Circles and the lowest point of the *sefirot* of straightness.

Just as dense concentrations of physical matter bend and distort space-time,[33] similarly these dark unactualized sparks, called *gevurot*, distort their surroundings, creating evil, that is, the illusion of separation. But as they actualize, they lighten and enlighten and exert less distortion on their environs. In this way evil dissipates, for it was only an illusion – a temporary wrinkle of space-time that will smooth out when the dark spark (or soul) at its center comes clean and returns to its source.

I.
Three primordial inequalities between *man* and *woman* produce the diminished moon and are the very source of evil.

II.
Why did God design the universe with these three defects?

A. Defect is a relative assessment.
B. Defect itself can accomplish things that perfection cannot.
C. The purpose of creation, for some mysterious reason, cannot be realized except via the agency of defect and evil.

III.
How does evil serve the purpose of creation?

A. Transformation requires a movement from flaw to perfection.
B. Purpose of creation is that there be an "other" with whom divinity can relate.
C. A true "other" must be a free agent with free choice.
D. Free choice, by definition, requires that options exist that are not God's will (i.e., evil).

IV.
How does God create evil?

A. The three disparities between *man* and *woman* cause the production of gevurot. the seeds of concealment and evil.

V.
The elimination of gender disparities.

---

33. This is part of Einstein's teachings on relativity and the meaning of e=mc^2

For many reasons (for example, their origin in the circular realms) the *gevurot* are called feminine lights.[34] When estranged from their masculine *chassadim* (the lights of conscious awareness), they become dark and dense. Their *tikun* entails a kind of matchmaking process between them and their corresponding masculine lights.

Practically, this means binding them back to their root on high by revealing the truth of their connection to God. Whenever a person acts in a way that reveals to the outer senses God's purpose for that moment and for all the elements within it, he elevates sparks and sweetens *gevurot*. The purer his intent, the more potent his act. Evil dissolves into nonexistence as the truth of God's oneness shines forth from the depths. The greatest mystery of all, however, is that, in the end, the layer of shards and concealment will become the most incandescent embodiment of this truth, outshining even the soul in its declaration of oneness.

To summarize, **free choice requires,** as its prerequisite, plausible options and that requires **the illusion of separation and independence from God.** The mechanism *HaShem* devised to conjure this illusion **is to manufacture *gevurot*,** dense knots of feminine light, **and to keep them separated from** their masculine counterparts among **the *chassadim*.**

The "diminishment of the moon" occurred anew at every stage of creation's unfolding. The shattering of vessels and appearance of *gevurot* is how it transpired in the World of Chaos.

שאחר שנתגלה אורות הגבורות למעלה וירדו ונשתלשלו למטה ונתפשטו הם לבדן בלתי חסדים הנה כאשר הגיעו מאחר אצילות ולמטה נברא הרע על ידיהם כמו שבארנו. והנה נעשה הגילוי דבחי' גבורות לבדן. ע"י המציאות דעולם הנקודות אשר מהם נעשה כל עולם התוהו שהוא בריאת כל הרע וכמו שבארנו שם. וכן גם אח"כ בעת התיקון דמעשה בראשית הנה לא

---

34. See "Kabbalistic Symbols of the Feminine," p. 25.

נתבטל הרע מכל וכל. ונשאר קיומו ליסוד הבחירה. ע"י הגילוי דהגבורות שנשאר אז ג"כ.

The roots of these *gevurot* are in the highest realms, and while they remain there, they only manifest holiness. Yet that is not how things stayed. Instead **they tumbled level after level, and when they fell out of the world of emanation** into the mental, emotional, and physical planes, **they became the source of evil** and its web of illusions.

The place where the *gevurot* first appear alone, separated from the tempering influences of **their *chassadim*** (or masculine lights) **is in the World of Points** (or Circles) as described previously. That world shattered **and its fallen state is called the World of Tohu (chaos), and it is there that evil first appears,** as the by-product of defiled *gevurot*. ***HaShem* repaired the situation** and cleared out much of the filthy debris when He fashioned our universe **in the six creation days.** He united most of the *gevurot* with their *chassadim* and the world shone with God awareness. **Nevertheless, because** *HaShem* willed that Adam and Eve have *free choice*, and because this requires the appearance of options, and because options require the semblance of "other-than-God," **He left some increment of evil** unrectified so that illusion would still hold sway even in the Garden of Eden. **Consequently, a portion of the *gevurot* remained unmatched** by their *chassadim,* **for**

I.
Three primordial inequalities between *man* and *woman* produce the diminished moon and are the very source of evil.

II.
Why did God design the universe with these three defects?

A. Defect is a relative assessment.
B. Defect itself can accomplish things that perfection cannot.
C. The purpose of creation, for some mysterious reason, cannot be realized except via the agency of defect and evil.

III.
How does evil serve the purpose of creation?

A. Transformation requires a movement from flaw to perfection.
B. Purpose of creation is that there be an "other" with whom divinity can relate.
C. A true "other" must be a free agent with free choice.
D. Free choice, by definition, requires that options exist that are not God's will (i.e., evil).

IV.
How does God create evil?

A. The three disparities between *man* and *woman* cause the production of gevurot. the seeds of concealment and evil.

V.
The elimination of gender disparities.

unsweetened *gevurot* **are the precursors to evil**, the raw materials out of which it congeals and upon which it feeds.

וכנודע שהשורש דכל מציאות הרע הנה הוא מבחי' הגבורות. והנה כ"ז יצא
בסיבת הג' חסרונות הנז'. כי הרי חסרון הא' מה שיצאו הדו"ן שהם בחי' חו"ג
בשני שמות מיוחדים שהם מ"ה וב"ן. הנה זה היה עיקר הסיבה לכל. כי יצא
הב"ן מתחילה והוא כל הגבורות דעולם הנקודות אשר מזה יצא כל עולם
התוהו וכנודע. וכן גם אח"כ בעת התיקון. הנה ע"י ב' חסרונות האחרים והוא
מה שלא נשתוו המ"ה וב"ן בכל פרצו'. הנה עי"ז אינם מתייחדים שניהם
בעוצם היחוד כהראוי. ועומד לעולם הוא גבוה ממנה. ועי"ז נשאר גם אחר
התיקון גילוי להגבורות בפנ"ע. ונשאר להרע שורש ומקום למציאותו וקיומו
בעולם עד ביאת המשיח. והרי ישנם עי"ז יסוד ומקום לבחירה כחפצו ורצונו
ית"ש. והרי נמצא כי אלו הג' חסרונות. הם כולם בכוונה ורצון ממנו ית"ש.

The primary mechanism that *HaShem* **employs for keeping the** *gevurot* **unmatched and thus available as a base for evil is** the disparity of stature and status between the masculine and feminine lights. **The three defects listed previously that** create a state of non-symmetry, and inequality between *man* and *woman*, are what **perpetuate the existence of evil in the universe.**

The first flaw, the fact that *man* **and** *woman* **(who also cor-**respondrespectively to the *chassadim* and the *gevurot*) emerge **from entirely different roots within Divinity,**[35] **is the primary inequality** and the second two derive from this. As a result of their disparity of roots, **the feminine came out alone** before the mascu-line, estranged and unmitigated by him. **Her** unsweetened *gevurot* **imploded, and the World of Circles shattered and tumbled into chaos. Thereafter, even in the rectified world** that followed, and even in its Garden of Eden, the masculine and feminine remained unsymmetrical and unequal on every level, even though *HaShem* repaired the situation to a significant degree.

As a result of the pervasive inequality and lack of symmetry

---

35. *Woman* is from ב"ן and *man* is from מ"ה. See footnote 15 of this chapter.

Map of the Unfolding of Worlds

(אין) עצמות הנעלם
Unknowable Essence

ע

אור אין סוף
Infinite Light
Light that is limitless in quantity, quality, and expanse.

ע

צמצום
Contraction and Concealment (of the Infinite Light) . . .
. . .from a circumscribed area within the vast expanse of Infinite Light to create an apparently vacant space that could hold
the entire created universe within its bounds.

ע

אדם קדמון
Primordial Man
Comprised of *sefirot* arranged both as circles and lines. The former, being "first in thought . . .", hold the higher vision.
The plane of pure and undifferentiated will, and source of all subsequent worlds.

ע

עקודים
Bound World
First era of creation; ten lights in a single vessel; forced communality with complete repression of individual expression;
unrectified world that was reabsorbed back into its source

ע

נקודים
World of Points (also called Circle World)[41]
Second era of creation; ten lights in ten *unconnected* and *un*-interincluded vessels (including both circles and lines);
psychotic individuality; "great lights with few and primitive vessels";
unrectified world that fell, shattered, and degenerated into the World of Chaos.
Of the eight primordial kings, seven of them "ruled and died." Their ruling was in the World of Points . . .

עולם התוהו
World of Chaos
. . . and their dying was in the World Of Chaos.
Shattered vessels from World of Points; origin of evil.   »

ע

עולם התיקון
Rectified World, Linear World, World of Tikun
Third era of creation. Ten lights in ten interconncected and interincluded vessels, thus integrating the values of both
communality and individuality; our universe; the universe described by the Torah; the eighth king who "ruled" and didn't die
and whose wife is mentioned; the era of evolving relationship between *man* and *woman*;
"an abundance of sophisticated vessels with lights that are few and small". Comprised of the following levels:

אצילות
World of Emanation
Spiritual plane; pure Divine archetypes; upper world.

בריאה
World of Creation
Mental plane; the highest of the three lower worlds.

יצירה
World of Formation
Emotional plane.

עשיה
World of Action
Physical plane.

קליפות
Klipot
Realm of shards, husks, and impure forces; fallen sparks and broken vessels from the World of Points (Circles and Chaos). ←

between *man* and *woman,* **they cannot meet in consummate union,** for they don't fit together quite right. To the extent that disparities of stature and status remain, there are always parts of one that don't match the other, **and *man* always stands higher than *woman.* Consequently, even in our World of *Tikun,*** there are many places where he does not meet her, and those **parts of her remain alone,** unsweetened, and **exposed.** It is precisely **there,** in the bare spaces that emerge from the inequalities between *man* and *woman,* that **evil thrives, and will continue to do so, until the messianic time.**

HaShem **wills free choice, which requires** options, which requires the illusion of other-than-God, which requires exposed *gevurot,* which requires the inequality of *man* and *woman.* Consequently, **the three lacks that** engender a state of inequality between *man* and *woman* **were introduced into the universe by design,** as was evil, its intended by-product.

Obviously, that is not the end of the story. We also know that *HaShem* created evil in order that it be eliminated. We are promised that in the end of days, "Evil will evaporate like smoke into nonexistence,"[36] and "Death will be swallowed up forever."[37] Every *thing* and moment, from the beginning of time until its end, has a portion in the world to come *except* evil.[38] Unlike all else, evil has no intrinsic purpose unto itself; it only serves as a means toward an end. Once its job gets done, it has no point, and immediately dissolves into oblivion. Every *thing* must have a purpose to justify its existence.

---

36. Standard Liturgy, Rosh Hashanah and Yom Kippur.
37. Isaiah 25:8. Death came into the universe after the first sin, when Adam and Eve ate from the Tree of Knowledge of Good and Evil. In a sin-free and perfected world there would be no death. And so, in the world to come, we will be reborn into eternal bodies.
38. *Leshem,* HDYH, 2:2:3:4.

Every act of choice transforms the soul, and each of its scenarios must include a bout with illusion. *HaShem* built into the structure of His universe that *good* cannot become *very good* except by encountering evil,[39] experiencing uncertainty as to which option holds the relevant truth, and freely choosing a response.

Two benefits accrue at the end of this sequence:

a.   Some increment of evil is eliminated from the universe.[40]

b.   The soul is transformed and enlightened.

These profits occur both from our "right" choices, and from enduring the purgating consequences that always follow in the wake of our "wrong" choices, which disabuse us of our illusions. Either way, at the end of the path, evil ceases, for the very wisdom that it catalyzed now becomes its undoing. Deception only has power where ignorance prevails. Consequently, each new expansion of consciousness dissolves another layer of illusion simply by seeing right through it. Any encounter with evil eventually engenders a deepened awareness of truth that, by definition, disempowers the very evil that produced it.

While the enlightenment and transforma-

I.
Three primordial inequalities between *man* and *woman* produce the diminished moon and are the very source of evil.

II.
Why did God design the universe with these three defects?

A. Defect is a relative assessment.
B. Defect itself can accomplish things that perfection cannot.
C. The purpose of creation, for some mysterious reason, cannot be realized except via the agency of defect and evil.

III.
How does evil serve the purpose of creation?

A. Transformation requires a movement from flaw to perfection.
B. Purpose of creation is that there be an "other" with whom divinity can relate.
C. A true "other" must be a free agent with free choice.
D. Free choice, by definition, requires that options exist that are not God's will (i.e., evil).

IV.
How does God create evil?

A. The three disparities between *man* and *woman* cause the production of gevurot. the seeds of concealment and evil.

V.
The elimination of gender disparities.

---

39. *Bereshit Rabbah* 9:2.
40. *Leshem*, HDYH, 2:4:17.
41. *Leshem*, "Treatise Addressing Confusions Surrounding the Circle and

tion catalyzed by evil will endure in our souls forever, evil itself will disappear from the universe, without even a pile of ash to mark its grave.

Our primary task as human beings is to eliminate evil and reveal the truth of God's oneness throughout the universe. Rav Elyashev shows that the illusion of other-than God (i.e., evil) derives from the inequalities between *man* and *woman*. Since evil's enchantments are what challenge the truth that God is one, it follows as a synonymous statement that the inequality between *man* and *woman* is what blocks our capacity to know the oneness of God.

DEBRIEFING

THE DIMINISHED MOON

What Do We Know?

1. The disparity of stature between *man* and *woman* is not an ideal, but a defect. This means that when measured against *HaShem*'s absolute standard of messianic perfection its blemished status is irrefutably apparent.

2. *HaShem* intentionally built the three flaws of gender disparity into the universe to serve an essential, though temporary, function. As the precursors to imperfection and evil, they enable the possibility of free choice, *HaShem*'s nonnegotiable imperative for creation.

3. *HaShem*'s unequivocal commitment to free choice proves that He seeks a non-narcissistic relationship with His creatures, whereby they operate as free agents and not as mere puppets to His will. *HaShem* does not want to be a ventriloquist with creation as His mouthpiece; He wants

---

Linear Worlds," 3:6. This treatise appears as an appendix to HDYH.

to be a freely chosen beloved, the true object of our hearts' desire.

4. The disparity of stature between *man* and *woman* is the hidden germ of evil. All that opposes the revelation of God's oneness, goodness, compassion, and perfection originate with the inequalities of gender that are their first cause.

5. The disparities of gender, along with evil, their intended by-product, will cease to exist in the messianic time.

What Don't We Know?

1. We still do not know what it will look like for *man* and *woman* to attain their equality of stature. In what ways will they become similar? In what ways will they remain different?

Logical Implications and Speculations

1. Rav Elyashev established that the disparities of stature between *man* and *woman* are inextricably linked to evil (defined as the illusion of separation and independence from God). This means that our holy task of "tending and keeping the garden," of removing evil and bringing the world to its fully actualized perfection, must include an active commitment to address the issues of gender disparity within the parameters of halacha. Lacking this, we may succeed in temporarily relieving a symptom or two, but as long as evil's roots remain intact, it is sure to be plotting a new assault with unrelenting vigor. Evil cannot contain itself and never stays repressed for long. This is evidenced on all fronts, from the personal to historical.

2. The *fact* of feminism is a good sign, for it means that we are starting to get to the root of things. The actual *expression* of feminism as a political movement uninformed by Torah and halacha, and unbeholden to God's truths, is cause for

adamant critique. Nevertheless, the fact that a movement now exists to address the inequalities of gender bodes well for civilization. It shows that our instincts are healthy and attuned, though their expression needs massive refinement.

3. We know that evil will not be finally eliminated until the end of days when *HaShem* Himself executes its demise. "R. Yehuda expounded: In the time-to-come the Holy One will bring the evil inclination and slay it in the presence of the righteous and the wicked...."[42]

Yet that final act, on that fateful day, culminates millenniums of accumulated effort. Each generation chips away at the vast (but finite) reservoir of evil that contaminates our universe.[43] No one can say: "Why should I bother with this dirty work, when *HaShem* promises to take care of it in the end?" No! The whole point is that we make our ongoing efforts below, working our knuckles to the bone, and *HaShem* matches each exertion with an abundance of assistance from above, amplified exponentially.

Similarly, this applies to the elimination of gender disparities that are evil's roots. They, too, will not cease before the messianic time, yet it remains our work to engage in the constant and committed effort to do whatever we can do here and now below, within the parameters of halachic stricture, to annul these defects and strive toward equality. This is God's work no less than the holy war against our evil inclination.

---

42. TB, *Sukkah* 52a.
43. *Leshem,* HDYH, 2:4:17.

6

TRANSFORMATION IS ONLY POSSIBLE AFTER A FALL

Perfecting and Perfection
A Series of Excerpts
from *Orot HaKodesh*

by R. Avraham Yitzchak Kook

BARE BONES LITERACY

SUMMARY

Perfection and Perfecting by R. Avraham Yitzchak Kook explores the cosmic function served by *woman's* ordeal. He shows that positive transformation cannot happen except via the jerky motion of one step back for two steps forward. There seems to be no other way to improve except by stumbling and recovering from that fall. This two-step sequence, as inefficient as it seems, eventually ends with the net gain of progress made. The moon's cycle of waning and waxing, of diminishment and re-attained stature, is the prototype for this cosmic truth and the means by which an absolutely perfect God manifests the elusive joy of perfecting.

VOCABULARY

7,000-Year Cycle of Biblical History – Tradition teaches that each creation day translates into 1,000 years of earthly history and the count begins from the appearance of Adam (a creature with specific spiritual capabilities that is *not* synonymous with *Homo sapiens*). The six weekdays are 6,000 years of refining ourselves and turning the world into a Temple that can hold and reveal the full Presence of God. This period culminates in the messianic time and then transitions into an entirely new era called the world to come, or seventh millennium and cosmic Sabbath. We are currently in the last quarter of this last millenium, as the Gregorian calendar settles into its twenty-first century.

evil – Literally, "broken" or "unstable." The illusion of existence as separate and independent from God.

Gan Eden – Garden of Eden. Paradise. The term that describes the nature of physical reality before the shattering and fragmentation that followed Adam and Eve's sin. Eden is the state where *HaShem*'s Presence visibly permeates reality, and all things express their perfection and exist in a state of union with God.

lights – *Lights* are always equivalent to consciousness in kabbalistic writings. Each *sefirah,* or spark, is a *light* that transmits a particular insight or capacity for awareness.

messianic era – The messianic era is a transitional time between *this* world and the next. It begins somewhere toward the end of the sixth millennium (we are now within the period of its likely beginnings) and will take us to the threshold of the world to come. It is the joyous stage of actualized perfection. Love of God, love of neighbor, and love of Torah reign.

TECHNICAL NOTES

The italicized terms: *man, woman, mother,* and *father* refer to kabbalistic archetypes (called *partzufim*) and, by extension, to the masculine and feminine attributes found in both men and women. The literal translation of the Hebrew text appears in bold print.

SYNOPSIS

PERFECTING AND PERFECTION

In these essays R. Kook explores the paradox of Divine perfection that rumbles at the heart of creation and instigates its forward motion. Two absolutely contradictory yet indispensable facts combine to create a dynamic perfection that is greater than the sum of its parts.

- Perfection – God is consummately perfect in a way that precludes the need for (and even possibility of) improvement.
- Perfecting – If God's perfection lacks nothing, it must also include the possibility of becoming *more* perfect.

Each statement negates the other, yet both are equally true. These two partners in paradox are none other than the cosmic sun and moon. Though R. Kook does not use those terms, the attributes he employs come straight from their compendium of correspondences. When *HaShem* directed the moon to diminish, He effectively assigned her the role (and labor) of perfecting, which includes change and transformation, shadow and light.

In these excerpts R. Kook presents an exquisitely articulate vision of the cosmic necessity (and glory) of *woman*'s role with its characteristic cycle of descent and re-attainment. All began with *HaShem*'s (so to speak) existential dilemma: It is an uncontestable principle of faith that God is infinite and that every attribute of Divinity partakes of that infinitude.[1] God is infinitely good, infinitely perfect, infinitely wise, and so on.[2] How then could *HaShem* express the infinite fullness of Himself in the finite realms? The answer is: through paradox. The irrationality of paradox makes it uniquely suited to house infinitude and to serve as its host in the lower worlds, for the jarring clash of paradox liberates new light not visible in either part alone.

These two components of Divine perfection, by virtue of their mutual contradiction, are not only paradoxical in relation to each other, they are also paradoxical in relation to *HaShem*. Each contains a heresy that is solved by the other, and only together, these two flawed truths embody the mystery of Divine perfection.

- The statement that God is consummately perfect inadvertently ascribes a limit beyond which God cannot go, because His maximum perfection has already been attained. This violates the principle of Divine infinitude.
- The heresy inherent in perfect*ing* is more obvious. To assert that there exists within Divinity an eternal process of transformation may solve the infinitude problem but introduces a different heresy: Perfect*ing*, which entails movement from lack to fullness, deficiency to completeness, ascribes *imper*fection and self-improvement to a God Who, by definition, was absolutely perfect all along.

---

1. Ramchal, *The Way of God* 1:1, 2.
2. *Zohar* 3:257b.

Nevertheless, when yoked together in unity, these two contradictory statements with their two complementary heresies expand luminously to contain the infinite truth of Divine majesty.

One of the features of paradox that makes it uniquely suited to this task is its capacity to generate a kind of electric current between its two poles. This happens automatically when the mind focuses in and discovers that it cannot make peace with either side. At the very moment the intellect savors the truth of one statement, the stink of heresy spoils its repose. Jolted, the mind scrambles for a solution, which it *does* find in the other side. But that statement, too, is also no safe haven, for its truth has problems of its own.

Back and forth, a reluctant nomad, the mind seeks peace to no avail until ... a wonder happens. Its oscillation triggers a kind of electric current that adds motion to the system. And once there is motion, there is time. And if the motion is perfectly symmetrical between truth and counter-truth (as here), then there is abovetime. Now, in addition to its static and opposing truths a dynamic element appears that fuses the system into a single coordinated whole that is greater than the sum of its parts and possesses the capacity to hold infinite truth.

R. Kook focuses here on the moon's half of this partnership, the mystery and practical expression of perfect*ing*, that is, *becoming* perfect, *progressing* toward wholeness. It appears to be built into the very fabric of reality from the start that it is impossible to make progress except through the back and forth motion[3] of "descent for the sake of progressing to an even higher place in the end."[4] Every forward step is preceded by a fall (or lapse of consciousness).

---

3. In Hebrew, רצוא ושוב.
4. In Hebrew, ירידה לצורך עליה; TB, *Makkot* 7b; R. Shneur Zalman of Liadi (*Rashaz*), *Likutei Torah* (LT), 3:87c, 4:2a.

This mechanism of perfecting applies on every plane of existence (physical, emotional, mental, spiritual).[5]

At the completion of each Creation Day (except the second),[6] *HaShem* considered His handiwork and "saw that it was good."[7] At the end of the sixth day *HaShem* employs a more superlative term: "*HaShem* observed everything that He had made and behold, it was very good."[8] What is unique about the sixth day, the *midrash* asks, that warrants His additional praise? What is the difference between *good* and *very good*?

The answers proposed by the *midrash* are most perplexing and seemingly the opposite of what logic (or philosophy) might presume. The *midrash* says:[9]

> *Good*, refers to the inclination toward good; *very good*, refers to the inclination toward evil....
>
> *Good*, refers to the dispensation of happiness; *very good*, refers to the dispensation of suffering....
>
> *Good*, refers to paradise; *very good*, refers to *gehenna* (hell)....
>
> *Good*, refers to the angel of life; *very good*, refers to the angel of death....
>
> *Good*, refers to the kingdom of heaven; *very good*, refers to the earthly kingdom....

---

5. *Leshem*, HDYH, MHY, 11 (first word *ve'nityased*).

6. Rashi, Genesis 1:7. "And why was the expression 'that it was good' not said on the second day? Because the work of creating the waters was not completed until the third day; for He had only begun it on the second; and a thing that is not completed is not at its perfection and at its best. On the third day, however, when the work of creating the waters was completed, and then He began and completed another work of creation, the expression 'that it was good' was repeated two times: once for the completion of the work of the second day and once for the completion of the work of the third day."

7. Genesis 1:4, 10, 12, 18, 21, 25.

8. Genesis 1:31.

9. *Midrash Rabbah, Bereshit* 9:7–13.

With these strange words the *midrash* reveals a great mystery and profound truth: growth always requires, as its catalyst, some encounter with evil (in one of its myriad forms, of which the *midrash* lists several) and this is exactly why God created it.[10] There are many options of response to this meeting, all of which eventually lead toward cleansing and perfection, though some routes are joyous and filled with inner peace, while others seethe with existential terror.

The fact remains that *good* cannot become better except via the catalyst of evil, whether as temptation or suffering, constriction, loss, lack, lapse of consciousness, stumbling, error, failure, injustice, sin, and so on. Its faces are legion. This whole package of fall – purification – transformation is the means by which an absolutely perfect God incorporates into Himself the experience of perfect*ing* (of perfection becoming even *more* perfect, of *good* becoming *very good*). This is the feminine expression of Divinity and R. Kook explores its mechanism and fragile beauty.

He explains: For the possibility of perfecting to exist within Divinity, some portion of absolute perfection had to forfeit its noble origins and descend into the depths. When the moon reluctantly agreed to this role, she accepted the most deplorable conditions of constriction, lack, and suffering. Then, from that lowly place, she embarked on a tireless journey back to her roots. Each step in her monumental trek (which extends from the beginning of time until its end) is a labor of garbage collecting, damage fixing, lack filling, and upward striving.

The effort, though immensely tedious, is not without its satisfactions. There is a particular type of exquisite joy that only comes from the experience of personal growth, and every soul longs for its

---

10. Isaiah 45:7. "I am the Lord and there is none else. I form light and create darkness. I make peace, and create evil. I the Lord do all these things."

sweetness. And there is a rare and precious beauty that only shines through the noble effort of choosing good no matter what it costs and making sacrifice to serve God. In addition to these unique pleasures that inhere in the process itself, the labor of perfecting will bear an infinitely greater bounty of reward at its end. Like a coiled spring compressed and released, the perfecting aspect of Divinity will eventually supersede the absolute perfection that was its starting point. The whole system inverts as it moves up a notch, *good* becomes *very good*, and the moon enjoys her newfound status at the top. Not only is she absolutely perfect as before, but the memory of where she's been and how she's struggled adds a whole new level of appreciation to her attainment. Now she enjoys perfection *plus* an ecstatic gratitude for being free of 6,000 years of pain.

The phenomenon of dynamic perfecting is extremely complex, for it starts in the lowest pits and reaches to exalted heights. The archetype that holds its presence has two polar opposite faces, one that shows its diminished beginning and one that shows its glorious end, and they are not obviously linked, except to one who knows the inside story, that achievement always begins with fall. To the uninitiated they appear as two separate entities altogether.

Exactly so is the feminine archetype, depicted both as the seductress who lures men into sin and the selfless nurturer who is a crown to her husband. She is the cause of lack, suffering, fear, and fall, as well as the holiest pleasure of achieved perfection and union with God. Any attempt to isolate the latter from the former must fail, for they are both one entity (i.e., *woman*) at different stages of her life cycle. The elimination of her dark side instantly chokes out all possibility of transformation.[11] That is the mystery

---

11. This is only true in our present, pre-messianic period of history. The world to come is characterized by growth through joy. We will no longer require evil and suffering as our catalysts.

of perfecting. It alone can turn *good* into very *good*, lead into gold, but there is no avoiding its toll. The challenge is to find the least damaging way to fall. Options include: sleep, dance, nature walks, exercise, music, chatting with a friend, summer vacation, existential questioning, picnics, trips to the beach, Purim, and so on.

The entire period of biblical history is a single moon cycle of diminishment and perfec*ting*, though this pattern plays out on every scale, and each of us passes through many such cycles in the course of our lives. Creation is that aspect of Divinity that is experiencing perfec*ting*. Each person receives a splinter of Divine perfection that has been compressed and diminished. Through the course of our lives we actualize its potentials, clean out its impurities, and restore it to the sublime perfection that is its truth and holy heritage. In this way we will all participate in the moon's labor and will all share in the fruits of her reward.

ANNOTATED TRANSLATION
PERFEC*TING* AND PERFEC*TION*

I[12]

מה אנו חושבים על דבר המטרה האלוקית בהמצאת ההויה. אומרים אנו,
שהשלמות המוחלטת היא היא מחויבת המציאות, ואין בה דבר בכח,
כי אם הכל בפועל, אבל יש שלמות של הוספת שלמות, שזה אי אפשר
להיות באלוקית שהרי השלמות המוחלטת האין סופית אינה מניחה מקום
להוספה, ולמטרה זו שהוספת שלמות גם היא לא תחסר בהויה, צריכה
ההויה העולמית להתהווה.

When contemplating the timeless question: **"Why did *HaShem* create the universe?" one observes** two contrary tendencies within Divinity.

---

12. R. Avraham Yitzchak Kook, *Orot HaKodesh (Lights of Holiness)* 2:531.

1. *Absolute* perfection requires the complete actualization of all potential. Unrealized possibility is always less than **perfect,** for it is *not yet* fully accomplished, it has *not yet* attained distinction.

2. And **yet,** there is a complementary (and seemingly contradictory) tendency in the universe: the holy **striving to become *more* perfect.** The nobility that shines when someone breaks through an old pattern and chooses good despite its costs **is also a type of perfection,** in spite of the still unactualized status of the person who revealed it. **Theoretically, it should be impossible for this** more delicate beauty **to co-exist with the absolute perfection of category one, for it violates the criterion of total actualization.** And yet, **it is equally impossible for creation to lack** this virtue, to not include in its repertoire of perfection the holy triumph **of self-improvement.**

Category one is a *state* of perfection, and category two is a *process.* The latter introduces dynamic content into the picture. There are two assertions, essential to Judaism's definition of God, that must be preserved in any theological discussion: *HaShem* is both perfect and infinite. Yet the absolute perfection of category one actually violates the criterion of infinitude, for it inadvertently creates a limit when it asserts that the paragon of excellence has already been reached and that no further improvement is possible. Consequently, **Divine perfection,** in order to be limit*less,* **must also include** the possibility of **infinite perfecting,** an eternal process whereby perfection becomes even more perfect.

ולהיות לפי זה מתחילת מתחתית היותר שפלה, כלומר ממעמד של החסרון
המוחלט, ושתלך תמיד הלוך ועלה להעליה המוחלטת. וההויה נוצרה
בתכונה כזה, שעדי עד לא תחדל מהתעלות, כי זאת היא פעולה אין סופית.

The mechanism by which this second, paradoxical attribute appears within Divinity is as follows: **Some portion** of absolute perfection **must** forfeit its noble origins, descend into the depths, and **assume an impoverished state of lack. Then, from that lowly place, it journeys back up** to its roots **in a ceaseless and eternal** odyssey of damage fixing, lack filling, and **upward striving. In this way creation incorporates into itself the** blessed joy of self-actualization. There is no end to this holy dance of **perfecting,** for (like its static counterpart) **it, too, partakes of Divine infinitude.**

וכדי להבטיח את העליה בעצמותה של ההויה נוצרה כולה בעילוי עליון,
והעילוי היה יותר מכדי השעור שתוכן מוגבל יכול להיות בפועל, אף על פי
שהוא יכול להיות בכח, על כן בהופעת ההויה בפועל נתקלקלו הדברים,
והכחות נסתבכו זה בזה, והנם עוסקים במלחמה חריפה, עד שתנצח
המחשבה המוחלטת האין סופית של טוב, ויתוקן הכל, בצירוף העילוי של
נתינת מקום להשלמתה של עליה בלתי פוסקת.

What guarantees that the transformations accruing from this descent **will be positive ones?** The mechanism is as follows:

Kabbalah[13] teaches that before creation, there arose within the mind of God a vision of the end and glorious perfection of the entire endeavor. This primordial glimpse of the most final future of the cosmos contained within its horizons both the universe as a whole and every individual within it – meaning, all the generations of all the peoples, races, and creatures that ever would be.

It was the utter and irresistible beauty of this vision that inspired the decision to create and propels the process forward even now. **Since this first thought derives from the loftiest source on high,** a gap exists between it and the physical plane that has a much more limited capacity to hold light. For this reason **the vision cannot slide smoothly into the world** and establish itself as a physical

---

13. *Pirkei d'Rebbe Eliezer* 283, as explicated by *Leshem,* HDYH 2:1:1; *Ari, Etz Chaim, Shaar HaClallim* 1, as explicated by *Leshem,* ChHB, *Drush Igulim V'nosher* 1:1 (*mahadura kama*).

fact, **for it simply doesn't "fit."** It can dwell below as a potential state but not as an actual one.

Consequently, **when it descended** into the physical plane, attempting to materialize, **it caused damage** instead of repair. The world could not contain its brilliance and shattered from the overload. In this broken state all its structure was lost and all **its elements discombobulated.** With no sense of higher unity or collective identity, only self-absorbed individuality remains. **Each** splintered **piece fights bitterly** for its turf. **Yet** from the midst of these warring factions **the original intention of infinite good** and boundless perfection takes shape and **prevails.** Paradoxically, these battles become the means by which that supernal vision of perfection (and peace) materializes. In this way the clashing of forces **and** creatures **effects positive transformation.** Like pebbles in a brook, their constant knocking smoothes jagged edges, and each eventually settles into the shape and position that is its place in the larger, collective vision. **This is the means by which absolute perfection creates the space inside itself to experience eternal perfecting.**

שזהו עדן מיוחד, שבזה הבריאה משלמת את כבוד נוראה.

The sweet pleasure of becoming more perfect is a singular joy. There is nothing that compares to its abiding gratification, for it includes the satisfaction of shifting from taker to giver in one's relationship with God. Each creature strives and struggles to become worthy, and **in so doing it perfects the glory of its Creator.**

II[14]

מבינים אנו בשלמות האלקית המוחלטה שני ערכים של השלמה. ערך אחד של השלמה, שמצד גדלה וגמירתה אין שייך בה הוספה של מעלה.

---

14. *Orot HaKodesh* 2:532.

אבל אם לא היתה האפשרות של הוספה היה זה בעצמו ענין חסרון, כי
השלמות ההולכת ונוספת תמיד יש בה יתרון ותענוג ואיזה מין העלאה,
שאנו עורגים לה כל כך, הליכה מחיל אל חיל, אשר על כן לא תוכל השלמות
האלוקית להיות חסרה זה היתרון של הוספת הכח. ועל זה יש באלוקות
הכשרון של היצירה, ההתהוות העולמית הבלתי מוגבלה, ההולכת בכל
ערכיה ומתעלה, ונמצא שהנשמה האלוקית העצמית שבהויה שבהויה המחיה
אותה הוא העילוי התמידי שלה, שהוא הוא יסודה האלוקי, הקורא אותה
להמצא ולהשתכלל ...

One discerns within the absolute perfection of Divinity two
paradoxical **features. The first is that God is absolutely perfect.** It
is impossible for there to exist, whether in reality or in imagination,
a perfection greater than His. **This aspect of Divine perfection
cannot become more perfect** for there is nothing beyond it, there
are no further levels to attain. And yet, this excellence conceals a
deficiency that mars the very perfection that it purports. **Perfection that lacks the possibility of becoming even more perfect**
is no longer completely flawless, for it **is missing something.** It is
perfection minus one small detail, the possibility of experiencing
dynamic perfect*ing*. Consequently, Divinity must also possess this
latter capability as well.

This second feature, **the possibility of positive transformation,
has certain fulfillments and gratifications and even a superiority
over** its more distinguished counterpart, the supreme (though
static) expression of **absolute perfection.** There is a particular
type of exquisite joy that comes from self-improvement, **and
every soul longs for its sweetness. The** exhilaration of personal
transformation, of **"ascending from strength to strength,"**[15] must
also be a Divine satisfaction. **It is impossible for the Creator to
lack this virtue.**

Consequently, there exists within Divinity a celebration of

---

15. Psalms 84:8.

creativity that manifests as the unceasing and universal unfolding of creation. Steadily and **relentlessly,** the universe and every
creature in **it presses toward perfection.**

The **soul of** each creature is a splinter **of pure Godliness that
dropped into the lowest world.** It is a spark of holy light, displaced from its home on high, trapped inside a physical body, **that
endeavors to return to its roots,** and in so doing, pulls all that
it touches along with it. In this way *HaShem* infiltrates the lower
realms and makes His will known from the inside out. **The Divine
soul serves as a heavenly messenger that calls each creature** back
to its roots, urging it to invest in the holy task of **self-discovery
and personal growth....**

III[16]

האיטיות שבסדר המציאות, ההגבלה שבטבע, הרשלנות החיצונית שלה,
הצמצום שבעליות רוחנית, הארעיות שבבניסים, כל אלה מחזיקי היסוד של
התעלות הבלתי פוסקת שהוא היסוד הפנימי של מציאות.

**The rule of gradual development that governs the material
universe, the** uncompromising **limitations imposed by natural
law and its apparently slipshod** approach to getting things done,
**the resistance of matter to the unfolding of spirit, the rarity of
miracle ... all these** seem to secure the reign of materialism. And
yet, the very opposite is true. They **actually serve the evolutionary
impulse** of spirit that rises **from the depths of the physical world**
and assures its success.

שיש לו גבול בתוך גבולו, שתספיק הירידה של התגלות המציאות העולמית,
עד עומקת היותר ירוד, ועד מחשכה היותר אפל, לעליה נצחית, בלא שום
הפסק. וכל תקופה איטית מכינה כוח לתקופה יותר מהירה בעליתה, עד
המהירות היותר עליונה.

---

16. *Orot HaKodesh* 2:529.

The fact that nature imposes limits on its own limits guarantees that the descent (and materialization) **of light into the thick darkness of *this* world will** reach the end of its tether and spring back into **an eternally enfolding ascension of spirit. This** 6,000-year **era of dense physicality, where** the properties of inertia and gradual development prevail, **is actually preparing** the world **for a new age of intensely rapid ascent.**

...ולעד לא תכלה הופעת ההתעלות, ותוספות האור העדן והחיים ההולכים ומתבסמים, ומתמלאים תמיד ערך יותר גדול ונשגב, עד שישתוו יחד צורת ההשלמה הגמורה, וצורת ההשתלמות הבלתי פוסקת, הבאה מסבת החסרון הקדום.

The Bible begins its creation chapters with the story of Adam and Eve. Kabbalah teaches that all the events of Genesis literally happened, and in a physical sense, but on an entirely different plane of reality than what we call the physical world today.[17] Only after Adam and Eve ate from the Tree of Knowledge of Good and Evil did the world turn inside out and upside down, and collapse into its now familiar form.

Jewish mysticism identifies four planes of existence, which it calls the four worlds because each contains an entire set of ten *sefirot* within it. From above to below they are:[18]

atzilut	אצילות	spiritual plane
briyah	בריאה	mental plane
yetzirah	יצירה	emotional (also psychic and astral) plane
assiya	עשיה	physical plane

It explains that in the Edenic era of Adam and Eve, the lowest and most material level of reality was the mental plane. This means that in those halcyon days bodies were made of thought. Even now,

---

17. *Leshem*, HDYH 2:4:3.
18. See Chapter 5, footnote 2.

ideas have a presence and exert influence in the world, although their impact seems mostly tenuous and speculative from our coarse and material vantage point. Not so in Eden. Adam and Eve's base of operations was the mental plane. Thought was the raw material of bodies. Eden is called the Garden of Delights because pure awareness constituted the molecules of existence and, as is known, the highest and most enduring ecstasies are those that come from expanding consciousness.

One of the primary tasks of our interim period of history (the 6,000 years between Eden and the world to come) is to repair the damage that transpired when our holy forebears ate from the forbidden Tree of Knowledge. Eventually, we will succeed in completing the quota of work that gains us entry into the messianic age. Then begins the reward phase of history with its eternally blissful process of deepening union with God. **This upward enfolding of creation will continue forever.**

One of the first milestones along the way is our reattainment of the level of beatific consciousness called the Garden of Eden. **The blissful light of Eden will suffuse all living things with intensifying sweetness, each moment more than the next. Eventually, the perfecting aspect of creation that has grown from lack to fullness,** flaw to wholeness, darkness to light, **will catch up to the transcendent-perfection-of-Divinity that was, by definition, absolutely perfect right from the start.** On that day there will no longer be a "small light and a great one,"[19] for the sun and the moon will have both grown great. Then will our prayer be fulfilled:[20] "May it be Your will, *HaShem* ... to fill the flaw of the moon that there be no diminution in it. May the light of the moon be like the light of

19. Genesis 1:16.
20. Standard Liturgy, *Kiddush HaLevana* (Sanctification of the Moon).

the sun[21] ... as it was before it was diminished, as it is said: 'Two great luminaries...'"[22]

All motion must have some "spring" that drives it forward and supplies its momentum. This is both a physical and metaphysical law. Since the entire universe exists within the absolute perfection of Divine light, flaw, lack, and darkness are energetically unstable states. As sure as water flows downhill, the pure light of God seeks to fill all the dark spaces of creation and dissolve its lacks. The disparity between Divinity's absolute perfection and the flaws of the material world instigates an unremitting effort (driven by natural forces) to eliminate that differential and restore the uninterrupted expanse of light that is *HaShem's* resting state. This affirmative action to eradicate lack in the lower world is called perfec*ting* and it is, paradoxically, an essential sub-feature of perfec*tion*. For perfec*tion* to lack absolutely nothing, it must also include within itself the possibility of becoming more perfect, that is, of growth and change and dynamic perfec*ting*, and these, by definition, cannot but build upon some previous state of lack, smallness, or *im*perfection.

Yet once its flaws have been remedied and its lacks filled, that aspect that was engaged in the active process of perfec*ting* becomes as impeccable as its holy counterpart, the perfection-that-always-was. What happens then, when it no longer has an impetus for growth, since there is nothing left to fix and nothing more to become? With equilibrium attained, there is no torque to drive the system forward. Perhaps it will now cease its upward spiral and merge back with the first category of perfection, having finally become identical with it. R. Kook says, "No." There still remains enough tension in the "spring" to drive the system forward in a never-ending process of perfec*ting*.

---

21. Isaiah 30:26.
22. Genesis 1:16.

ויספיק הזכר של חסרון העבר לתן דחיפה תמידית להשתלמות הולכת
ונוספת.

Now the **mere** *remembrance* **of the previous state of lack sustains** the vector of growth. Yet its front of transformation shifts from the repairing of defect to a deepening appreciation of the blessed gift of perfection and closeness to God. The memory of millennia in darkness and exile, now contrasted with the bliss of Eden, initiates **an infinite unfolding** of gratitude that becomes the new front **of** growth and change and **perfect*ing*.**

Like a rubber band stretched and released, it now overshoots its starting block. Not only is it as faultless as the absolute perfection of its reference point, but it has the possibility of becoming even more perfect, by virtue of its now infinitely deepening capacity for appreciating its perfection.

ותהיה הצורה של השתלמות הבילתי נפסקת מתעלה על ההשלמה הגמורה.
אשת חיל עטרת בעלה, וצדיקים יושבים ועטרותיהם בראשיהם ונהנים מזיו
השכינה, ההולכת ומתגברת תמיד, עליה אחר עליה, לאין קץ ותכלית. ברוך
ד' לעולם אמן אמן, וישתבח שמו לעד ולנצח נצחים.

The perfecting aspect of Divinity will then supersede the pole of absolute perfection. "The woman of valor becomes the crown to her husband." Just as a **crown sits** *above* the head, so has perfect*ing* moved beyond perfect*ion*. *Tzaddikim* sit with their crowns on their heads and bask in the radiance of the *Shekhinah,* who continues to unfold her beauty in a never-ending spiral of perfect*ing*. The Blessedness of *HaShem* is forever deepening, which means that the beholder's awe intensifies from each moment to the next. He or she must say, **"Amen," and again, "Amen," and again . . . ,** for each new revelation prompts its own exclamation. **His name will** continue to inspire praise that magnifies with each instant, from now unto eternity. There will be no end to the revelation of glory. There will never be a moment that does not expose an absolutely new facet of Divine beauty.

IV[23]

מגמת ההויה כולה, מצד החפץ הכמוס האין סופי, היא כפי הגלותה לנו, עצה
גדולה של התעלות והוספה נצחית, שאם אין מציאות של קוטן וחסרון לא
יוכל להיות רק גדול ומילוי, אבל לא התגדלות, ודריכה תדירית לתוספת
ברכה.

Creation's purpose, as evidenced by the persistent longing that
daily rises from its hidden core, **is to** serve as the means by which
Divinity **manifests eternal growth and perfecting. It is obvious
that without** a starting point of **lack or immaturity, there would
be no possibility of improvement, change, and joyful transformation. Everything would already be full and realized. All** the
lack and imperfection in the universe **is only a means toward
this** end and the luxurious **flow of blessing** that accompanies its
realization.

ואף על פי שאין קץ להעילוי של השלמות המלאה, שאין בה עילוי מצד אין
סופיותה, מכל מקום כלול בה גם כן זה הכח הנשגב של התעלות תדירית,
וזה נחשב כאלו השלמות המוחלטה משתלמת על ידי ההשתלמות, הבאה
על ידי הופעת הקוטן הבא אל הגדול, ועבודה זו היא צורך גבוה.

**Although the perfection of Divinity is consummate beyond
measure, it does not adequately manifest the attribute of infinitude** because it conceals a limit in its very assertion of ultimate
attainment. Consequently, Divinity **must also include** *within*
**Itself a capacity for infinite transformation. It is as if absolute
perfection were itself becoming more perfect** by means of the
perfecting process happening within it. And yet, perfecting, by
definition, **requires that lack and immaturity exist as the raw
materials of its craft. This** possibility of growth and dynamic
unfolding, with all its messy prerequisites of darkness, defect, and
imperfection, **is** in some mysterious way, **a Divine necessity.**

---

23. *Orot HaKodesh* 2:530.

DEBRIEFING

PERFECT*ING* AND PERFECT*ION*

What Do We Know?

1. Divine perfection is the summation of two contradictory and irreconcilable states of being:
   - Perfect*ion* – which only permits *full* actualization and *absolute* impeccability into its sphere.
   - Perfect*ing* – which has no meaning except in response to a preexisting state of lack and imperfection.

   This crushing paradox lives at the heart of the universe and the energy released from the sparks that fly as its polarities resist fusion quietly powers creation's unfolding.

2. Although Rav Kook does not mention the moon explicitly, it is clear that perfecting corresponds to the talmudic (and kabbalistic) archetype of lunar diminishment.

3. It is impossible to rank these two complementary elements of Divine perfection. Each is superior in some ways, and inferior in others, and each has a heretical underside.
   - Perfect*ion*'s heresy is that it inadvertently sets an upper limit of ultimate attainment that contradicts the principle of Divine infinitude.
   - Perfect*ing*'s heresy is that it ascribes imperfection, lack, and defect to *HaShem*.

4. Perfecting:
   - is a dynamic process of unfolding, as opposed to a static state;
   - enables creation to move from *taker* to *giver* in relation to *HaShem*. The struggle and sacrifice entailed in choosing good, despite its cost, gives something back to *HaShem* (as it were) by perfecting His glory in the universe;

- shines with a unique and exquisite beauty that is nowhere else to be found.

5. The aspect of Divinity actively engaged in perfect*ing* is the soul-stuff of creation. That portion of absolute perfection that forfeited its noble roots and descended into the depths of lack and defect is what then splintered into the sparks of soul that enliven created things.

6. Just as the moon has a bipolar cycle of waning and waxing, so is the diminishment phase of perfect*ing* just one half of its oscillation. The constriction entailed in collapse acts as a compressed spring that powers an eternal process of perfect*ing*, which culminates in the infinitely deepening ecstasy of the world to come. The 7,000 years of biblical history (which include both *this* world and the *next*) are a single moon cycle, of waning and waxing.

7. The perfect*ing* aspect of Divinity will eventually supersede the perfect*ion* pole. Not only does it attain an equally consummate perfection, but its sojourn in darkness will instill an eternally deepening gratitude for redemption and for the blessed gift of Divine embrace.

8. In some mysterious sense, *HaShem* "needs" there to be a below, with lack and imperfection, that strives to improve its condition. This is no less a Divine necessity than the theological assertion that God is absolutely perfect.

7

THE EXPANSION OF CONSCIOUSNESS AND DISSOLUTION OF HIERARCHY

Miryam's Circle Dance[1]

By R. Kalonymous Kalman Halevi Epstein (the *Meor V'Shemesh*)

BARE BONES LITERACY

SUMMARY

Miryam's Circle Dance by *Meor V'Shemesh* on *Parashat Beshalach* presents a glorious vision of the things that will change when *woman* recovers her full stature, and feminine consciousness, now matured, exerts greater influence on the world and its values.

---

1. R. Kalonymous Kalman HaLevi Epstein (*Meor V'Shemesh*), *Parashat BeShalach* (first word, *Od*).

VOCABULARY

dinim (**also called** *gevurot*) – These terms mean, literally, "severities" and refer to the dark knots of unrectified potential that are the driving force behind our universe. *Dinim* and *gevurot* are generally associated with unconscious lights.

Hoshanna Rabbah – (literally, "Great Call for Redemption"). The seventh (and last) day of Sukkot, marked by elaborate beseechings for rain and redemption. On that day congregants circle the table that holds the Torah scroll seven times.

lights – *Lights* are always equivalent to consciousness in kabbalistic writings. Each *sefirah*, or spark, is a *light* that transmits a particular insight or capacity for awareness.

malchut – The lowest of the ten *sefirot* is called *malchut*, which means, literally, "royalty" and "kingship." It corresponds to the physical plane and represents the final stage in light's congealing into matter.

messianic era – The messianic era is a transitional time between *this* world and the next. It begins somewhere toward the end of the sixth millennium (we are now within the period of its likely beginnings) and will take us to the threshold of the world to come. It is the joyous stage of actualized perfection. Love of God, love of neighbor, and love of Torah reign.

sefirah / sefirot – The ten channels of Divine flow and emanation that link the Transcendent Light with Its evolving and apparently finite creation.

Shemini Atzeret – (literally, "Eighth Day of Closure"). A holiday that immediately follows the seven days of Sukkot. The eighth day, Shemini Atzeret, is the simplest festival of the Jewish calendar. It, in itself, has no special observances beyond the standard celebratory meals that mark each holiday.

Simchat Torah – (literally, "Rejoicing of Torah"). In the Diaspora, where each holiday lasts two days (instead of one, as in Israel), the second day of Shemini Atzeret (the ninth day of Sukkot) becomes Simchat Torah, a time of joyous celebration for the gift of Torah. The day is spent circle dancing around the Torah scrolls, which are held by the congregants. In Israel, both Shemini Atzeret and Simchat Torah occur on the eighth day.

Sukkot – (literally, "Tabernacles"). The fall harvest festival where Jews voluntarily exile themselves from the security of their homes and live for a week in fragile dwellings beneath the stars, to remind themselves of the impermanence and unreliability of the material world. Special prayers are recited throughout that week, and in the morning liturgy, congregants, in procession, circle the table that holds the Torah scroll.

world to come – The seventh millennium and period following the messianic era that marks an entirely new state of existence, where physicality dissolves and souls (with their new light bodies) experience an infinitely deepening ecstasy of relationship with God.

worlds – refers both to the four planes of reality – physical, emotional, mental, spiritual – and to the sequential stages in creation's unfolding (see "Map of the Unfolding of Worlds," p. 167).

TECHNICAL NOTES

The italicized terms *man*, *woman*, *mother*, and *father* refer to kabbalistic archetypes (called *partzufim*) and, by extension, to the masculine and feminine attributes found in both men and women. The literal translation of the Hebrew text appears in bold print.

SYNOPSIS

MIRYAM'S CIRCLE DANCE

R. Epstein comments on a brief passage from the Torah that
transpires after the miraculous parting of the Red Sea. With everyone safely secured on the other side, Moshe led the people in a
hymn of thanksgiving. Immediately afterward the Torah describes
Miryam gathering the women for a celebration of music, song,
and dance.

> And Miryam the prophetess, the sister of Aaron, took the
> timbrel in her hand; and all the women went out after her with
> tambourines and with circle dances. And Miryam answered
> them: "Sing to the Lord, for He has triumphed gloriously; the
> horse and his rider has He thrown into the sea."[2]

R. Epstein builds his commentary on two hints in that passage.
First, he observes that the Torah presents information about the
particular type of dance performed, that it was a circle dance.
Second, he notes that Miryam sang her thanksgiving song in the
present tense while Moshe formulated his nearly identical praise
in the future.[3] Based on these clues, R. Epstein demonstrates that
Miryam, in her dance, accessed a higher state of consciousness
than did Moshe through his song. R. Epstein bases his argument
on kabbalistic teachings about the unfolding of worlds.

It is known that creation passed through several eras before
settling into the stable and familiar form that is our world. The

---

2. Exodus 15:20–21.

3. Miryam says, "Sing to the Lord, for He has triumphed gloriously; the horse
and his rider has He thrown into the sea." Moshe speaks nearly identical words,
except in the future tense, "I *will* sing to the Lord for He has triumphed gloriously; the horse and his rider has He thrown into the sea..." (Exodus 15:1).

stage immediately preceding ours is called the Circle Universe,[4] while ours is the Linear World of straight lines and hierarchy.[5] These terms are both technical and metaphorical. They describe their arrangement of *sefirot* (the former as concentric circles, the latter as three parallel lines),[6] and the divergent nature of their worldviews.

Kabbalah explains that just as creation emerged from the depths of Divinity, so will it return there in a single cycle of extension and retraction. Its worlds will unfold downward until their endpoint of emanation and then begin a reverse course back toward their roots (and beyond). Yet, unlike a yo-yo whose motion is similar, the universe undergoes profound transformations at each stage.

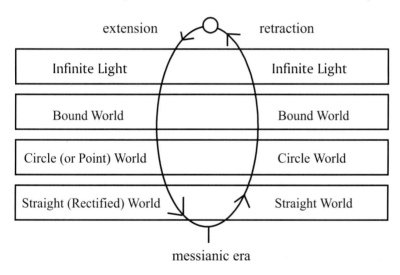

The creation that returns has metamorphosed through its experience. It has been fixed, actualized, cleansed, and transfigured along the way. Nevertheless, its return route is the exact reverse

---

4. Also called the World of Points.
5. Also called the Rectified World.
6. See diagram p. 206.

of its original emanation. We are still approaching the maximum point of extension, which will be unmistakably marked by the messianic age, and then we will begin our journey back up to our roots.[7] The first stop will be the World of Circles, the stage that immediately preceded ours on the way down.[8]

Looking toward the future, the Circle World is a more evolved and rectified state of consciousness than our present linear reality. Its lights are just becoming visible on the horizon, signaling our approaching transition from this era to that. R. Epstein explores the worldviews of these two realities and the divergent psychologies that characterize each.

In the Linear World everything occupies a unique position along a continuum extending from above to below. Each value imposes a hierarchy that orders the world according to its preferences. The Torah also ranks its members by the standards that it holds dear. A higher soul is one that is awake, is in continuous communion, and always chooses the most spiritually productive option; a lower soul is ignorant of spiritual truths and wallows in the entangling repercussions of wrong action. This hierarchy of spiritual status marks a descending flow of enlightenment. Each person receives teachings from the level above and passes them on to the level below. Everyone is a student to those above and a teacher to those below.

This Linear World, with its multitude of intersecting hierarchies, creates an encompassing network of incentives (both positive and negative) that motivate the resource-demanding

---

7. *Leshem*, HDYH 2:4:17:5 (first word, *V'achor*).
8. *Leshem* explains that although this is technically called the World of Points, it is also correct to refer to it as the Circle World because relative to the worlds that follow, its organization is circular. "Treatise Addressing Confusions Surrounding the Circle and Linear Worlds," 3:6. (This treatise appears as an appendix to HDYH).

labor of self-improvement. Hierarchy of status defines a pecking order that keeps everyone striving to keep up with the Joneses. People occupying higher ranks become role models who inspire others to invest the effort required to obtain similar success. The whole point of the era of hierarchy is to create a context of values, inducements, constraints, and coercions that press out the full potential of each soul down to its last drop. Its straight line presents a clear direction of growth and compelling enforcements to assure forward motion.

Eventually, and hopefully quite soon, we will complete this consuming labor of self-development. All potential will be actualized, all impurities cleansed, all deprivations enriched, and all ignorance eliminated. At that point hierarchy will cease, for it will have grown obsolete. Its whole point was to instigate the grueling work of self-actualization and to establish clear lines of authority to facilitate the downward flow of teachings. Its worldview, though built on a shaky foundation of relative truths, was (and is) remark- ably successful in achieving its goals. But, explains R. Epstein, its days are numbered, its truths will pass, and a new and more rectified order of consciousness will reign, called the Circle World.

Just as a circle has no beginning or end and every point is equidistant from its center, so is this true for souls. Truly, it is impossible to rank them, for each is the most beloved in the scale of values that is its perfected virtue.

Each creature will eventually attain its full potential and shine with the unique revelation of Divine beauty that only it can manifest. The spiritual bliss of the world to come is the intensely abiding joy of finally becoming who you are. When that happens, the distorting veneer of hierarchy will melt away and, behold, we will find ourselves standing in a circle with *HaShem* at its center, and we will dance together in holy celebration.

In the future the Holy One will make a circle dance for the *tzaddikim*. He will seat Himself among them in the Garden of Eden and each one of the *tzaddikim* will point with his finger and say, "This is our God for whom we have waited, that He might save us. This is the Lord for whom we hoped; we will be glad and rejoice in His salvation."[9,10]

In the Circle World, it will be gloriously clear that every soul is equally precious and singularly beautiful in a way that cannot be ranked. Similarly, it will not anymore be possible to look to one's neighbors for guidance in serving God, for each person has a unique soul-specialty, and in that area he or she is the world's foremost expert. There is nowhere to look for instruction except straight from *HaShem*, who metaphorically sits at the circle's center, equidistant from all its holy points.

On that eternal day, everyone will be satiated with knowledge of God to the fullest capacity of his or her joy and all hierarchies of status will dissolve. In wonderment people will discover that on the scale of enlightenment, all have become equal.

The paradigm shift goes deeper still, for R. Epstein explains that the conventions of gender in kabbalah echo the physical differences between men and women. Bestowal is a masculine role, receiving is a feminine one. Consequently, in the linear scheme, the teacher is masculine in relation to the student who is influenced by him. In the Circle World these hierarchical rankings between human beings will end, for no one will receive spiritual guidance from neighbors, spouses, or even teachers. All will turn straight to the Holy One for inspiration, and on that day, says R. Epstein, all power disparities will cease, including the archetypal source of

---

9. Isaiah, 25:9.
10. TB, *Taanit* 31a.

them all, the hierarchy of gender, with its asymmetrical distribution of authority and dependency.

All this Miryam knew and intended when she led the women in their circle dance. Miryam drew the future into the present, initiating the Jewish nation into the secret truth, promise, and yearning of the Circle World: The day will come, blessed and welcomed by all, when power disparities will cease and perfect equality reign, when every soul will shine with its glory, and all will become the most dearly beloved of their Creator.

Miryam phrased her song in the present tense, for she was actually holding that consciousness within herself as she sang and danced. The lights of the Circle World are so vast that they cannot fit into the brain as an isolated organ of consciousness. They require full body participation (for example, in dance), and even a collection of them in coordinated activity (in this case, all women) to create a container sufficiently spacious to hold their revelations. Moshe spoke in future tense, for he knew *about* circle consciousness and that it would eventually reign, but he could not, in the present, access that state himself.

ANNOTATED TRANSLATION
MIRYAM'S CIRCLE DANCE

ותקח מרים הנביאה אחות אהרן את התוף בידה ותצאנה כל הנשים אחריה
בתופים ובמחולות ותען להם מרים שירו לה' כי גאה וגו'.

And Miryam the prophetess, the sister of Aharon, took the timbrel in her hand; and all the women went out after her with tambourines and with circle dances. And Miryam answered them:

"**Sing to the Lord,** for He has triumphed gloriously; the horse and his rider has He thrown into the sea."[11]

After 210 years the Jews finally (and supernaturally) escaped from slavery in Egypt. Their renowned string of miracles culminated in the greatest wonder of all: the Red Sea parted to allow their passage while miraculously drowning the Egyptians who were following in close pursuit. When safely secured on the other side, Moshe led the nation in a jubilant hymn of thanksgiving. The Torah records the words of that song and continues at once with the verses above that recount Miryam's celebration with the women. Rav Epstein **asks** several questions **on that passage:**

יש לדקדק מה בא להשמיענו בזה שהוציאה כל הנשים ולהיכן הוציאתן. גם קשה על מלת ובמחולות שנראה כמיותר, ובתורתינו הקדושה אינו מיותר אפילו אות אחת. עוד יש לדקדק מפני מה אמר משה אשירה לה' שהוא לשון עתיד והיא אמרה לשון הוה הוה שירו לה'.

1. **Why is the verse informing us that "all the women went out after [Miryam]"?** What is it teaching us by this fact?

2. **Where exactly did** Miryam and **the women go?**

3. It would have been enough to mention that "the women went out after her with their timbrels..." **Why must it add the seemingly superfluous detail about their dancing?** Since **the Torah never wastes a letter,** let alone a word, this added information must be significant.

4. **Why do** Miryam and Moshe use nearly the same language when they sing to *HaShem,* yet **Moshe employs the future tense** ("Then I will sing..."[12]) while Miryam speaks in the present ("Sing to the Lord...")?

ונראה לרמוז בזה על פי מה דאיתא בגמרא (תענית לא:) עתיד הקב"ה

---

11. Exodus 15:20–21.
12. Exodus 15:1.

לעשות מחול לצדיקים והוא יושב ביניהם בגן עדן, וכל אחד מראה באצבעו,
זה ה' קוינו לו, ופירש רש"י מחול סביב, כמו מחול הכרם.

This curious **passage is alluding to** a mystical teaching in **the
Gemara** about the world to come.[13]

**In the future the Holy One will make a
circle dance (מחול)[14] for the *tzaddikim*.
He will seat Himself among them in the
Garden of Eden and each one of the
tzaddikim will point with his finger and
say, "This is our God for whom we have
waited,** that He might save us. This is the
Lord for whom we hoped; we will be glad
and rejoice in His salvation."[15]

להבין הדבר נראה דהנה כשעלה ברצונו הפשוט לברוא
את העולם צמצם אלקותו יתברך שמו ונעשה עיגול וכל
העולמות ממשיכין אלהותו יתברך שמו בשוה, ואחר
כך ברא את העולמות בקו הישר, ונעשו צמצום עד
שנתגשם העולם והתחיל להיות ברורי עולמות, דהיינו
בעולם העליון צמצם אלהותו מעט, ובעולם התחתון
ממנו צמצם יותר, וכן עד סוף כל העולמות. ואנו משיגים
אלוהותו מתתא לעילא שצריכים אנו לברר הניצוצות
הקדושות וילך ממדריגה למדריגה.

The idea is as follows: In the stepwise sequence
of creating our universe, of crystallizing the
material world out of pure undifferentiated

I.
Questions on the biblical passage
that prompted this commentary.

II.
One can only answer these questions by knowing the history and
structure of the universe.

A. Sequence of creation's unfolding, particularly its transition
from circles to straight lines.

B. The continued presence and
influence of circles in our
straight-line universe.

III.
The linear world: its structure,
worldview, mechanism, and
purpose.

IV.
The circle world: its structure,
worldview, mechanism, and
purpose.

V.
Symbolic enactments of circle
consciousness in Jewish ritual
practices.

VI.
The original questions now
get answered by knowing that
Miryam was initiating the nation
into circle consciousness.

---

13. TB, *Taanit* 31a.
14. The Hebrew word מחול (translated "circle dance") is somewhat ambiguous
and could also mean "chorus" or simply a generic dance. Rashi notes the similarity of this word to a related term that means "an unsown belt of land that
marks the perimeter of a field" (*Kilayim* 4:1) and so defines it as a circle dance.
15. Isaiah 25:9.

light, creation passed through a series of consecutive stages extending from above to below.[16] In brief: Before the *beginning,* God's Infinite Light was everywhere. Creation simply could not happen for there was no room for worlds to emerge: every nook and cranny was already filled with Presence.

***HaShem*'s first step was to withdraw His light** from a circumscribed place, **creating a spherical void** now free to be filled by something else. This vacated space became the primordial womb for creation's unfolding. Into its hollow depths *HaShem* **emanated a single ray** of light (from its radiant surroundings), the unfolding and dissipation of **which is the history and evolution of creation** as we know it.

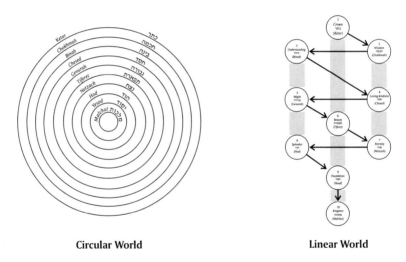

Circular World   Linear World

This transition from Infinite Light to present reality did not happen smoothly but rather in two trials.[17] **The original emana-**

---

16. This subject is elaborated in great detail here and summarized in the diagram called "Map of the Unfolding of Worlds," pp. 167.

17. Actually three, though the first is not immediately relevant to the discussion at hand. See the "Map of the Unfolding of Worlds," which includes an earlier stage that precedes these two, called the Bound World. Thus the actual

tion first formed ten **circular** and concentric channels of flow (or *sefirot*). For reasons explained, this Circle World could not bear the subsequent influx of radiations and shattered under their strain. Instantly, it was replaced by an alternative emanation of ten *sefirot* arranged along parallel lines, which was built from its shards.

Though the epoch of *points* and *circles* has passed and the hierarchy of *lines* and *straightness* now rules, circle truths still permeate our reality and are felt in at least four ways:[18]

1. The boundary that holds back the surrounding light and maintains the dark expanse of creation's womb is called the Great Circle, for it defines the spherical geometry of our universe. Upon its bulwark all life depends, for were it to lapse for even a millisecond, the Infinite Light would flood in, dissolving creation out of existence.

2. Since this newly fashioned Linear World was built from the recycled debris of shattered circles, it carries a primal memory of that event in every molecule of its being.[19] Consequently, though the era of circles is long gone, a

I.
Questions on the biblical passage that prompted this commentary.

II.
One can only answer these questions by knowing the history and structure of the universe.

A. Sequence of creation's unfolding, particularly its transition from circles to straight lines.
B. The continued presence and influence of circles in our straight-line universe.

III.
The linear world: its structure, worldview, mechanism, and purpose.

IV.
The circle world: its structure, worldview, mechanism, and purpose.

V.
Symbolic enactments of circle consciousness in Jewish ritual practices.

VI.
The original questions now get answered by knowing that Miryam was initiating the nation into circle consciousness.

sequence of the creation of worlds passes through three epochs: the Bound World (which was reabsorbed back into the Infinite Light); the World of Points (which shattered); and the Rectified World (which is the universe within which we live).
18. *Etz Chaim* 1:1–3.
19. R. Yaacov Lainer, *Beit Yaacov, Vayikra* 1.

permanent imprint, etched into the subconscious depths of the universe, continues to exert a covert influence on all matters, great and small.

3. The universe is holographic, which means that every piece contains aspects of every other piece inside itself. This applies both to objects and to processes. Consequently, the straight line that organizes the rectified world into a hierarchy of ten *sefirot* reenacts the primordial history of creation as it fashions **each** *sefirah* (and **world**). It **begins by forming a circle and then extends downward in a linear expression** that defines that attribute. Consequently, even in the world of lines and hierarchy, there exists an invisible web of circles that quietly impacts upon the unfolding of our personal and collective lives.

4. The Map of the Unfolding of Worlds on p. 167 illustrates the stepwise sequence by which Divinity formed our material world out of pure undifferentiated light. Its arrows all point downward. Yet it is equally true that creation follows that same path, though now from below to above, in its return journey toward perfection, enlightenment, and consummate embrace.

On the way down, the Circle World was flawed and so it shattered. Yet, paradoxically, its truths (or lights) are actually higher than those of the Linear (Rectified) World that replaced it. Kabbalah teaches that in their early stages of development the circular vessels were too immature to hold the magnitude of consciousness that shone there and so they crumbled. Though our world has more sophisticated vessels, curiously its lights emanate from a lower source. Its truths are dull and time-limited, compared to the resplendent and eternal awarenesses of its circular predecessor.

And still, the fulfillment of creation's purpose requires

a temporary sojourn in the linear realms to develop its cisterns to maximum capacity. Vessel-stretching is the specialty of *this* world. Once this preparatory work is done and all potential actualized, creation will return to the level of circle consciousness, yet this time equipped with proper vessels to hold its scintillating lights.

The primal direction of growth, built into the fabric of creation, that steers each moment "forward" in the most cosmic sense of that word, is back up toward the Circle World and the re-realization of *its* holy truths.

It is clear that the terms Circle World and Linear World not only describe arrangements of *sefirot* but present entire worldviews and value frames. **In the Linear World** everything occupies a unique position along a continuum extending from above to below. **The terms upper and lower are determined as follows:** In the stepwise sequence of creating our universe, *HaShem* underwent a gradually intensifying series of concealments. **Step by step, the Infinite Light withdrew Itself from creation and the extent of Its absence defines the hierarchy of worlds: the less concealed, the higher the world; the more, the lower. The task of human beings is to raise the shards** from the shattered Circle Era.[20] In so doing, they force *HaShem*

I.
Questions on the biblical passage that prompted this commentary.

II.
One can only answer these questions by knowing the history and structure of the universe.

A. Sequence of creation's unfolding, particularly its transition from circles to straight lines.
B. The continued presence and influence of circles in our straight-line universe.

III.
The linear world: its structure, worldview, mechanism, and purpose.

IV.
The circle world: its structure, worldview, mechanism, and purpose.

V.
Symbolic enactments of circle consciousness in Jewish ritual practices.

VI.
The original questions now get answered by knowing that Miryam was initiating the nation into circle consciousness.

---

20. The detailed mechanics of this process are described here.

out of hiding by witnessing, despite appearances to the contrary, that there is only God, and that He is one. **When successful, the status of that world** jumps notches for its concealment quotient inverts. Once God is seen, that place becomes "holy ground" and **enters the** prestigious assembly of **higher worlds.**

וכל העולמות וכל הברואים הם בבחינת דכר ונוקבא בחינת משפיע ומקבל, כי העולם היותר גבוה משפיע לעולם התחתון ממנו, וכן הקטן צריך לגדול ללמוד ממנו, כי כל דבר שהוא בקצוות יש לו סוף וראש, ומראשו עד סופו הוא רחוק, וכל שהוא למעלה מן הסוף הוא קרוב יותר להראש, כן כל שהוא למעלה למעלה מעולם התחתון הוא קרוב יותר לאין סוף ב"ה. ולכן הקטן צריך לגדול ללמוד ממנו עבדות השם, כי הוא משיג יותר ומשפיע לקטן ממנו.

Our physical plane that is the habitation of rocks, plants, animals, and humans is now among the lowest of worlds. An opaque, leathery skin encases its lights and conceals their glow. The outer eyes report multiplicity, with oneness nowhere to be found. Only a penetrating vision can tunnel through appearances and behold the pattern of unity that hides beneath.

The physical plane, with its multifarious range of life forms, actually comprises a single, cosmic hierarchy. Its scale of status calibrates as follows: The more complex an organism, the more sophisticated the soul manifesting through it.[21] Each level of life is a wider-angle lens that brings a new increment of consciousness into focus. Divinity, alone, possesses infinite consciousness, most simply defined as the range of a being's capacity to react and interact with its environment. The higher the creature, the more expressions of awareness (and so of God) can manifest through it. Since the measure of Divine concealment defines the hierarchy of worlds, that creature obtains an eminent rank.

---

21. *Soul* and *consciousness* are equivalent terms. There are five levels of soul and each indicates a particular capacity for consciousness.

Since higher creatures possess more light and awareness (for that is what defines them as higher), their role is to share that spiritual bounty with those below, whose way is to receive from them. The conventions of gender in kabbalah echo the physical differences between men and women. **Bestowal is a masculine role; receiving is a feminine one. Consequently,** kabbalah personifies **the higher realms as masculine in relation to those below, since they impart and the others imbibe.**

Creation began when the Infinite Light withdrew from Its center, forming a hollow womb that could hold worlds. The progression of history is the undoing of that concealment, the re-illuminating of that dark void by revealing God's Presence there. Each moment draws another trickle of Infinite Light back into the "empty" space that holds our world. This happens via the agency of mitzvot (and right-action), as well as through sufferings, for both are consciousness-raising experiences. Lessons are learned and wisdom absorbed from the school of hard knocks as surely as from the study of holy texts. And, since "*HaShem's* seal is truth,"[22] both, in the end, reveal God.

An elaborate machinery exists to package this influx of light into a form that matches the capacities of its recipients. **In the hierarchy of worlds,** each creature participates in this relay of illumination, according to its position along the continuum. **Each receives** a

I.
Questions on the biblical passage that prompted this commentary.

II.
One can only answer these questions by knowing the history and structure of the universe.

A. Sequence of creation's unfolding, particularly its transition from circles to straight lines.
B. The continued presence and influence of circles in our straight-line universe.

III.
The linear world: its structure, worldview, mechanism, and purpose.

IV.
The circle world: its structure, worldview, mechanism, and purpose.

V.
Symbolic enactments of circle consciousness in Jewish ritual practices.

VI.
The original questions now get answered by knowing that Miryam was initiating the nation into circle consciousness.

---

22. TY, *Sanhedrin* 2a.

drop of light (or **teaching**) **from the level above,** digests it, refor-mulates it, **and passes it on in a** modified **form that befits the level below it.**

In this way, through the course of time, the Infinite Light increases its presence in the lower worlds. The evolution of culture, knowledge, and consciousness are the visible fruits of this gradual enlightening.

In the World of Straightness, each level draws from the one above it. Everyone has a rank in the hierarchy, which extends from above to below with a whole range of points in between. **The top is closest to the Infinite Light, the bottom is farthest away.** Translated into human terms, a higher soul is one that is awake, is in continuous communion, and always chooses the most spiritually productive option; a lower soul is ignorant of spiritual truths and wallows in the entangling repercussions of wrong action. Now, in the Linear World, this hierarchy is real and serves two purposes.

1. It defines a descending flow of teaching that draws the Infinite Light down, level after level, from above to below.
2. Its hierarchy of status provides incentives for the resource-demanding labor of self-improvement. *HaShem* placed each soul in the world with a unique potential and the holy chore of assuring that it gets actualized.

   Self-development is a labor-intensive process. No one spends that amount of effort without very compelling inducements, both positive and negative. *HaShem* hangs a carrot in front and a fire behind to assure that the work gets done. One of His most successful motivating tools is "the rule of the Joneses." Implanted in the human soul is a natural drive to keep up with one's peers, and in the World of Straightness this is a healthy and functional tendency, especially if one's Joneses are spiritually striving folk.

Hierarchy of status defines a pecking order, whereby each strives to improve his position and defend it from encroachments. Self-worth, for better or worse, is often linked to one's position on the particular hierarchy that measures success in the area of one's values and ambitions.

People occupying higher ranks become role models that inspire effort. One looks at them and thinks, "Since they did it, I know it's possible. If I work hard enough, there is no reason that I can't do it, too."

The whole point of the era of hierarchy is to create a context of values, inducements, constraints, and coercions that press out the full potential of each soul down to its last drop. Its straight line presents a clear direction of growth and compelling enforcements to assure forward motion.

I.
Questions on the biblical passage that prompted this commentary.

II.
One can only answer these questions by knowing the history and structure of the universe.

A. Sequence of creation's unfolding, particularly its transition from circles to straight lines.

B. The continued presence and influence of circles in our straight-line universe.

III.
The linear world: its structure, worldview, mechanism, and purpose.

IV.
The circle world: its structure, worldview, mechanism, and purpose.

V.
Symbolic enactments of circle consciousness in Jewish ritual practices.

VI.
The original questions now get answered by knowing that Miryam was initiating the nation into circle consciousness.

אבל לעתיד יתקן כל אחד חלק נשמתו עד שרשו,
ויעלו הניצוצין הקדושים, והחיצוניות יתבטלו מכל
וכל, ויופיע אז אור בהירות אלהותו בכל העולמות ויהיה
העיגול והקו שוה, ולא יהיה אז בחינת דכר ונוקבא כי
כולם בשוה ישיגו אור אלהותו יתברך שמו כמו בדבר
עגול שאין ראש וסוף, ולא יצטרך עוד שום אדם ללמוד
מחבירו, כמו במחול הכרם, שהוא מקו האמצעי קרוב
לכל העיגול בשוה, כן אז ישיגו כולם מאור הבהירות
אלהותו בשוה כדכתיב (ירמיה לא, לג) ולא ילמדו עוד
איש את רעהו כי כולם ידעו אותו מקטנם ועד גדלם.

Every soul will eventually actualize its potential. The utopian end of days is exactly that; **all the fallen sparks will be raised,**

all the *gevurot* sweetened, all potentials actualized, **all illusions neutralized. God's light will shine through the world,** dissolving hierarchy **as it turns the line into a circle.**

A possible mechanism for this configurational transformation of line into circle is as follows: A circular disk (like a coin) when viewed along its edge can appear as a single line. When viewed from an angle slightly above its edge, it begins to look like an oval.[23] Finally, when observed from above, it appears as the circle that it really is. Nothing has changed except the viewer's perspective. This is a three-dimensional analogy of an infinitely more complex process taking place in our ten-dimensional world. Nevertheless, the difference between the World of Hierarchy and the Circular World remains a matter of perspective. An immature and narrow-minded consciousness has a constricted field of vision that perceives the universe as a line. As the mind evolves and enlightens, its perspective expands. From its now more elevated orientation the world assumes a circular form. Nothing has changed except the mind's visual field and its expanded capacity to integrate multi-dimensions of complexity.

When that happens, the distinctions between higher and lower, giver and receiver, masculine and feminine, will cease. Everyone will know God in a way that is perfect and unique. In the World of Lines, quantity is the primary yardstick of value, for it lends itself easily to comparisons. In the World of Circles, quality is what counts, and, like apples and oranges, qualities are not easily ranked. Each person is a unique entity, incalculably complex, intrinsically worthy, who fulfills an absolutely necessary and irreproducible function in the universe.

---

23. One could even say that the Tree of Life, with its three parallel pillars, defines a kind of bisected oval, which provides a glimpse into a more expanded perspective of the world than ordinary (linear) vision generally allows.

In the World of Hierarchy, value is peer-referenced. Everyone looks around to see where others are aiming and what they are achieving, and then measures him- or herself to that. In the Circle World, where absolute value is an inalienable right and an intrinsic property of each soul, worth is completely self-referenced, which actually means God-referenced. "Am I realizing the full potential of my soul with its unique combination of talents and sensitivities? Am I fulfilling what God wants from me?" These are the only questions that will matter, and in the world to come their answer will always be yes. Each soul will eventually attain its full potential and shine with the unique revelation of Divine beauty that only it can manifest. The spiritual bliss of the world to come is the intensely abiding joy of finally becoming who you are. Deep down, this is all anyone wants. The problem is the near impossibility of knowing what that is. Our potential is not only hidden from others, it is generally hidden from ourselves as well. The remedy is our extended training period in the world of lines and straightness. Its mechanism is as follows: Each person looks around at the Joneses and the beautiful things they possess, and this triggers drives, lusts, and desires inside them to acquire similar things. *HaShem* cleverly implanted a lock-and-key mechanism into the universe, whereby a soul is attracted to exactly those beauties that resonate with some unactualized potential inside itself; as the popular saying observes, "There is no accounting for taste." Each soul is programmed to respond to the specific "attractors" which,

I.
Questions on the biblical passage that prompted this commentary.

II.
One can only answer these questions by knowing the history and structure of the universe.

A. Sequence of creation's unfolding, particularly its transition from circles to straight lines.
B. The continued presence and influence of circles in our straight-line universe.

III.
The linear world: its structure, worldview, mechanism, and purpose.

IV.
The circle world: its structure, worldview, mechanism, and purpose.

V.
Symbolic enactments of circle consciousness in Jewish ritual practices.

VI.
The original questions now get answered by knowing that Miryam was initiating the nation into circle consciousness.

through its laboring to possess them, "coincidentally" allow it to realize its own potential.

In this way *HaShem* motivates the grueling work of self-actualization, leading us along right paths and persuading us to invest the enormous effort required to underwrite the endeavor. In the end, all will find their place around the circle's edge and celebrate with overflowing joy the pleasure of finally becoming who they really are. There is no greater delight than this. It is the heavenly elixir of the world to come.

When we arrive at this stage, the distorting veneer of hierarchy (and line consciousness) will melt away, for it will no longer have a purpose. It was a temporary and utilitarian truth, though in its heyday it was the most relevant truth, for the whole point of that era was to get massive amounts of work done. Soul actualization is a labor-intensive exertion that requires the irresistible incentives provided by the web of intersecting hierarchies and status-rankings in the Linear World. Still, its days will pass and we will return to the era of circle consciousness that proclaims a more exalted and eternal truth: every creature is one of a kind, uniquely fashioned to reveal a distinct facet of Divine beauty. On its scale of values, everyone is *HaShem*'s most favored one and **all will have become completely equal.**[24] In that world the baker will not look to his neighbor, the rabbi, or even to Mashiach, and feel less accomplished or worthy than he. Everyone will be filled to overflowing with the joy of having discovered who he or she really is. It will be absolutely clear to the baker that it would not augment his pleasure to stand in his neighbor's more prestigious or affluent shoes; rather, the opposite. It would dampen his ecstasy, for he would suffer from not being true to his own soul and its Divinely ordained mission to be the best baker possible.

---

24. *Etz Chaim* 1:1:1–2:3.

For everyone, whether baker, rabbi, or housewife, it takes lifetimes of grinding labor to accomplish one's soul-purpose. That curious fact becomes the great equalizer, based on the well-known principle that "the reward is in proportion to the toil."[25] On the scale of effort everyone comes out equal.

The **consciousness** of the world to come **is symbolized by a circle,** a perfectly symmetrical object **that has no beginning or end,** no up or down, and each of its points is equidistant from the common center toward which it faces. Similarly **in the circle world,** it will be gloriously clear that every soul is equally precious and singularly beautiful in a way that cannot be ranked. **It will not anymore be possible to look to one's neighbors for guidance in serving God,** for each person has a unique soul-specialty, and in that area he or she is the world's foremost expert. **There is nowhere to look for instruction except straight from** *HaShem,* who metaphorically **sits at the circle's center, equidistant from all its holy points.**

On that eternal day, everyone will be satiated with knowledge of God to the fullest capacity of his or her joy and all hierarchies of status will dissolve. In wonderment people will discover that on the scale of enlightenment all have become equal.

All this Jeremiah prophesied:[26] "I will put My Torah in their inward parts and write it in their hearts, and will

I.
Questions on the biblical passage that prompted this commentary.

II.
One can only answer these questions by knowing the history and structure of the universe.

A. Sequence of creation's unfolding, particularly its transition from circles to straight lines.
B. The continued presence and influence of circles in our straight-line universe.

III.
The linear world: its structure, worldview, mechanism, and purpose.

IV.
The circle world: its structure, worldview, mechanism, and purpose.

V.
Symbolic enactments of circle consciousness in Jewish ritual practices.

VI.
The original questions now get answered by knowing that Miryam was initiating the nation into circle consciousness.

---

25. Ethics of the Fathers 5:22.
26. Jeremiah 31:32–33.

be their God and they will be My people. **And they shall teach no more every man his neighbor** and every man his brother saying, 'Know the Lord.' **For they will all know Me, from the least of them to the greatest of them,** says the Lord. And I will forgive their transgression and I will remember their sins no more."

וזהו פירוש הגמרא, עתיד הקב"ה לעשות מחול לצדיקים, והקב"ה יושב ביניהם בגן עדן, פירוש לעתיד לבא ישיגו הצדיקים השגה גדולה מאור העליון אשר אין שם בחינת דכר ונוקבא, ואין שום אחד מהם יצטרך ללמוד מחבירו, כי אז יתגלה אור בהירות אלהותו בכל העולמות, ויהיה עיגול עם הקו בשוה כמו מחול הכרם שמקו האמצעי הוא קרוב לכל העיגול בשוה.

This serves to explain the passage from the *Gemara* cited previously:

In the future the Holy One will make a circle dance (מחול) for the *tzaddikim.* **He will seat Himself among them in the Garden of Eden** and each one of the *tzaddikim* will point with his finger and say, "This is our God for whom we have waited, that He might save us. This is the Lord for whom we hoped, we will be glad and rejoice in His salvation."[27]

In the future everyone will be cleansed of sin and **attain full knowledge of God,** thereby **entering the category of** *tzaddik.* The accumulated labor of lifetimes of striving and suffering will end in collective perfection. This path toward sainthood is equally a journey toward circle consciousness, for the knowledge of God acquired en route is what dissolves the illusions of hierarchy **and will ultimately eliminate gender roles altogether,** which serve as the archetypes for all other power disparities.

If one associates the masculine role with an enlightened master who imparts knowledge and the feminine role with an unlearned

---

27. Isaiah 25:9.

novice who receives instruction, **then gender will cease in the world to come, for no one will be learning from neighbors, spouses, or even teachers. Truth will shine through the world,** its light as plentiful as the air we breathe, and all will have the taste buds to enjoy (and comprehend) it.

Hierarchies will cease and merge into the more expanded and rectified circle consciousness that will rule that new age. **Like the perimeter of a vineyard where each point is equidistant from Its** *center,* so will all be equally close to the Infinite source of light and consciousness, the Blessed Holy One.

וזה כוונת ההקפות שאנו מקיפין בהושענא רבה ובשמיני עצרת, אנו עושים הקפות בסוד (ירמיה לא, כא) נקבה תסובב גבר, להמשיך על ידי הקפות את אור העליון אשר אין שם בחינת דכר ונוקבא, וזאת היתה כוונת מרים הנביאה שהוציאה כל הנשים אחריה ועשתה עמהם הקפות, בסוד נקבה תסובב גבר, כדי להמשיך אור עליון, אשר אין שם בחינת דכר ונוקבא. ולכן אמר משה, אשירה לה' מפני שמשה אמר בבחינת דכר ונוקבא שלא הופיע עדיין אור הבהירות העליון, לכן אמרו אשירה שעדיין לא השיגו משלם השגת אלקותו, לכן אמרו לשון עתיד. כשאשיג אז אשיר, אבל מרים המשיכה בהקפתה אור עליון והשיגו אז אשר אי אפשר להשיג יותר, לכן אמרה שירו עתה שהשגתם היה מה שאי אפשר להשיג יותר. וזהו פירוש הפסוק ותקח מרים וגו'. ותצאן כל הנשים אחריה בתופים ובמחולות, פירוש שעשתה עמהם הקפה כמחול הכרם, בסוד נקבה תסובב גבר, ובזה המשיכה אור עליון, אשר אין שם בחינת דכר ונוקבא. ותען להם מרים שירו לה', פירוש שעתה

השגתם השגה גדולה כל כך מה שאי אפשר להשיג יותר, לכן שירו עתה לה'.

This circle **truth is reenacted each year on the two festivals of Sukkot and Simchat Torah.** Among the practices of those days is **the custom to dance in a circle** around the Torah. **On** Sukkot (which includes **Hoshanna Rabbah**) the movement is slow **and** stately; **on Shemini Atzeret** (which includes Simchat Torah) the dance is vigorous and celebratory.

The verse that describes the deeper symbolism of this practice reads, **"The Lord has created a new thing on the earth, woman shall surround man."**[28,29] **Its words hearken to the era described previously where circle consciousness supersedes hierarchy and replaces it as the greater and more encompassing truth.**

The circle dancing that happens on Sukkot and Simchat Torah **draws the lights of that sublime era down** into our constricted world of lines and hierarchy. For those moments **gender disparities cease** and the soul encounters circle lights. Now it knows how to orient, for having glimpsed the larger landscape, it identified the center to which it must face. With this experience the soul is primed to discriminate *holy* sweetness and pure teachings by their consistency with circle truths.

All this Miryam knew and intended when she led the women in their circle dance. Miryam drew the future into the present, initiating the Jewish nation into the secret truth, promise, and yearning of the Circle World: The day will come, blessed and welcomed by all, when *"woman* **will encompass** *man."* **The highest lights will fill the world,** insights that cannot be imagined by minds confined by hierarchy. On that day **gender disparities will cease,** and perfect equality will reign.

Moshe phrased his celebratory *song of the sea* **in the future tense ("I** *will* **sing to** *HaShem . . .* "), **because his vision** was more limited than Miryam's. His conceptual **mind could not** break the

---

28. Jeremiah 31:21.
29. Rashi actually translates this as "Woman will turn into a man."

gender-barrier to **access the infinitely sweeter lights that lie on the other side. And so he sang in the future tense, accepting that he could not, in the present, access those future truths,** as if to say, **"Then, when** my mind has evolved to the next level, and I **become able to hold those holy circle lights,** **then** I *will sing."*

Miryam, conversely, was able to touch those lights and bring them down into the present **through her circle dance.** This exalted task required the participation of her entire body. Circle World lights are so intensely bright and complex that they do not fit into the delimited spaces of brain and mind. These sufficed as organs of awareness for straight line consciousness, but no amount of upgrade will equip them to hold circle lights. Like trying to run a complex graphics program on an antiquated laptop, there is not enough space in the computer's brain to hold the complexity of operations, to allow the images to form or move through their transformations. Similarly here, circle awareness is so vast that it takes an entire body to hold it. Each cell must participate in the effort and share in the load. The final "knowing" is a visceral experience where awareness permeates every limb and organ in the body. It is this body-based feature that makes these truths ecstatic.

I.
Questions on the biblical passage that prompted this commentary.

II.
One can only answer these questions by knowing the history and structure of the universe.

A. Sequence of creation's unfolding, particularly its transition from circles to straight lines.
B. The continued presence and influence of circles in our straight-line universe.

III.
The linear world: its structure, worldview, mechanism, and purpose.

IV.
The circle world: its structure, worldview, mechanism, and purpose.

V.
Symbolic enactments of circle consciousness in Jewish ritual practices.

VI.
The original questions now get answered by knowing that Miryam was initiating the nation into circle consciousness.

…Every mouth shall offer thanks to You; every tongue shall vow allegiance to You; every eye shall look toward You; every knee shall bend to You; every erect spine shall prostrate itself before You; all hearts shall fear You, and each of my internal organs and kidneys shall sing praises to Your name, as it is written: "All my bones shall say: *HaShem*, who is like You?[30] . . . Let all my internal organs bless His holy Name."[31] [32]

Through her dance Miryam attained a visceral state of knowing the highest and most mysterious truths of the universe, and from inside that knowing she rejoiced, *"Now* I sing. . ." **All that we will discover in our eternally deepening journey toward knowledge of God, Miryam knew then. This is what the Torah teaches when it describes her celebration: "And Miryam the prophetess,** the sister of Aharon, **took the timbrel in her hand; and all the women went out after her with timbrels and with circle dances.** And Miryam answered them: 'Sing to the Lord, for He has triumphed gloriously; the horse and his rider has He thrown into the sea.'"[33]

When Miryam gathered the women to dance in a circle (like the untitled ground surrounding a vineyard), she embodied, as a physical reality, the abstract and incomprehensible concept of *"woman* surrounding *man."* **In that moment the lights of that truth actually descended below and imparted their secret knowledge to all present. In the deepest recesses of soul, all understood that hierarchy is an illusion** and that gender disparities, **their primary expression,** must eventually cease.

Miryam answered the women in the present tense, "Sing, *now,* to the Lord . . ." for in that moment she apprehended and embodied circle truths, **the highest secrets of the universe. She merited**

---

30. Psalms 35:10.
31. Psalms 103:1.
32. Standard Liturgy, Shabbat morning prayers, *Nishmat Kol Chai,* which appears at the end of the section called *Pesukei d'Zimra.*
33. Exodus 15:20–21.

to sing her song in the present tense, while even Moshe (the greatest prophet who ever lived) **could only know those words as distant truths.**

DEBRIEFING
MIRYAM'S CIRCLE DANCE

What Do We Know?

1. The Circle World is not just a particular arrangement of *sefirot*, but an entire worldview and value frame. It regards every soul as a unique entity, incalculably complex, intrinsically worthy, which fulfills an absolutely necessary and irreproducible function in the universe. In the Circle World, every soul is equally beloved to *HaShem* and there is no hierarchy of greatness between them.

2. The hierarchies and rankings of the Linear (Rectified) World are time-limited and partial truths. The nonhierarchical, circle perspective will ultimately prevail as the final word.

3. Our sojourn in the Linear (Rectified) World, laboring beneath its yoke of narrow judgments and partial truths, serves an absolutely critical function. By pressing out the full potential of each soul, it prepares light-vessels that will, for the first time in the history of the universe, be able to absorb and integrate Circle World consciousness.

4. Miryam's Circle World lights were brought down through dance, and in particular, a circle dance. It is known that in the higher states of consciousness described by kabbalah, the entire body becomes an instrument of awareness. Their state of "knowing" permeates every cell and cannot be confined to the organs of brain and mind. Similarly here,

the vessel that Miryam employed to draw circle lights into the world possessed two features:

   a. It required bodily participation, in the form of dance.

   b. It needed to be a collective effort. No individual can stretch sufficiently to contain circle consciousness fully. A proper vessel for this purpose must integrate the capacities of a multitude of souls, in this case, the women.

5. Miryam and the women were able to access these lights of higher consciousness while Moshe, the greatest prophet that ever lived, could not.

Logical Implications and Speculations

1. The fact that Miryam and the women were able to access these lights of higher consciousness while Moshe, the greatest prophet that ever lived, could not implies that the particular knowledge that comes from the Circle World may be more accessible to women than men.

2. What does one do with this information? How does one balance the conflict of perspective between the Linear and Circular Worlds? Wisdom requires:

   a. An awareness of both orientations and a true appreciation of their respective merits.

   b. An understanding of their sequence of applicability and the position of one's own generation along that timeline. It seems that we are currently in the linear phase of history, though fast approaching the era when circular truths will begin to take precedence.

   c. It is said about the perspectives of Hillel and Shamai,[34]

---

34. Hillel and Shammai were the two most illustrious Sages of their time (c. 40 B.C.E.) and they generally arrived at opposite conclusions, both on matters of law and philosophy. Concerning them, the *Gemara* teaches, "A voice from heaven announced, 'These [opinions of Hillel] and these [contradictory opin-

"these and these are true words of the living God yet the opinions of Hillel should be followed as practical halacha" in this period of history (except with minor exceptions). Similarly here, wisdom requires that one affirm both truths and yet lean toward Linear World values when making practical decisions. Yet, also here, one must recognize exceptions to the rule, situations that call for the emphasis of circle values in their practical decision. (The very capacity to contact the unique features of a moment and identify it as an exception is itself a Circle World skill.)

d. Kabbalah teaches that in the messianic period Shammai's opinions will become more relevant than Hillel's and we will rule according to his conclusions.[35] Similarly in the transition from lines to circles, wisdom requires that one be attuned to this shifting and make decisions accordingly.

3. Why is the Circle Era considered an unrectified world on the way down (and so it shattered) while on the way up it is a *super*-rectified world, even more so than our present universe, which is actually titled the Rectified World?

---

ions of Shammai] are both true words of the living God but the practical law follows Hillel'" (TB, *Eruvin* 13b). Interestingly, the positions of Hillel could be characterized as more compatible with circle consciousness, the opinions of Shammai with a more linear worldview. Perhaps the decision to follow Hillel's conclusions was an affirmative action to include circle perspectives in an era that would be primarily linear. The fact that Shammai's orientation will gain prominence in the messianic time (see paragraph d. above) is perhaps the same pattern. To assure that the Circle Era includes the linear and to counterbalance its polarity, Shammai's stricter and seemingly narrower opinions will apply.
35. *HaMikdash Melekh, Parashat Bereshit* 17b; *Rashaz, LT,* Numbers 54b–c; R. Tsadok, Chanukah 8; Mikdash Shmuel to Avot, 5:19.

As explained, circle consciousness includes the appreciation of each soul as an absolutely perfect, unique, and intrinsically worthy entity. This awareness has a different effect on souls as they are "coming down" versus going up. On the way down, souls are just bundles of potential waiting to be actualized. If circle consciousness were to rule, a soul, even in its unactualized state, would be appreciated as already perfect, "as just fine the way it is." There is not much incentive to engage in the grueling labor of self-development when the message from every direction is, "You're so beautiful. You are already perfect exactly the way you are." Consequently, the danger in a world where circle values rule is that growth and actualization will not happen, for there is nothing to be gained by the effort. One is already basking in unconditional positive regard.

Consequently on the way down, the Circle World was unrectified, for the urgent mission of soul-actualization could not happen to its full extent within an exclusively circular frame. And so it shattered, to be replaced by the Rectified, Linear World of hierarchies and coercive growth incentives. With all its failings, its half-truths, and narrow-minded judgments, the work gets done, potential does get actualized, and the results speak for themselves. Gradually, throughout the entire six-millennium history of the Rectified World, circle consciousness (via the *partzuf woman*) has been slowly infiltrating the larger cultural milieu. The seven-stage sequence outlined by the *Ari* describes this progression.

At first circle values were hardly visible, and only recently have they built a momentum and accumulated a substantial presence. Now, in this postmodern era of democracy, psychology, spiritual awakening, and human rights awareness, circle lights are fast approaching their full stature, and exerting a profound impact on the conceptual paradigms of contemporary history.

Once our potential has been actualized and humanity has become the best it can possibly be, the most rectified perspective and the truest attitude is that informed by circle values. Every soul really is the best and most beloved. Each fulfills an absolutely unique and critical function and shines with incomparable beauty. It is impossible to rank them, silly even, for there are as many standards of excellence as there are souls. Each sits at the top of the scale that measures *its* specialty.

The purpose of the world to come is different from *this world*. *Here*, now, is the work-phase of history. *There*, will be the reaping of reward, the ecstasy of an ever deepening relationship with *HaShem*. The expanded vision of the Circle World is exactly what will facilitate the full realization of our individual and collective beauty, enabling us to enter a deeper level of intimacy with *HaShem* and not shatter from the force of His Infinite Light.

Furthermore, circle consciousness on the way up is actually an integration of both linear and circular paradigms that together form the vessel that can hold infinite blessing.

4. The *sefirah* of *malchut* (and its *partzuf woman*) can be characterized as a splinter of light from the Circle Era that dropped into the Rectified World, and as it fell it imploded, until it hit bottom as a densely compacted knot of unactualized potential. The seven stages of woman's development become the path by which this splinter of circle light reconstitutes itself and integrates its profound awareness into the Linear World, which it eventually supplants as the prevailing ideology.

5. In the *Ari's* seven-stage sequence of *woman's* development, the latter stages describe a phase whereby *woman* comes into her "brains." It is clear that *woman's* brains will be different from *man's*, for their specialty is circle truths. All disciplines and areas of study will benefit from incorporating the enriched and expanded perspective of circle awareness into their thought patterns and problem-solving paradigms.

8

THE MESSIANIC VISION OF EQUALITY AND BEYOND...

The Voice of the Bride[1]

By R. Shneur Zalman of Liadi (*Rashaz*)

BARE BONES LITERACY

SUMMARY

Voice of the Bride by R. Schneur Zalman of Liadi takes the *Ari*'s model a step beyond and shows how the polarities of masculine and feminine will eventually invert. There will come a time, blessed and welcomed by all, when the feminine will have greater access to transcendent consciousness, and when that happens she will bestow and **man** will receive from her.

---

1. R. Shneur Zalman of Liadi, *Tefilot Lkhol HaShana*, pp. 138–139.

VOCABULARY

Amidah – (literally, "standing"). Another term for the **Shemoneh Essrei** (or Prayer of Eighteen Blessings). See *Shemoneh Essrei.*

Arikh Anpin – The second (lower) root of soul, in the *sefirah* called *crown.* It faces downward toward creation and generates a constant will-toward-good in the personality.

Atik Yamin (Atika) – The highest root of the soul. The innermost point of the *sefirah* called *crown*, which actually touches the Infinite Light and dwells in the pleasure of that union.

halacha – (literally, "walking"). The vast system of Jewish law derived from the Torah as received by Moses and explicated by the Sages, which defines the entirety of Jewish life. There is no area of experience that is outside the jurisdiction of halacha.

integrated lights – truths and understandings that have been apprehended by mind or heart.

katnut – (literally, "smallness"). A term referring to an immature or constricted state of consciousness.

lights – Lights are always equivalent to consciousness in kabbalistic writings. Each *sefirah*, or spark, is a *light* that transmits a particular insight or capacity for awareness.

malchut – The lowest of the ten *sefirot* is called *malchut*, which means literally "royalty" and "kingship." It corresponds to the physical plane and represents the final stage of light's congealing into matter.

man and *woman* – Kabbalistic archetypes of male and female in their prime, as opposed to *father* and *mother*, which signify their later stages of life.

messianic era – The messianic era is a transitional time between *this* world and the next. It begins somewhere toward the end of the sixth millennium (we are now within the period of its likely beginnings) and will take us to the threshold of the world to come. It is the joyous stage of actualized perfection. Love of God, love of neighbor, and love of Torah reign.

mother – The higher (or elder) feminine archetype associated with the *sefirah* of *understanding* (*binah*).

partzuf / partzufim – The set of six kabbalistic archetypes that coalesce into a family system, with each filling a unique role, for example: *father, mother, man, woman*. Equally frequently, these *partzufim* function as different "voices" or sub-personalities within a single individual.

sefirah / sefirot – The ten channels of Divine flow and emanation that link the Transcendent Light with Its evolving and apparently finite creation.

Shemoneh Essrei – (literally, "eighteen"). The group of originally eighteen, but now nineteen, blessings that form the core and backbone of Jewish worship. Under most circumstances the obligation to pray three times a day is only fulfilled by reciting the *Shemoneh Essrei*. This prayer is recited silently, while standing, feet together, facing Jerusalem.

surrounding *lights* – Truths and understandings that are too deep or great for the mind (or vessel) to grasp.

Mishnah – First recording of the Oral Law compiled by Rabbi Yehuda HaNasi in 180 C.E. Primarily legalistic in content, the Mishnah consolidates the Oral Tradition as it had evolved from Sinai through the Second Temple period. It forms the basis of the *Gemara*.

TECHNICAL NOTES

The italicized terms *man, woman, mother,* and *father* refer to kabbalistic archetypes (called *partzufim*) and, by extension, to the masculine and feminine attributes found in both men and women. The literal translation of the Hebrew text appears in bold print.

SYNOPSIS

VOICE OF THE BRIDE

When a Jewish man and woman wed, seven marriage blessings are recited for them beneath the bridal canopy. R. Schneur Zalman comments on the last of these special prayers, which heralds an idyllic time when "the jubilant voices of both groom and bride will be heard on the streets of Jerusalem . . . and the groom will rejoice *with* his bride."[2] R. Schneur Zalman reads these lines in the context of his encyclopedic knowledge of Jewish teachings, where even the most subtle hint reverberates in ever-widening circles of association. He interprets this prayer as depicting a profound transformation of gender relations that will culminate in messianic times.

R. Schneur Zalman identifies two shifts in status quo anticipated by the prayer's carefully selected words. First is the emergence of woman's voice from passive silence to full expression (as indicated by the blessing's unnecessary repetition of the word *voice* both in relation to groom *and* in relation to bride). Second is a reversal of polarities between *man* and *woman*. Now when consciousness (and its associated joys) descends from above to below, it passes first to *man* and from him to *woman*. In this sequence, he gives and she receives. In messianic times the polarity will invert and consciousness will move in the opposite direction; it will pass first to *woman*, and from her to *man* (as derived by comparing this prayer's closing words to a nearly identical line in the sixth blessing

---

2. The full text is as follows: Blessed are You, *HaShem*, our God, King of the universe, Who created joy and gladness, groom and bride, mirth, glad song, pleasure, delight, love, brotherhood, peace, and companionship. *HaShem*, our God, let there soon be heard in the cities of Judah and the streets of Jerusalem the sound of joy and the sound of gladness, the voice of the groom and the voice of the bride, the sound of the grooms' jubilance from their canopies and of youths from their song-filled feasts. Blessed are You, *HaShem*, Who gladdens the groom with the bride.

that precedes it). R. Schneur Zalman elaborates on these remarkable teachings and explores their implications, both for Israel's relationship to God, and *woman's* relationship to *man*.

He compares this messianic progression to Judaism's two-stage process of marital relationship, which defines a stepwise sequence of deepening intimacy, called betrothal and marriage. These are precisely defined terms in Jewish law. Betrothal is a legally binding commitment to marry. Though the couple is not permitted to relate sexually, in most other respects they are as if legally married and the dissolution of their engagement requires a divorce. The second level of matrimonial commitment occurs when the bride formally enters her husband's home. The wedding canopy symbolizes their coming together under one roof and so effects this change of status. The marriage is finalized by its physical consummation. These legal categories have metaphysical correlations as well. In betrothal the couple's outer layers of soul engage; in marriage their core selves touch and bond.

Betrothal requires one of several specific deeds to activate the obligations associated with that commitment. The Mishnah states, "A woman is [betrothed] in three ways: When she receives a sum of money [or a gift of equivalent monetary value ...]"[3] Nowadays, this is fulfilled by the exchange of a ring,[4] a gold band that *encircles* her finger.

This model also applies to the relationship between *HaShem* and Israel, where He is the groom and they are the bride. Their commitment evolves through a similar progression of intimacy. R. Schneur Zalman proves that the Torah's revelation effected *HaShem's* betrothal to Israel, the first stage of intimacy where

---

3. TB, *Kiddushin* 2a. The passage continues,"... or by a document, or by sexual relations."
4. *Shulchan Arukh, Eben HaEzer (IH)* 31.

externalities engage. Their relationship will consummate in messianic times.

Just as man effects betrothal with a ring, so did *HaShem*, for the ring's circular form parallel's the metaphysical concept of surrounding lights. In kabbalah, lights that can be grasped and integrated are called inner and internalizable (אור פנימי); lights that are present but too "high" or "deep" or "vast" to be contained within their vessel of consciousness are described as surrounding or hovering (אור מקיף). Both types descended at Sinai.

According to Jewish tradition, the Torah's revelation was the most profound manifestation of God that ever transpired on the planet. An estimated four million people experienced that historic event. A searing revelation of Presence engraved the souls of an entire nation with the-truth-of-the-universe compressed into a single burst of light. Its impact continues to impel their generations to be seekers and servants of God and will do so until the end of time.

Sinai is different from all other prophetic encounters, not only in its amount of light but also in its quality. Other biblical prophesies only accessed the aura of Divinity, the glow that surrounds the Blessed Luminary. At Sinai the Infinite Light itself, the actual source of illumination, was manifestly present. And yet, the people could not contain that intensity of revelation. Its bolt of insight impacted their souls, but only a fraction integrated as conscious awareness. The rest overflowed into a ring of surrounding light that holds all the possibilities of future consciousness within its glow. With each passing moment the vessel of awareness expands and a drop of surrounding radiance slips inside and integrates there. Eventually, all the encircling lights will be internalized by our infinitely expanded capacity to know God.

R. Schneur Zalman defines both integrated and surrounding lights by their relationship to Torah. Integrated lights are truths and teachings that are accessible to us now, at this point in our development. All the accumulated wisdom of the Jewish people, its Torah commentaries, legal rulings, moral lessons, and mysticism are integrated lights to the extent that they are known and incorporated into life.

Conversely, the inner dimension of Torah, the repository of secrets hidden within the text elucidating the deeper reasons behind its laws, stories, and textual structure, came down at Sinai but was not actually *revealed* at that time. Embedded within each letter, word, and story are all the unrealized possibilities of interpretation daily elucidated. These ungraspable lights (along with the higher states of consciousness that accompany them) form a shimmering halo around the integrated lights of the revealed Torah, enclosing them as if in a sphere of radiant consciousness. With this encircling band as His engagement offering, *HaShem* betrothed the Jewish people at Sinai and secured their commitment to marry at the end of days.

Throughout their engagement period, Israel's relationship to *HaShem* daily ripens. It is not a time of passive waiting; only active preparation will do. Our task is to labor in Torah, to release its hidden teachings and allow ourselves to be transformed by its truths. Each day Israel exposes another layer of concealed lights and soon there will be no secrets left. The Torah's soul-satisfying wisdoms will illuminate every question, resolve every doubt, and explain every suffering.

The fullness of Divine light will shine through the Torah and fill Israel's collective heart, bones, cells, and spaces with Holy Presence. There will be no place inside them that is not permeated with God and nothing of God that does not fit inside them. A perfect marriage, a consummate union of glory and awe.

This transition from betrothal to marriage happens through the gradual integration of surrounding lights. The transfer of consciousness from above to below, from its infinite source on high to its final expression as expanded awareness in the minds of mankind, follows one path of descent now, in the engagement period, and will follow an alternative route in messianic times. Now, this stepwise relay of consciousness begins with *mother*, who passes it on to *man*. He internalizes what he can and the rest spills over as surrounding light. *Man* then separates out a portion of his newly integrated lights and passes them on to *woman*.

The rule is stated thus: The higher the *partzuf*, the greater its capacity to hold light. Consequently, at each transfer only some illumination actually fits into the vessel below. The rest gets displaced into a ring of transcendent awareness that holds all the possibilities of future apprehension and that encircles the head of the lower *partzuf*. In this way each upper level becomes a crown to the level below.

This is the order of descent in pre-messianic times, while the moon is diminished and *woman*'s stature is less than *man*'s. In this configuration *woman* cannot access her own transcendent lights, for she cannot reach them on her own. She needs *man* to draw them from *mother* and pass them to her.

Woman's preparation for marriage requires that she heal all traces of diminishment and re-attain her full stature. Consummation can only happen when *man* and *woman* match from the crown of their heads to the soles of their feet, and this is only possible when they meet as equal statures. As long as *woman* remains diminished, their union can never consummate and "marriage" cannot happen.

Then, explains the Rav, their relationship evolves to a higher level still. *Woman* recovers her full stature and then supersedes *man*. When this happens, their polarity inverts. Now she becomes "the crown to her husband," holding the superconscious lights that are destined for him but that he cannot reach on his own. Like a rubber band stretched and released, she springs beyond *man* and becomes the intermediary in their relationship, a service he will have provided for 6,000 years. Since she can now access levels that he cannot, she transfers their illuminations to him, some of which he integrates and some of which he cannot, for his vessel of consciousness is too small to contain them. Instead they encircle his head as a crown, fulfilling the verse that states "the woman of valor will become a crown to her husband."

The seventh marriage blessing depicts this shift in the polarity of *man* and *woman* with its closing words, "...Blessed is *HaShem* Who rejoices the groom *with* the bride." Its use of the word *with* (as opposed to the word *and* in the sixth blessing) indicates that *woman* is now the primary source of joy and *man* comes along *with* her. In the first six millennia of history, consciousness (and its joys) flows from *man* to *woman,* but this dynamic will change in messianic times. The supersconscious lights of God awareness will pass first to *woman,* and then, afterward, to *man.*

Rav Schneur Zalman depicts this gender transformation as a two-step process. First *woman* comes into her voice. Her current lack of voice manifests in two ways. Now her betrothal happens through a one-way flow of speech. The groom talks while the bride stays silent. He pronounces his intention, "Behold you are sanctified [betrothed] to me..." and she does not respond. Her silence expresses her lack of protest, which establishes the criteria of mutual consent. Their engagement, with all its contractual responsibilities, activates by her muteness. Second, the *Shemoneh Essrei,*[5] the epitome of prayer and *woman*'s essential expression of Divine service (as opposed to Torah study, which is *man*'s), is a silently offered prayer.

The seventh marriage blessing reads, "Let there soon be heard...

5. The *Shemoneh Essrei* is the central prayer of Jewish worship. See Glossary.

the voice of the bride." R. Schneur Zalman reads this as an invocation: Let the bride come into her voice. Let her express herself and project herself in fully audible speech, the very opposite of the whispered prayers we now employ in our *Shemoneh Essrei*.

In the future *woman* will return to her roots and receive her lights straight from the very source of consciousness itself, the inwardness of the Infinite Light. The relationship between groom and bride, God and Israel, will then be fully consummated, as *woman* attains her full stature and they now meet at every level of their beings. *Woman* will recover her voice, and the roles of *man* and *woman* will invert. *Man* will receive his light and bounty from the transcendent levels of *HaShem* via the agency of *woman* as his intermediary, a state described by the seventh marriage blessing, "Blessed are You, *HaShem*, Who rejoices the groom *with* the bride." All the promised pleasures of the messianic times are merely effects of this profound shift in gender relations.

ANNOTATED TRANSLATION

VOICE OF THE BRIDE

ברוך אתה ה' אלקינו מלך העולם אשר ברא ששון ושמחה חתן וכלה גילה רנה דיצה וחדוה אהבה ואחוה ושלום ורעות. מהרה ה' אלקנו ישמע מהרי יהודה ובחוצות ירושלים קול ששון וקול שמחה קול חתן וקול כלה קול מצהלות חתנים מחופתם מערים ממשתה נגינתם ברוך אתה ה' משמח חתן עם כלה.

Blessed are You, *HaShem,* our God, King of the universe, Who created joy and gladness, groom and bride, mirth, glad song, pleasure, delight, love, brotherhood, peace, and companionship. *HaShem,* our God, **let there soon be heard** in the cities of Judah and the streets of Jerusalem the sound of joy and the sound of gladness, **the voice of the groom and the voice of**

the bride, the sound of the grooms' jubilance from their canopies and of youths from their song-filled feasts. **Blessed are You, *HaShem*, Who gladdens the groom with the bride.**

This is the last of the seven marriage blessings (*sheva brachot*), the special prayers recited under the wedding canopy and at each of the seven celebratory meals in the week following. The language of its bolded lines is curious for several reasons:

הנה יש להבין מה ששינה בחתימת ברכת שמח תשמח מחתימת ברכה האחרונה אשר ברא כו' ששם אמר משמח חתן וכלה ובחתימת ברכת אשר ברא אומר משמח חתן עם הכלה[6]. וגם מהו עניין הבקשה באמרו מהרה ישמע כו' קול חתן וקול כלה מה שייך עניין הרמת קול לחתן וכלה בשמחתם וגם למה דווקא לעתיד ישמע קול חתן ולא עתה וגם מהו שכפל לומר שני קולות קול חתן וקול כלה כו'.

1. **Why is the closing line of this blessing** only subtly **different from the one that precedes it?**[7] **The sixth**[8] *sheva bracha*

---

6. The closing line of a blessing, expressed in the formula of "Blessed are You...," is called a *seal*. It condenses the thoughts that precede it into a single statement of prayerful affirmation.

7. The entire sixth blessing reads, "Gladden the beloved companions as You gladdened Your creatures in the Gan Eden from aforetime. Blessed are You, HaShem, Who gladdens groom and bride."

8. The blessings are said in a different order under the *chupa* than at the celebratory meals. Under the *chupa* the prayer over the wine is said as the first *sheva bracha*

I.
Questions raised by the seventh marriage blessing.

II.
Preview of the essay's thesis: that the perfected Messianic vision of **man** and **woman** includes a reversal of their role polarities.

III.
The underlying mechanism of this reversal follows the sequence of engagement and marriage as it applies...
A. to men and women,
B. and to Israel and *HaShem*

IV.
Metaphysics of Israel's marital relationship with *HaShem*. Betrothal – The union of externalities and comprehension of outer lights.

V.
The transition from betrothal to marriage marks a quantum shift in *woman's* development.
A. She will then have independent access to her own flow of lights.
B. *Man's* and *woman's* roles will reverse and she will pull their lights from above.
C. The metaphysical laws underlying this transition.

V.
The seventh marriage blessing's vision of Messianic transformation.
A. Stage 1: woman recovers her voice.
B. Stage 2: woman becomes a crown to her husband with greater access to their joint account of superconscious resources than he.

ends with the prayer, "Blessed are You . . . **Who gladdens** the
groom and **bride**," while the **seventh ends** with, " . . . **Who
gladdens the groom** with **the bride**."

The difference between them must be significant
enough to warrant both blessings. Otherwise, one of the
prayers would be redundant and its recitation would violate
the prohibition of taking God's name in vain.

2. **Why is the blessing stated with such urgency: . . . let there**
   soon **be heard . . . the voice of the groom and the voice of
   the bride?"**

3. **What is the connection between the raised voices of
   groom and bride and their joy** at coming together?

4. **Why is the blessing stated in the future tense, as if only
   then will their voices be heard, but not now in the present?**

5. **Why is the prayer careful to explicitly mention the word**
   voice, **both in relation to the groom and in relation to the
   bride: "Let there soon be heard . . . the** *voice* **of the groom
   and the** *voice* **of the bride,"** when it could more simply have
   said, " . . . the voices of groom and bride."

The answer to these questions draws its illumination from the
body of kabbalistic teachings called the *Diminished Moon*, a collection of mystical writings that elucidate the mystery of gender.

אך הנה מה שאומר משמח חתן וכלה קאי עתה בזמן הגלות ומה שאמר
משמח חתן עם הכלה קאי לעתיד דהיינו איר שישמע קול חתן וקול כלה
אז לעתיד דווקא משמח חתן עם הכלה אבל עכשיו שלא נשמע עדיין קול
חתן וכלה משמח חתן וכלה.

---

and then the six special blessings follow. At the celebratory meals, the six
special blessings precede the prayer over wine so the numbering changes.
What is here called the *seventh* becomes the *sixth*. What is here called the
sixth becomes the *fifth*.

The sixth *sheva bracha*, which ends with the phrase "…**Who rejoices** the **groom and** the **bride**," describes the relationship of male and female in our **present**, fallen, and **exiled state.** The seventh blessing, which reads… **Who rejoices** the groom *with* the bride," applies to **the future** and presents the ideal and perfected endpoint of the collective marriage between men and women as cosmic archetypes evolving through time. The blessing describes a two-step process of realizing its vision.[9] The first shifting of relationship is described by the phrase "**then will be heard…the voice of the groom and the voice of the bride.**" Only once both **voices are heard can the last phase of history begin, where "the groom now rejoices with the bride." Since at present the voices of bride and groom are not both heard,** the reality of the sixth blessing applies instead, and a lower state of **joy binds the groom** and **the bride.**

וההפרש ביניהם ידוע שכשאומר משמח חתן עם הכלה היינו שהשמח' באה מצד הכלה וממנה עיקר השמחה לשמח את החתן אבל כשאומר משמח חתן וכלה היינו שהחתן משמח לכלה ואל החתן בא עיקר השמחה בתחילה ולכך אומר משמח חתן ואחר כך כלה כו'.

The difference between these two blessings and the three-step sequence of relationship

---

---

9. In the prayerbook containing the essay here translated, there also appears another essay, entitled, "*Ki Al Kol Kavod, Chupa*" ("Above Every Glory Is a Canopy"), where this point is explicitly elaborated.

they describe **is known** to all versed in kabbalah. In the future era described by the seventh blessing, **when "the groom rejoices with the bride,"** their polarity of giving and receiving will invert. While generally the male bestows and the female receives, then **the awakening of joy will originate with the bride and only afterward spread to the groom.**

Conversely, in the sixth blessing, which describes our present, fallen state by the phrase "… **Who rejoices the groom _and_ the bride,"** the situation is reversed, **and the arousal moves from groom to _bride_.** Since the kindling of **joy starts** with him, the verse describes the sequence of joy as starting **with the groom** and **afterward the bride.**

ולהבין ביאור הדברים ושיש הטעם אה למה עכשיו השמחה בחתן ואחייב בכלה ולעמיד יהיה עיקר השמחה מן הבלה בוי. הנה יש *להקדים* תחלה שרש עניין אירוסין ונישואין.

To understand the reason behind this shifting of the polarity **of joy's flow, that now it passes from groom to bride yet soon it will emanate from bride to groom, one must first understand** the difference between **betrothal and marriage as** sequential stages of connubial commitment. Besides their literal application in every wedding ceremony, they also mark the path of Israel's evolving relationship with God and Torah.

Betrothal and marriage are precisely defined terms in Jewish law. Betrothal is a legally binding commitment to marry. Though the couple is not permitted to relate sexually, in most other respects they are as if legally married and the dissolution of their engagement requires a divorce. The second level of marital commitment occurs when the bride formally enters her husband's home. The wedding canopy symbolizes their coming together under one roof and so effects this change of status. The marriage is finalized by its physical consummation.

דהנה צמיג תודה אמה לנו משה מורשה א"ת מורשה
אלא מאורסה.

Several *midrashim* employ the metaphor of engagement and marriage to describe Israel's evolving relationship with *HaShem* through history:

> **Moshe commanded us the Torah, a *morasha* (inheritance)** to the congregation of Jacob."[10] [The *Gemara* derives a homiletical teaching based on the similarity between two words, one of which appears in this verse.] **Don't read *morasha* (inheritance), rather** substitute a different but similar sounding word, *me'orasah* (**act of betrothal**). With this substitution the verse now reads, "Moshe commanded us the Torah as an engagement token to the congregation of Jacob."[11]

Two teachings emerge from this *Gemara*.

1. The relationship between Israel and *HaShem* parallels the relationship between groom and bride.
2. The Torah's revelation at Sinai bound Israel to *HaShem* through the first stage of matrimonial coupling, called betrothal (*airusin*).

I.
Questions raised by the seventh marriage blessing.

II.
Preview of the essay's thesis: that the perfected Messianic vision of **man** and **woman** includes a reversal of their role polarities.

III.
The underlying mechanism of this reversal follows the sequence of engagement and marriage as it applies...
A. to men and women,
B. and to Israel and **HaShem**

IV.
Metaphysics of Israel's marital relationship with *HaShem*. Betrothal – The union of externalities and comprehension of outer lights.

V.
The transition from betrothal to marriage marks a quantum shift in *woman's* development.
A. She will then have independent access to her own flow of lights.
B. **Man's** and **woman's** roles will reverse and she will pull their lights from above.
C. The metaphysical laws underlying this transition.

V.
The seventh marriage blessing's vision of Messianic transformation.
A. Stage 1: woman recovers her voice.
B. Stage 2: woman becomes a crown to her husband with greater access to their joint account of superconscious resources than he.

---

10. Deuteronomy 33:4.
11. TB, *Pesachim* 49b.

וכן אמרו בעטרה שעטרה לו אמו ביום חתונתוזו מ"ת שהוא בחי' אירוסין
בלבד שנקרא חתונתו ולא בחי' נישואין:

And similarly another *midrash* teaches:[12] "Go forth, O you daughters of Zion, and gaze upon King Solomon, even **upon the crown
wherewith his mother crowned him on the day of his espousals...**"[13] The *midrash* [reads this verse as metaphorically referring
to the union of *HaShem* with the Jewish people and] identifies
the Torah's revelation at Sinai as the historic event corresponding
to "the day of His espousals." It further proves that this dramatic
encounter effected betrothal (and not marriage) by another verse
[where Moshe commands the people to prepare for the Torah's
revelation]: "And you shall sanctify yourselves today and the
day following."[14] [Since the word here for "sanctify" (**kidashtem**
/ קִידַשְׁתֶּם) shares the same root as the word for "engagement"
(*kidushin*/קִידּוּשִׁין), this proves that the Sinaic bond was betrothal
and not marriage.]

כי בחי' נישואין יהיה לעתיד דווקא בביאת הגואל כמ"ש כי ובועליך עושיך
כו' אבל עכשיו אינו אלא בחי' אירוסין בלבד.

The final consummation of Israel's relationship with *HaShem* as
marital union will only happen in the future, when the messianic **redeemer comes** to lead the world through its final stages of
transformation. **Then will** Isaiah's **prophesy be fulfilled: "Your
husband is your maker."**[15] The term for "husband" in this verse
emphasizes the physically consummated union of man and wife.

Rambam depicts this joyful era of redemption with the following words:

---

12. *Bamidbar Rabbah* 12:10; *Mishnah, Taanit* 4:8; *TB, Taanit* 26b.
13. Song of Songs 3:11.
14. Exodus 19:10.
15. Isaiah 54:5.

In that time there will be neither famine nor war, envy or competition. Good will flow in abundance and all delights will be [as common] as dust. The occupation of the entire world will be solely to know God. Therefore the Jews will be great sages and know hidden matters, attaining knowledge of their Creator to [the full extent] of human potential as Isaiah states, "The world will be filled with the knowledge of God as the sea fills the ocean bed."[16]

In addition to these more familiar features of that yearned-for time, kabbalah adds another blessing to the list. The messianic era will bring a profound transformation of gender relations, which it explicitly depicts as an equalizing of stature between man and woman, groom and bride. This is the subject of Rabbi Shneur Zalman's essay *The Voice of the Bride,* translated here.

During this interim **period** until the messianic time, Israel's spousal relationship with *HaShem* is daily ripening. Yet since it remains unconsummated, **the term** that most accurately describes their level of intimacy is **betrothal,** a preparatory period wherein the couple readies for wedlock.

וההפרש הזה בין אירוסין לנישואין הוא עניין ההפרש בין בחי' פנימית לבהמי חיצוניות בו' דהיינו במ"ת הגם

---

16. Rambam, *Mishneh Torah, Hilchot Melachim* 12:5.

שהיה בחיי גילוי אא"ס בחכמה שבתורה בעשרת הדברות אפל היה האוד
הזה מבחי' חיצונית בלבד ועי'כ לא ניתנה התורה אז דקבבחין' חיצוניות
והוא עניין חלק הנגלה שבתורה כי אורייתא סתים וגליא כידוע.

Kabbalah is the body of Jewish teachings that elucidates the esoteric layers of implication in every story, sentence, word, and law
of the Torah, as well as its customs and rituals. **The sequence of
betrothal and marriage** as a stepwise progression of relationship
has mystical significance that is likewise explicated by kabbalah.

In betrothal, **the external layers** of the couple engage, but their
"insides" do not yet touch. As above, so below. When they marry
and begin their physical relationship, a **core-level bonding** of soul
simultaneously occurs.

Although **the inner essence of Divinity called** the Infinite
Light revealed Itself at Sinai as the **radiant** wisdom of the Torah,
and condensed Itself into **ten infinitely compact seeds of teaching called** the Ten Precepts, nevertheless, only **the more external
layers of the** Infinite **Light** were actually manifest in that encounter. **Consequently**, the relationship between *HaShem* and Israel
created by **that revelation of Torah was** an **external** bonding.
Though their attachment was profound, their insides were not yet
engaged.

The **Torah has** infinite layers of **teachings, some of which
are visible** while **others lie** deeply **concealed** beyond the grasp
of human comprehension. **At Sinai only its more accessible layers** actually **shone** forth **as explicit teachings** and visible lights.
HaShem limited Himself to what would be apprehensible to that
generation, at that point of history.

אבל בחי' פנימית התורה שהוא כל בחי' הסוד הגנוז בנגלה שבתורה הנק'
טעמי תורה כידוע לא נתגלה כלל בזמן מ"ת בהר סיני אלא לעתיד דווקא

יתגלה אור פנימית טעמי התורה כולה לפי שלעתיד
יהיה גילוי אא"ס בתורה מבחינ' פנימית אא"ס.

Conversely, the inner dimension of Torah, the repository of secrets hidden within the text elucidating the deeper reasons behind its laws, stories, and textual structure, was not revealed at Sinai. Yet it initiated a process of unfolding that assures its eventual release, for each generation from that point hence peers into the Torah and exposes another layer of its hidden light. **By the end of days** there will be no secrets left. **The Torah's inner recesses will blaze forth, and all will behold** the glory of **its every detail. The most inward** and abstract **beauty of the Infinite Light will shine through the Torah** like a holograph, **rendered visible** by the perfectly ground lens of its Oral Teachings embodied as the living community of Israel.

וענייין בחי' פנימיות וחיצונית הללו היינו בחי' פנימית
דעתיקא שנק' עוגג העליון של עצמות המאציל בידוע
הוא הנקרא עתיקא דעתיקין.

As explained, each of the ten *sefirot* and six *partzufim* have a distinguishing trait that is their contribution to the soul. A person's nature and level of spiritual development determines which of those traits are integrated in strong and healthy ways, and which are under- or over-developed. The Tree of Life marks a ten-step path from below to above that each soul follows in its journey toward perfection and reunion with its Creator.

The last stop in its trek is the *sefirah* called *crown* (*keter*), which contains two *partzufim*: an upper one called *Atik Yamin* (*Ancient of Days*) and a lower one called *Arikh Anpin* (*Long Countenance*). The trait associated with *Atik* is spiritual bliss (תענוג), and the trait associated with *Arikh* is will (רצון), for it is the source of all motivating impulses within the personality. For various reasons, sometimes these two *partzufim* are considered a single level, in which case *Arikh* is absorbed by *Atik*, which now comprises two layers, one outer and one inner. In this essay, Rav Shneur Zalman employs this latter model (see diagram on following page).

IN SUMMARY

When it says that only the outer layers of the Infinite Light were revealed at Sinai, while its inner lights stayed hidden, encased within the text as unrealized possibilities of interpretation, **the terms *inner* and *outer*** refer to specific levels in the kabbalistic map of reality. In this context they **indicate the two layers of *Atika*,** the deepest root of soul and the point where it is hewn from the pure simple oneness of the Infinite Light. *Atika* is the place where man touches God (so to speak).

The inner, hidden lights of the Torah form the inner **layer of *Atika*,** whose trait is spiritual bliss. This is the highest level of consciousness available in this world (as opposed to the world to come). It is defined as a pure, unselfconscious pleasure that comes when the self is nullified **before the** consuming fire of **Divine Presence** and yet, like Moshe's bush, is not consumed. Rather, in this self-nullified state, awareness permeates every cell of the body; no longer is it limited to the organs of brain and mind. **As is known** to all who are studied in kabbalistic literature, this exalted state of

consciousness awaits all who reach the last milestone of their journey, called *Atika d'Atikin* (**Most Ancient One**). And yet, like all
the promised rewards of the next world and nether realms, a taste
(diluted as it may be) is always available in this world as well.

Sefirah	Partzufim Terminology		This Essay		Trait	Inclusive Term In This Essay
Crown - כתר	עתיק יומין Ancient of Days	=	עתיקא דעתיקין Most Ancient One	=	תענוג Spiritual Pleasure	עתיקא Atika
	אריך אנפין Long Countenance	=	עתיקא Ancient One	=	רצון Will	

ובחינת חיצונית הוא בחי' עתמיקא סתם שהוא בחי' מקור וכתר לנאצלים
כנדוע.

The outer aspect of the Infinite Light revealed at Sinai, which congealed into the visible letters of the Torah, is called Atika, Ancient
One (as opposed to *Most Ancient One*). This outer layer of *Atika* **is
the earliest beginning of the emanated** worlds **and serves as their**
crown, **which means that it holds the vision of their perfection
and motivates them to realize that end.**

ועכשיו אין גילוי עונג המאציל בתוכה רק מבחינת חיצונית העונג העליון
וע"ב לא נגלה למטה רק בחי' חיצונית מתורה אבל לעתיד שיתגלה בתורה
בחי' פנימית העונג העליון (הנקרא שעשועי המלך בעצמותו כמ"ש בס' עמק
ממלך) וכמ"ש ואהיה אצלו שעשועים כו' לבך יתגלה אז למטה בחי' פנימית
הנק' טעמי התורה כי הטעמים שרשם בבחי' התענוג כו' וד"ל.

Now, since many of **the Torah's** enlightening teachings remain
locked away inside itself, the pleasure that comes from knowing
them **is not available** to us. **Only a surrounding** glow is visible **and**

the lower-order pleasure that comes from beholding that outer layer of truth. Although **only the external teachings of the Torah are** actually **revealed now,** this is a temporary condition. Each generation daily mines new jewels from its rich quarry and **eventually** our tunneling **will reach the** bedrock **core** of consciousness itself. **The pure ecstasy** of *Atika* will erupt into the world and infuse all living things with rapture, inaugurating a new era of blissful union with *HaShem* **called "the delight of the King in His essence," as described in the book *Emek HaMelekh*.**

This phrase can be read in three ways:

- The otherworldly **delight that comes when** creation (who will then be called *king*, having completed its perfection and assumed the role of *HaShem*'s royal emissary, i.e., king) reunites with its source (essence) in the Infinite Light.
- **The delight of** the Creator **(the King** of kings) **when He reunites with** the lost pieces of **His essence** that were strewn throughout creation at the primordial cataclysm called the shattering of the vessels. These shards of light are the sparks of soul that are finally completing their 6,000-year pilgrimage back to their source.
- The "rest state" of Divinity, the "natural" vibration of His being, is delight. This phrase thus refers to **the delight of the King (***HaShem***) that pervades His essence** and characterizes it. Anyone who accomplishes the feat of making contact with Divine essence is instantly electrified by that rapture called the King's delight.

This idea is conveyed in a verse from Proverbs,[17] which depicts the Torah as *HaShem*'s beloved child. The Torah reminisces, "I was by Him a nursling, **and I was daily His delight.** Playing always

---

17. Proverbs 8:30.

before Him, playing with the universe, His earth; and my delights were with the sons of men."

In the end of days **the inwardness of the Torah will be revealed below; its hidden,** soul-satisfying **truths** will illuminate every question, resolve every doubt, **explain** every suffering. **These explanations of Torah have their root in the** highest **level** of *Atik,* **called spiritual delight,** for pleasure always reduces to an expansion of awareness. As Israel absorbs the deeper and more mystical teachings of the Torah, they become en*light*ened, literally. Their minds illuminated with the holy radiance of Torah wisdom, they will again "see from one end of the world to the other"[18] and this itself will be their bliss.

והנה הגם שבזמן מ"ת לא נגלה רק בחי' חיצוניות ההארה בלבד מ"מ גם בחי' פנימית האור נמשך ובא גם הוא למטה כמ"ש וירד ה' על הד סיני וכשירד ירד בכל עצמותו

While it is true that **only the outer layers of** the **Infinite Light were actually revealed at Sinai, nevertheless the inwardness of the** Infinite **Light did come** forth **into the lower worlds** at that time, **as the Torah** itself **attests, "And HaShem came down upon Mount Sinai."**[19] When the verse anthropomorphically describes HaShem **coming down, it is teaching that the**

---

18. TB, *Hagigah* 12a.
19. Exodus 19:20

actual source of light, that is, the Infinite Light, itself "came down" into this world. This is qualitatively different from all other revelations that are encounters with the aura surrounding the "luminary" but not with the actual body of light itself.

וגם הרי אמר אנכי מי שאנכי זה הוא בחי' פנימית הכתר כידוע.

Another proof that the inwardness of the *Infinite Light* came down at Sinai, although it was not actually revealed at that time, is the fact that *HaShem* began His revelation of the Torah with the word *Anochi* (I am). The first commandment **reads, "I am** *HaShem* your God, Who brought you out of the land of Egypt, out of the house of bondage."[20] That aspect that *HaShem* refers to as **"I" is the** level of consciousness identified with the **innermost point of the** *sefirah* **of crown (***keter***) as is known.** The *partzuf* associated with this point is *Atika d'Atikin,* the Infinite Light hidden *inside* the Torah, the source of holy pleasure and infinitely expanded awareness.

אך ורק שלא באה בחי' הארה הפנימית לידי גילוי גמור בבחי' א"פ אלא
נשאר למעלה בבחי' העלם הנקרא אור מקיף השוכן ושורה על בחי' א"פ
בהעלם מכל צדדים כו'.

Nevertheless, although **this inner light** of *Atika* came down into the world, it **did not enter** the visual field of those beholding the **revelation. Instead, it hovered beyond** the edge of conscious perception, **effectively invisible.**

Lights that can be grasped and integrated are called inner and internalizable (אור פנימי). *Lights* that are present but too "high" or "deep" or "vast" to be contained within their vessel of consciousness are **described as surrounding** or hovering (אור מקיף). **The lights** of *Atika d'Atikin* that held the inner secrets of the Torah **could not integrate** into the nation at that time. It literally could not "fit" into their minds, even at the Edenic level of development that

---

20. Exodus 20:2.

they attained at Sinai.[21] **Displaced, the light** of *Atika d'Atikin* **formed a kind of invisible halo around the integrated lights** of the revealed Torah, **enclosing them as if in a sphere** of radiant consciousness.

וזהו עניין בחי' אירוסין כמ"ש ביום חתונתו וכנ"ל כי הרי עניין האירוסין למטה ג"ב הוא בבחינה זאת דהיינו בבתי' אור מקיף בלבד כידוע בעניין טבעת הקידושין שהוא דבר עגול מקיף לאצבע היד כי באמרו הרי את מקודשת לי ממשיך לה רק בהי' אור מקיף בטבעת זאת וזהו פי' מקודשת גבבחי' קדש העליון כו' וזהו א"ת מורשה אלא מאורסה בבחי' אירוסין בלבד.

This is why the Talmud describes the relationship formed between Israel and *HaShem* at Sinai as **betrothal,** interpreting, **"The day of his espousals (engagement)** ... as a reference to the revelation at Sinai. **In both cases** (engagement and Sinai) only the more superficial layers of the couple enter into active relationship, while their inner essence stays *un*engaged and assumes a position of surrounding light. The vessel of their relationship is not developed enough to hold the full intensity of their inner selves. For this reason **the** classic **symbol of betrothal is a ring, a circular ornament that** surrounds **the finger. And when** the groom proposes, and **speaks** the halachic formula of engagement, **"Behold you are sanctified**

---

21. TB, *Shabbat* 146a.

(מקודשת) **to me (i.e., betrothed) by this ring…"**[22] he effects
two mergers:

1. The superficial layers of himself and his beloved enter into
   active and committed relationship.
2. Their respective core levels of soul bond to the vessel of
   relationship as **surrounding lights.**

This is **symbolized by the ring** that he places on his fiancée's
finger.

The reason that **he uses the language of sanctification**
(מקודשת) instead of the actual term for "engagement" (מאורסת)[23]
is to **link** his action up **to the supreme holiness** (קדש עליון)[24]
associated with the *sefirah* of *keter* (crown), also a circular ornament that sits upon the head and surrounds the primary organ of
consciousness, the brain.

---

22. *Mishnah, Kiddushin* 3:1.

23. A clarification for those less familiar with Hebrew. The Mishnah presents
a formula for effecting halachic engagement that includes the statement,
"Behold you are *sanctified* to me… Why doesn't the groom say a more explicit
and straightforward statement, "Behold, you are engaged to me"? The paragraph explains that the Hebrew word for "sanctified" has other associations
that the Sages wished to bring into the process.

24. *Zohar* 2:121b, 122; 3:66a, b. This is the term for the point where the *sefirah*
of *chokhmah* contacts the *sefirah* of *keter*.

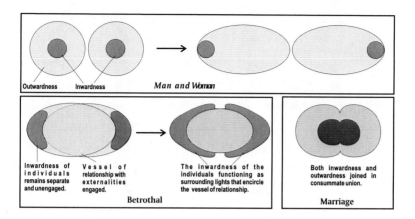

This is the basis for the *Gemara*'s **comment: "Don't read** *morasha*, **inheritance, rather read** *me'orasah*, **fiancée," thereby implying** that the Torah's revelation was **an engagement ceremony** between *HaShem* and the Jewish people, the transcendent lights serving as the circular ring effecting betrothal.

אבל בחי' נישואין היינו שבא אור השפע מן המשפיע במקבל בגילוי גמור כמו הייחוד והזווג בביאה עד שעושאה כלי שעושאה כלי בביאה זו כמאמר אין אשה כורתת ברית אלא למי שעשאה כלי כו' וכמ"ש כי בועליך עושיך כו' ולא בבחי' מקיף בלבד.

Marriage, on the other hand, is a deeper state of union. **The** flow of **bounty and revelation passes from bestower to receiver completely.** There is nothing of the revealer that cannot be seen, held, and contained by the perceiver. Their union is consummate **and parallels the physical relationship between husband and wife.**

There are thirty-nine categories of prohibited work on Shabbat, each of which constitutes a particular type of creative labor. One of these categories is called building, and included within it is the prohibition against opening containers. While the container is factory sealed (for example, the can of tuna or bag of sugar), it is not actually functioning as a vessel since its contents are not available to the outside world. Halacha defines *vessel* as a container *with an opening* that allows access to the product within. Consequently, when a person opens a can of tuna he or she is effectively creating a vessel in that moment. Until the person removed the bonded metal top, the tin was a partially constructed vessel-in-potential. By someone cutting away the top, its contents become accessible to human usage, and it enters the category of vessel proper. It is thus true to say that the "opener" of the vessel is its "maker."

Similarly, the first time a woman has physical relations, she becomes a "vessel" in the fullest sense of the word. And "as below, so above," her capacity to "receive" on every level of soul is similarly awakened. Her contours of spiritual receptivity are molded into shape by that encounter. A metaphor that describes this idea is an embossing stamp. The metal has a design engraved, in bas-relief, and when pressed against the paper or wax it creates a negative image that perfectly matches the original design. The outward projecting metal die actually carves out a custom "vessel" of perfectly suited proportions to hold its unique image.

Similarly, an inner covenantal bond of spirit forms between a woman and her husband in their first relations. A man who lacks the strength of soul to impact his bride in this way will not succeed in forming the bond that defines marriage on all its inner levels, and their union will likely not succeed. **This is what the Sages mean when they say, "A woman does not bind herself in a covenant** of marriage **except with one that can make her a vessel."**[25]

And so it says regarding the end of days, when Israel and *HaShem* finally consummate their union, **"Your husband is your maker."**[26] *Your husband* (i.e., the one whose revelation of light and beauty has entered into your soul and carved out a space that

---

25. TB, *Sanhedrin* 22b.
26. Isaiah 54:5.

can hold the full content of that revelation), *He is your maker* (i.e., you have become your full self by this experience). Now you can fulfill your highest function. The pleasure of consummation is the pleasure of becoming who you really are. It is as if you were "made" in that moment, while before you were a "partially constructed vessel-in-potential." "Your husband is [truly] your maker."

In marriage proper, the inner lights are **no longer** displaced to a **surrounding** position; rather, they return to their centers, which have now merged into a common core.[27]

וכדוגמא זאת יהיה לעתיד כאשר יתגלה בחי' פנימית אא"ס בתורה בגילוי גמור וע"כ אמרו ביום חתונתו בזמן מ"ת שהיה רק בחי' אירוסין וביום שמחת לבו לעתיד שיהיה בחי' נישואין בהתגלות טעמי תורה כי האשה נקנית בשלשה דרכים בכסף כו' וידוע דכנ"י נקרא' אשה ונקנית בבחי' מקיף בטבעת קידושין כו'.

Similarly in the future, the full radiance of the Infinite Light will shine through the Torah, its soul no longer hidden by the coarse materiality of ink on parchment that cloaks it now. Every wisdom, insight, and mystical reverie will radiate forth for all to see.

Consequently, the Sages equate "the day

---

27. Israel is defined as a creature, unique in the universe, by virtue of its capacity to know, contain, and reveal the full range of existential possibilities that exist within Divinity Itself. At present this is only a potential, but a potential that *will* be realized.

I.
Questions raised by the seventh marriage blessing.

II.
Preview of the essay's thesis: that the perfected Messianic vision of *man* and *woman* includes a reversal of their role polarities.

III.
The underlying mechanism of this reversal follows the sequence of engagement and marriage as it applies …
A. to men and women,
B. and to Israel and *HaShem*

IV.
Metaphysics of Israel's marital relationship with *HaShem*. Betrothal – The union of externalities and comprehension of outer lights.

V.
The transition from betrothal to marriage marks a quantum shift in *woman's* development.
A. She will then have independent access to her own flow of lights.
B. *Man's* and *woman's* roles will reverse and she will pull their lights from above.
C. The metaphysical laws underlying this transition.

V.
The seventh marriage blessing's vision of Messianic transformation.
A. Stage 1: woman recovers her voice.
B. Stage 2: woman becomes a crown to her husband with greater access to their joint account of superconscious resources than he.

of his espousals" to the giving of the Torah at Sinai, for there began the engagement bond between *HaShem* and Israel. They vowed to wait for each other until the end of days, when their time would be ripe for wedlock. The entire verse reads, "Go forth, O you daughters of Zion and gaze upon King Solomon, even upon the crown wherewith his mother crowned him on the day of his espousals and on the day of his gladness of heart." The phrase "... day of his gladness of heart" refers to the future when the marriage between *HaShem* and Israel will finally be consummated. The fullness of Divine light will shine through the Torah and be received by Israel, filling their collective heart, bones, cells, and spaces with Holy Presence. There will be no place inside them that is not permeated with God and nothing of God that does not fit inside them. A perfect marriage, a consummate union of glory and awe.

Jewish law defines betrothal as a legal contract of intention to marry that requires one of several specific deeds to activate the obligations associated with that commitment. The Mishnah states, "A woman is betrothed in three ways: When she receives a sum of money [or a gift of equivalent monetary value ...]"[28] Nowadays this is fulfilled by the exchange of a ring,[29] an ornament that encircles her finger. Similarly, Israel is called "woman" in relation to *HaShem*, and she was betrothed by the encircling light that descended at Sinai and served as her engagement ring.

והנה ידוע בע"ח דעכשיו בחי' המ"ל מקבלת האור מבחי' ז"א שהוא יחוד הוי"ה אלקים כו' ובחי' ז"א מקבל מוחין לעצמו מבחי' אימא וז"ש בעטרה שעטרה לו אמו.

According to kabbalah, the role relations that characterize mar-

---

28. TB, *Kiddushin* 2a.
29. *Shulchan Arukh*, IH 31.

ital union are evolving through time. The model that describes our present stage of development is slowly shifting and after passing through several intermediate milestones will eventually invert. R. Isaac Luria identifies seven developmental stages in the evolving relationship of men and women from Eden to the end of time.[30] **Until the final stage, *woman* receives** her cosmic flow of **light,** bounty, and consciousness **via the intermediary of her spouse.** Her relationship to the transcendent aspects of God is mediated by her *husband* and all of her Divinely bestowed gifts must first pass through him. His work is to identify which of his spiritual bounties truly belong to him and which are *her* rightful inheritance that he must release into her possession.

The masculine in turn **receives his flow of** light and **consciousness from** the *partzuf* directly above him, called *mother.* His "brains"[31] derive from there and remain rooted within her. She thus serves as his crown, for her lights sit above his head and encircle it with transcendent brilliance. Always, the integrated awareness of a higher *partzuf* is superconscious and

I.
Questions raised by the seventh marriage blessing.

II.
Preview of the essay's thesis: that the perfected Messianic vision of *man* and *woman* includes a reversal of their role polarities.

III.
The underlying mechanism of this reversal follows the sequence of engagement and marriage as it applies ...
A. to men and women,
B. and to Israel and *HaShem*

IV.
Metaphysics of Israel's marital relationship with *HaShem*. Betrothal – The union of externalities and comprehension of outer lights.

V.
The transition from betrothal to marriage marks a quantum shift in *woman's* development.
A. She will then have independent access to her own flow of lights.
B. *Man's* and *woman's* roles will reverse and she will pull their lights from above.
C. The metaphysical laws underlying this transition.

V.
The seventh marriage blessing's vision of Messianic transformation.
A. Stage 1: woman recovers her voice.
B. Stage 2: woman becomes a crown to her husband with greater access to their joint account of superconscious resources than he.

---

30. *Ari, Etz Chaim, Shaar Miut HaYareach.*
31. *Brains* is a literal translation of the Hebrew word מוחין and is a frequently used term in kabbalah. It refers to the upper three *sefirot, keter, chokhmah, binah* (and sometimes *daat*), and thus indicates the faculties of conscious and superconscious awareness, i.e., *intelligence* in the broadest sense of the term.

ungraspable by the one below it. **This further explains** the verse from Song of Songs that describes betrothal with the words " ... **the crown wherewith his mother crowned him** on the day of his espousals." The *mother* in this verse is *binah* and the crown is her integrated lights, which exceed the capacity of his brains and so surround his head like a crown.

This relationship system, where the flow of influence passes from the Infinite Light to *mother* to *man* to *woman*, **is** kabbalistically **expressed by** a particular form of **the union between** two names of God, י / ה / ו / ה (**the unpronounceable name** of God) **and** א / ל / ה / י / ם (pronounced **Elohim**).[32]

כי בחי' החתן למעלה הוא בחי' ז"א דאצילות שנקרא משפיע כידוע בפי' חתן
לשון נחות דרגא נחית ויורד מלמעלה למטה ובחי' מ"ל דאצי' נקרא כלה
בחי' מקבל כידוע ובחי' בינה דאצי' ממשיך מוחין לז"א וע"י אורות דאימא
שמקבל הוא שיש בכחו להשפיע למלכות אח"כ.

Kabbalah identifies four planes of reality, which it calls the four worlds because each contains an entire set of ten *sefirot* and six *partzufim* within it. From above to below they are:[33]

atzilut	אצילות	spiritual plane of pure Divinity
briyah	בריאה	mental plane
yetzirah	יצירה	emotional (also psychic and astral) plane
assiya	עשיה	physical plane

---

32. Generally, this combination of names refers to the endpoint and rectified expression of masculine and feminine in their equal-statured, face-to-face relationship. Sometimes, however, it expresses this less mature state of relationship where the feminine remains dependent upon the masculine. See *Zohar* 1:20a (R. Ashlag's commentary, paragraphs 110–115), where both of these usages appear. Another explanation appears in *Sharei Ora* by R. Yosef Gikatilla, *Shaar Chamishi*.

33. See Chapter 5, footnote 2.

Atzilut, the highest and most spiritual world, is the plane of cosmic archetypes and the first appearance of *partzufim*. The "**heavenly groom**" discussed in this **essay indicates the level of** man **in the world of** *atzilut*. He embodies **the force of divine bestowal** and heavenly **influence** upon the lower realms.

The Hebrew **term for "groom,"** חתן (*chatan*), **relates to the phrase** נחות דרגה, to "drop rank," suggesting movement from above to below, fall and descent. This semantic derivation emphasizes his role as holy envoy, pulling transcendent lights from above and transferring them to his spouse below. **The** Hebrew **term for "bride,"** כלה (*cala*), **relates to the root** כלל, "to include," and highlights her trait of receptivity.[34]

The flow of consciousness in the world of *atzilut* thus passes from *mother* to *man* to *woman*. ***Mother* (*binah*) pulls wisdom down and passes it to her son. The lights *man* receives from *mother* empower him to extend bounty to** his own wife, **the *sefirah* of *malchut*,** and *partzuf* of *woman*.

---

34. The word *cala* also relates to a similar root, כלה, which means "to complete, finish, perish," as in the phrase כלות, a state of fatal rapture where the soul actually leaves the body because of its insatiable longing to unite with its Beloved above.

וזהו בעטרה שהוא בחי' המוחין שעטרה לו אמו דוקא ביום חתונתו כו' וכל זה עכשיו דוקא.

Thus, when the verse describes "**the crown** which his mother crowned him on the day of his espousals...," **it refers to the enlightened insights that** *mother* **brings down** from the higher realms and transfers to her *son*. These lights, however, exceed his mental capacity at that time and so, unable to fit "inside," **they hover around his head** as surrounding lights, appearing as a "crown." **This was** his *mother's* **engagement gift**, to assure that he would have the necessary resources to function as a true husband and holy envoy to his bride. **All this still applies today.**

אבל הנה לעתיד כתיב אשת חיל עטרת בעלה הרי בחי' מ"ל שנק' אשת חיל תהיה עטרת לבעלה שהוא בחי' ז"א ונמצא בחי' העטרה שעטרה לו אמו ביום חתונתו בזמן מ"ת הנה לעתיד יבא לו העטרה זאת דוקא מבחי' מלכות הנק' מקבל מפני שאור המלכות תתעלה אז למעלה מעלה מבחי' ז"א לפי שנעוץ סופן בתחילתן כי סוף מעשה דוקא עלה במחשבה תחלה וכמ"ש ביאור דבר זה במ"א באריכות.

This hierarchy of flow describes the relationship between *man* and *woman* in their earlier stages of development. Just as each day brings Mashiach one step closer, so does the relationship of groom and bride daily mature into its ideal of equal-statured union. **The verse that describes its future and perfected state is "A woman of valor is the crown** (עטרה) to her husband."[35] **This source depicts the bride as a valiant** or mighty **woman who now assumes the position of** crown **to her husband (the groom).** Their roles have reversed. Until this stage he served as her crown, holding the lights that were ultimately destined to her but still too "big" for her vessel. Here she becomes his crown and holds the consciousness that eludes his now more limited grasp.

---

35. Proverbs 12:4.

One could summarize the entire 6,000-year odyssey of biblical history as the progressive enlightening of the lower realms. Each instant some increment of Infinite Light trickles down into the world and integrates into the minds of its inhabitants. An elaborate production line exists, extending from above to below, that packages the Infinite Light into a form that can be absorbed by the lower worlds. One key feature of this cosmic chain of descent is that the higher level always functions as a crown to the world below it.

In the betrothal period initiated at Sinai, the flow of consciousness passed from *mother* to *man* to *woman*, and each served as the crown to the one below it. The verse that describes this arrangement is **"the crown wherewith his mother crowned him on the day of his espousals**...for **at Sinai** the *man* received his superconscious inheritance of lights from *mother* as an engagement gift. He internalized a portion and passed a fraction on to his fiancée as a betrothal token, as an engagement ring.

In the future, this crown of superconscious lights that *man* received from **mother** **will instead come from woman (i.e., his *wife*). She, who had previously been below** him in stature and "intelligence," **will now surpass him,** and their roles will reverse. She will be holding their higher lights and he will receive his portion from her.

The mechanism that underlies this turn of

events is a metaphysical law that has two formulations. *Sefer Yet-zirah* states, "**The end is enwedged in the beginning.**"[36] The last (and lowest) point of creation was actually the first and essential reason for it. Similarly, a verse from the Shabbat liturgy states, "**The final outcome was the first thought.**"[37] These ideas are discussed at length in other places.[38]

Kabbalah teaches that this *first thought* was a piercing vision of the accomplished purpose of creation. Its utter and compelling beauty inspired *HaShem* (as it were) to begin His "labor" of materializing that dream. It is the whole point of creation and yet it is the last to come forth. Everything else is an intermediate building block toward its one culminating end, the perfect embodiment of that original vision. The last piece of handiwork in the six days of creation was woman. This means, according to these principles, that her "root" is higher than all that preceded her, for "the last and lowest **end derives from the** first and highest **beginning.**" It follows that her trait of receptivity must be the ultimate and eternally enduring purpose of creation.[39]

When the universe is a work in progress, *HaShem* needs builders to complete the millennia-sized task of perfecting the world. This downward-facing work is a masculine skill and when *it* is in demand, power and status reside with those that have it.[40] But eventually (and actually quite soon, in the relative scheme of things), the world will be built, the job will be done, Shabbat will come. And then the trait in high demand will be receptivity, the

---

36. *Sefer Yetzirah* 1:7.
37. Standard Liturgy, *Kabbalat Shabbat, L'Cha Dodi*.
38. *Rashaz, Lt Torah* 3:13:1; 4:5:3; 4:10:3; 4:27:2; 4:35:2; 4:45:4.
39. *Rashaz, Tora Or* (TO), *Parashat Vayigash* (first words, *Biur al*)
40. TB, *Berachot* 64a. "'And all your children [literally, sons] shall be students of *HaShem* and your children [sons] will have abundant peace.' Don't read [*banekha*] 'your sons,' but [*boniekh*] 'your builders.'"

capacity to receive the Divine revelation of love and light and Presence that is the pleasure of eternity. This upward-facing activity is a feminine skill and, apparently, the ultimate purpose of creation.

In the world of appearances, woman is lowest; in the world of roots, she is highest. When creation returns to its roots and its hierarchy rules, the polarity of masculine and feminine will reverse and she will become the crown to her husband. Now the opposite is so.

ולהיות כן יובן ענין מאמרם ז"ל בימות משיח באמרם עתידים צדיקים שיאמרו לפניהם קדוש כי שורש נשמת הצדיקים מבח' מל' שתתעלה למעלה מעלה בבח' הכתר שנק' תחילתן ולכך יאמרו לפניהם קדוש וד"ל.

This also explains the mysterious **statement by** Chazal **concerning the messianic time:**[41]

Now the angels gather before *HaShem* and worship Him with the formula of adoration that we imitate in our *Kedusha* prayer when we say, "Holy, holy holy is the Lord of hosts."[42] **There will come a time when** the heavenly **hosts will recite "holy, holy, holy ... before the righteous** *tzaddikim* as it is now said before the Blessed Holy One. This is the mystical interpretation of the verse,[43] "And it shall come to pass that

---

41. TB, *Bava Batra* 75b.
42. Isaiah 6:3.
43. Isaiah 4:3.

---

he that is left in Zion, and he that remains in Jerusalem shall be called Holy."

This switch **happens because the souls of the** *tzaddikim* (the righteous and pious ones) **are,** surprisingly, **rooted in the** lowest *sefirah* **called** *malchut,* which forms the *partzuf* of *woman,* whereas the *partzuf* indicated by the title *Blessed Holy One* is *man.* Consequently, **when** the universe returns to its roots and **woman rises to her holy beginnings in the highest** *sefirah* **called** *crown,* she will be manifesting a higher octave of Divine majesty than *man,* also called Blessed Holy One, and **the angels will** address **their adoration** to her, and **to the** righteous *tzaddikim* who embody her traits.

ובכל זה יובן מה שאנו אומרים עתה משמח חתן וכלה ולעתיד משמח חתן עם הכלה כו' כי הנה עתה בחי' מ"ל הנק' כלה מקבלת מבחי' ז"א הנק' חתן כו' לכך השמחה תחלה בחתן ואח"כ החתן משמח לכלה כי שפעה בא לה מבחי' ז"א ע"י מוחין שקיבל מאור אימא כנ"ל בפי' עטרה שעטרה לו אמו כו'.

It is now possible to answer the essay's original five questions regarding the last two marriage blessings.

The sixth *bracha,* which applies to the relationship of *man* and *woman* **in their present,** unperfected state, closes with the words "Blessed are You, *HaShem,* **Who rejoices the groom** *and* **bride."** The seventh blessing, which applies **to the future, reads instead,** "...**Who rejoices the groom with the bride."**

Now, *woman,* **who is called bride, receives her lights from** *man,* **who is called groom.** His larger stature affords him greater access to the transcendental realms and she is dependent upon him for this. He pulls their lights down from *mother* and afterward transfers hers to her. Since lights and consciousness are always synonymous with joy, the sixth marriage blessing describes the present as a time when **gladness passes from groom to bride, and he is the agent of her joy.**

This hierarchy of descent begins with **mother, who passes superconscious** and surrounding **lights to her son,** *man,* an act **described by the verse "the crown wherewith his mother crowned him** on the day of his espousals." **He** internalizes some of that light, separates out a portion, and **conveys it to** *woman,* his wife.

אבל לע"ל שנא' אשת חיל עטרת בעלה שתתעלה המ"ל בכתר ויהיה מדריגתה למעלה במחי' ז"א אז יאמר משמח חתן עם הכלה דהיינו שעיקר השמחה יהיה מן הכלה שהיא בחי' מ"ל סוף כל דרגים מפני שנעוץ סופן בתחילתן ומן הכלה יבא אור שפע שמחה זאת אל החתן כמ"ש אשת חיל עטרת בעלה וכמו כן כתיב הנני בורא חדשה כו' נקיבה תסובב גבר כו' וד"ל.

This hierarchy of flow is not the ideal and will not always be so. **Eventually, "The woman of valor [will become] the crown to her husband."** Like a rubber band stretched back and released, when *woman* completes her *tikun,* **she will spring beyond the level of** *man* **up to the level of** *crown* (the first and highest *sefirah*). **When this happens,** their gender polarity of higher and lower, giver and receiver, will reverse and she will bestow consciousness to him. The seventh blessing describes this turn of events with **the phrase, "…Who rejoices the groom** *with* **the bride." The essential source of joy** (and consciousness) **will originate with the bride,** *woman,* who has reattained her full stature after nearly 6,000 years on **the lowest rung of creation. This is what it means that

"**The end is enwedged in the beginning.**" When "the end" finally reattains its beginning, the lowest becomes the highest and **the groom will receive his flow of light and joy from the bride,** who has become his crown, **as the verse foretells, "A woman of valor is the crown to her husband."** This future era **is also alluded to by another verse** in Jeremiah, **"Behold I will create a new thing . . . the woman will surround the man."**[44] Now, since his "intelligence" is higher than hers, his lights are the surrounding ones, for her vessel of consciousness is too limited to hold them. In the future the opposite will be true. Her consciousness will supersede his, spilling over as surrounding lights to his more limited vessel at that time.

וזהו מהרה ישמע בערי יהודה כו' קול חתן וקול כלה כי הנה עתה בזמן הגלות אין לבחי' מ"ל רק מה שמקבלת מבחי' ז"א בעלה כי לית לה מגרמה כלום ולכך התפילה נק' צלותא דבלחש מפני שאין לכלה הנק' מלכות בחי' דבור בבחי' התפשטות וכמ"ש נאלמתי דומיה בבחי' הקטנות שהוא בבחי' שתיקה וכמ"ש אדני שפתי תפתח פי' תפתח אתה אבל מצד עצמה אין לה בחי' דבור בקול כי בטלה עם כל כוחותיה להיות בבחי' נקודה אחת בלבד באצילות כו'.

This also **explains** why the seventh blessing expresses impatience with the present and seeks to hurry its envisioned end, "**. . . Let there soon be heard in the cities of Judah . . . the voice of the groom and the voice of the bride . . .**"

Now, in our fallen and **exiled state, the** *woman* **only has what she receives from her husband, "she has absolutely nothing that is intrinsically her own."**[45] She is completely dependent on him. This model of gender relations plays itself out on other planes as well.

Every level of reality displays gender. There is always a giver and a receiver, a masculine and a feminine. It is certainly possible (if not probable) that within a given "couple" these roles would

44. Jeremiah 31:21.
45. *Zohar* 1:140a, and many others.

switch from situation to situation. For example, in certain contexts, one of the pair assumes the role of active bestower while in another context he becomes the more passive receiver and vice versa. Nevertheless, in every field of focus gender exists. Consequently, if one examines the subject of Divine service, Torah study is considered a masculine expression, and prayer, a feminine one. There are many reasons for these associations.

Among the variety of prayer forms found in Judaism (praise, request, thanksgiving, affirmation, the *Shema*, etc.) the most complete and essential expression of prayer is the *Shemoneh Essrei* (literally, eighteen), the Prayer of Eighteen Blessings (though it actually has nineteen, for one was added at a later period in history). This prayer is the heart of each worship service. All other liturgy is either building up to or winding down from it. When the word *prayer* appears unqualified in Jewish writings, it refers to the *Shemoneh Essrei* (also called the *Amida*, or standing prayer). Halacha derives many of the laws regarding its recitation from Chana, the mother of Shmuel, whose prayer for a child appears in the first book of Samuel.[46] The most distinctive rule is that it must only be whispered. Nearly all other liturgical expressions are pronounced with full voice. Conversely,

I.
Questions raised by the seventh marriage blessing.

II.
Preview of the essay's thesis: that the perfected Messianic vision of *man* and *woman* includes a reversal of their role polarities.

III.
The underlying mechanism of this reversal follows the sequence of engagement and marriage as it applies ...

A. to men and women,
B. and to Israel and *HaShem*

IV.
Metaphysics of Israel's marital relationship with *HaShem*. Betrothal – The union of externalities and comprehension of outer lights.

V.
The transition from betrothal to marriage marks a quantum shift in *woman's* development.

A. She will then have independent access to her own flow of lights.
B. *Man's* and *woman's* roles will reverse and she will pull their lights from above.
C. The metaphysical laws underlying this transition.

V.
The seventh marriage blessing's vision of Messianic transformation.

A. Stage 1: woman recovers her voice.
B. Stage 2: woman becomes a crown to her husband with greater access to their joint account of superconscious resources than he.

---

46. 1 Samuel 1:1–2:10; TB, *Brachot* 31a, b.

the *Shemoneh Essrei* is enunciated just loud enough for one's own ears to hear, no more.

Since prayer is a feminine mode of worship, and **the essential expression of prayer is** the *Shemoneh Essrei,* **the whispered prayer,** then its thrice-daily recitation symbolically **reenacts the bride's absence of voice** at this point in history. Speech is a human being's primary tool for projecting him- or herself out into the world. The hidden content of one's thoughts becomes heard by another, and even more, once spoken, they influence the subsequent actions of those that heard them. Since speech is an outward projecting extension of influence, it is a masculine mode of expression, while the more receptive, listening role is feminine. One who has no "voice," whether literally or metaphorically, **lacks the** normal **channels of exerting** power and **influence** over his or her environment and must resort to nonverbal methods, which often include violence or passive-aggressive protest.

King David describes this voiceless state by the verse, **"I was struck mute with silence."**[47] Kabbalah identifies this phrase from Psalms with a profoundly regressed developmental **state that it calls** *katnut*[48] (literally, "smallness"), conveying the idea of narrow-minded and constricted consciousness. **A primary feature of** *katnut* **is the inability to express oneself in words.** A chasm exists between awareness and speech, due to one's inadequate capacity of articulation (whether chronic or momentary).

---

47. Psalms 39:3.

48. The term *katnut* describes an immature state, generally corresponding to the soul's preadolescent period of development, "where the individual is only able to understand the externality of things..."The term applies both to the natural growth process when the soul is passing through *katnut* for the first time, and it is an age-appropriate condition, as well as regressed expressions of *katnut,* where an adult lapses into age-inappropriate immaturity. The verse from Psalms, "I was struck mute with silence..." refers to the latter.

One's depth or intensity of thought cannot be conveyed through the insufficiently developed instrument of speech. Instead one retreats into frustrated silence.

And so the *Shemoneh Essrei* begins with the words, "*HaShem,* **open my mouth** that my lips may declare Your praise." *HaShem,* if You want my prayers, if You want a dialogue of communion, then You must assist the process. **You must help me speak.** On my own I lack the skill. I have regressed to such a point that **I have lost my voice and capacity for self-expression, along with** many **other powers** that associate with maturity and expanded consciousness. I cannot even stand upright. I am a puddle. All of my upper nine *sefirot* (representing my higher levels of awareness) have collapsed into the lowest one (*malchut*), and **I am reduced to a single point occupying the lowest level of the emanated world.**

וזהו שהחתן אומר להכלה הרי את מקודשת לי והכלה שותקת ובשתיקה זאת היא מקודשת ולכאורה היה מהראוי שתדבר בפיה בפי' שמסכמת בקידושין הללו.

For this reason engagement happens through a one-way flow of speech. **The groom** talks while the bride stays silent. **He pronounces his intention, "Behold you are sanctified (betrothed) to me…" and she does not respond.** Her silence expresses her lack of protest, which establishes the criteria of mutual consent. **Their engagement,** with all its contractual responsibilities, **activates by her muteness. Why doesn't she speak at least a word of verbal consent?** That would seem to be more consistent with the mutually binding character of their relationship.

אך הענין הוא לפי שבחי' המלכות הנק' כלה היא עכשיו בחי' טפל ובטל לגבי החתן ולכך קולה לא ישמע לא בתפילה ולא בקבלת קידושין אלא גם בשתיקה מתקדשת כו'.

The reason for this custom is that the engagement ceremony models the earlier developmental stages in the evolving relationship of *man* and *woman.* In those stages **the bride** is just beginning to recover from her fall and diminishment. Her **stature remains severely decreased and overwhelmed to the point of near non-existence before the groom.** The most obvious symptom of this disparity in stature **is her lack of "voice," both in** her associated form of worship, that is, **prayer,** and in her mute **acceptance of engagement. Each** reflects her *katnut* and **is** thus **performed in silence.**

אבל לעתיד כשתתעלה בחי' המלכות בכתר ותהיה עטרת בעלה כנ"ל שאז תהיה בחי' משפיע לז"א בעלה הרי יהיה לה אז בחי' קול בהתפשטות בפ"ע וזהו קול כלה שיהיה לכלה בחי' קול בחי' התגלות והתפשטות הדבור בקול רם היפוך בחי' צלותא דבלחש דעכשיו וד"ל.

However, the time is rapidly **approaching when** *woman* will complete her journey of perfecting. Fully recovered from her "fall," **she will return to her root in the** *sefirah* **of** *keter* **and manifest as "a crown to her husband,"** having now superseded him in stature. Their roles will have inverted **and she will be drawing down** their light, bounty, and consciousness **and passing it on to him** (a service he has provided for millennia). All this will follow an earlier shift **when the bride comes into her voice,** both literally and metaphorically, for voice **symbolizes the more general activity of projecting herself out into the world as an independent agent.** The seventh marriage blessing reads, "Let there soon be heard**...**

the voice of the bride." **Let the bride come into her voice.** Let her **express herself and project herself in fully audible speech, the very opposite of the whispered prayers we now employ** in our *Shemoneh Essrei.*

וזהו ישמע כו' קול כלה פירוש מהרה ישמע לשון עתיד דוקא כי דוקא לעתיד יהיה בחי' קול כלה העליונה וכל עיקר הטעם הוא לפי שעכשיו אינו אלא בחי' אירוסין שהאור אינו בא אלא בבחי' חיצונית בלבד ובחי' הפנימית שורה רק בבחי' מקיף והוא ענין הקידושין בטבעת כנ"ל לכך בשתיקה דוקא מתקדשת דהיינו בהיותה דוקא בבחי' ביטול בצלותא דבלחש כו'.

This is what it means that "the voice of the bride **will be heard,"** meaning, **"Let it** *soon* **be heard."** Both **phrases indicate a future state when the supernal bride will** finally attain her full stature and **recover her voice. Now we are still in the era of engagement, and the bonding** between *man* and *woman* only **incorporates their more external layers of light** and consciousness. Their inner selves are displaced. Prevented from entering into direct contact, they **surround** the couple instead, exerting an indirect influence **and serving as their** cosmic **engagement ring. Reflecting this** cosmic stage of development, **where** woman (and all things feminine) **is still** profoundly **diminished, a bride accepts her engagement in silence and prayer is whispered.**

אבל לעתיד שתתעלה המלכות בבחי' הכתר ותקבל מבחי' פנימית אא"ס שהוא בחי' נשואין דהיינו שנעשית

כלי בפ"ע ע"כ ממילא יהיה למ"ל בחי' קול בהתפשטות ואדרבא מן המ"ל

יבא אור שפע לבחי' ז"א כנ"ל בפירוש משמח חתן עם הכלה דקאי לעתיד

דוקא כנ"ל וד"ל:

But in the future *woman* will return to her root as crown and receive her lights straight from the very source of consciousness itself, **the inwardness of the Infinite Light. The relationship** between groom and bride, God and Israel, **will then be fully consummated, for woman will become a vessel unto herself,** a freestanding, independently acting partner in marriage. **She will recover her voice and project herself out into the world to such an extent that** the roles of *man* and *woman* will invert. *Man* **will receive his light and bounty** from the transcendent levels of *HaShem* **via the agency of *woman*** as his intermediary, **a state described** by the seventh marriage blessing, "Blessed are You, *HaShem*, **Who rejoices the groom *with* the bride."** This shifting of dynamic between *man* and *woman* underlies all of the promised messianic blessings that await Israel **in the end of days.**

DEBRIEFING

THE VOICE OF THE BRIDE

What Do We Know?

1. The role relations between *man* and *woman* are going to experience a drastic shift in messianic times.
2. This transition will culminate in a reversal of "traditional" polarities; the feminine will become the primary agent of bestowal, and the masculine will receive from her, at least in the area of lights and consciousness.
3. This shifting of role relations is an unequivocally good thing. It is one of the yearned-for transformations of the messianic time.

4. While Israel is betrothed to *HaShem* (i.e., from Sinai until the messianic end of days), the masculine aspect of Israel predominates; when Israel finally consummates its marital union with *HaShem*, its feminine half will predominate.

What Do We Not Know?

1. We do not know anything about the sequence of getting from here to there. Is it a gradual turning? Is it a quantum shift? Or perhaps a combination of the two?

2. We do not know what the implications of these ideas are (or will be) in real life. How will this shifting of polarities translate into the reality of people's lives?

3. We do not know how or whether to consciously participate in this process. Should we actively facilitate its unfolding or passively receive it as it happens?

4. We are now within the era called "the birth pangs of Mashiach." The question becomes, "Is it a time to resist the urge to push, or has parturition proceeded to the point that pushing is good and necessary?" How can we know the answer to this question?

Logical Implications and Speculations

1. Underlying this shift in the polarity of *man* and *woman* is an even deeper (and more fundamental) shift in the purpose of creation. When the universe is a work in progress, *HaShem* needs builders to complete the millennia-sized task of perfecting the world. This downward-facing work is a masculine skill and when *it* is in demand, power and status reside with those what have it. But eventually (and actually quite soon, in the relative scheme of things) the world will be built, the job will be done, and Shabbat will come. When that happens, the trait in highest demand will be *receptivity*, the capacity to receive the Divine reve-

lation of love and light and Presence that is the pleasure of eternity. This upward-facing activity is a feminine skill and, apparently, the ultimate purpose of creation.

9
TWO GREAT LIGHTS... *REVISITED*

Babylonian Talmud (*Chullin 60b*)

BARE BONES LITERACY

SUMMARY

The moon's dialogue with the Blessed Holy One, recorded in the Babylonian Talmud, conceals paradigm-shifting insights about the essential nature of relationship and the rectified expression of gender. In particular, it clarifies *man's* role in this cosmic drama of lunar collapse and the way he can (and must) assist its *tikun*.

The rise of the *Shekhinah* is a welcomed transformation that will finally enable the full and joyous union of male and female. Only as equals do *man* and *woman* truly match. This perfect marriage has been our (perhaps unconscious) yearning for 6,000 years, and from its consummation flow all the promised blessings of the world to come.

VOCABULARY

Back-to-back relationship – An immature and self-absorbed mode of relating, in which neither partner ever really "sees" the other, except as an object whose sole purpose is to satisfy his or her own narcissistic needs. Adam and Eve's relationship before their *nesira* was back-to-back.

front-to-front relationship – A relationship of true and healthy love. The couple bonds from mutual desire and shared vision. This possibility of relationship only arises after *nesira*.

gadlut – (literally, "greatness"). Expanded, mature, and God-centered consciousness.

katnut – (literally, "smallness"). Immature, narrow-minded, self-centered, and constricted consciousness.

man and *woman* – Kabbalistic archetypes of male and female in their prime, as opposed to *father* and *mother*, which signify their later stages of life.

mitzvah – One of the 613 commandments of the Written Torah. It is also used colloquially to refer, in general, to good deeds.

nesira (surgical uncoupling) – Tradition teaches that Adam and Eve were originally created as a single, bi-gendered creature with male and female halves fused together like Siamese twins. God then severed this bond, releasing them to meet face-to-face as freestanding individuals for the first time. This is how Jewish tradition interprets the biblical story of Eve's formation.

Principle of Interinclusion – A distinguishing feature of our present universe is its holographic structure. Every piece includes something of every other piece inside itself. This is always true. No matter how small the fragment, no matter how many subdivisions one executes, the resulting particles always contain a complete set of the whole.

Talmud – The main repository of the Oral Tradition, scribed in 499 C.E., that interprets and elaborates the Torah.

teshuva – (literally, "return"). Return to the service of God. The inner, all-consuming commitment to devote one's life to serving God. The process of lower *teshuva* involves acknowledging sins, regretting them, and committing to change.

tikun, tikunim – A word that means "rectification, healing, repair, perfection, elevation" ... all of these at once.

tzaddik / tzaddikim – (literally, "righteous, perfect"). A person who has purged his or her entire being of all impurity and of every inclination (even subconscious) to act contrary to spiritual law.

TECHNICAL NOTES

The italicized terms *man, woman, mother,* and *father* refer to kabbalistic archetypes (called *partzufim*) and, by extension, to the masculine and feminine attributes found in both men and women. The literal translation of the Hebrew text appears in bold print.

SYNOPSIS

TWO GREAT LIGHTS (CHULLIN 60B) ... *REVISITED*

R. Shimon ben Pazzi pointed out a contradiction between two halves of the verse in Genesis describing the formation of the sun and moon. It begins by stating, "and God made the two great lights," and continues with the phrase "the great light to rule by day and the small light to rule by night."

The moon said to the Blessed Holy One, "Master of the universe, is it really possible for two kings to share one crown?"

He replied, "Go, and make yourself small."

"Sovereign of the Universe!" cried the moon; "Because I suggested something proper, must I diminish myself?"

He replied, "Go and you will rule by day and by night."

"But what is the value of this?" cried the moon. "Of what use is a lamp in broad daylight?"

He replied, "Go. Israel shall reckon by you the days and the years."

"But it is impossible," said the moon, "to do without the sun for reckoning the days, as it is written, 'And let them be for signs and for seasons, and for days and years.'"

"Go. The righteous shall be named after you as we find, Jacob the Small, Samuel the Small, David the Small."

On seeing that she would not be consoled the Blessed Holy One said, "Bring an atonement for Me for making the moon smaller."

This is what R. Shimon ben Lakish meant when he declared, "What is different about the he-goat offered on the new moon, that concerning it the Torah writes, '...for the Lord'? The Blessed Holy One is saying by that phrase, "Let this he-goat be an atonement *for Me*, for making the moon small."[1]

---

1. TB, *Chullin* 60b.

This talmudic tale of sun and moon, which inspired all of the teachings here compiled, yields a whole new body of insights when revisited now, at the end of the path. Two innocent questions crack the text open and expose new landscapes of implication.

- To whom is the moon addressing her complaint? The title Blessed Holy One could refer to the Transcendent One (who outranks both kings) or to her male cohort, the sun himself. Kabbalistic sources permit both interpretations.[2]
- The story ends with the Holy One bringing a sin offering for making the moon small. What exactly is the sin he seeks to atone? Doesn't sin always imply that one had options and chose the low road? What could that possibly mean in this scenario?

In general, the term *Blessed Holy One* refers to the *partzuf, man.*[3] In the standard formula of affirmation recited before performing a mitzvah, the term *Blessed Holy One* refers to that aspect of God in spousal relationship with the *Shekhinah* (or moon).

"For the sake of the unification of the Blessed Holy One with His *Shekhinah* ... I am ready to fulfill this holy command."

It is explained in chasidut that all of the lights from God's essence find their consummate expression in *zeir anpin* [*man*]. For this reason *zeir anpin* [*man*] may be referred to as "the Blessed Holy One."[4]

Similarly, in the previous chapter R. Schneur Zalman brought a talmudic passage describing how the angels address their worship

---

2. *Leshem,* HVS 1:1–7, 7:4–7.
3. The *Ari* states this association explicitly in *Etz Chaim, Shaar HaClalim, perek* 12. This is based on the association between the title, Blessed Holy One, and the Tetragrammaton. *Leshem,* ibid.
4. Ginsburgh, Yitzchak. www.inner.org.

to the aspect of God called Blessed Holy One, which kabbalah equates with *man*.[5] In the future, when even higher levels of Divine majesty manifest in the world, the angels will shift their attention there. The aspect of God called Blessed Holy One will no longer be the focus of their worship.

We direct our prayer to the Tetragrammaton, or four-letter name of God, which expresses the Infinite entirety of Divine Being but which manifests primarily through the level associated with the *partzuf, man*.[6,7] The Blessed Holy One, which is the source of God's (lower) providence, is the highest level of God accessible to us on a constant basis. In exceptional moments, and with extraordinary merit, an individual may enlist levels of Divine assistance that originate beyond the Blessed Holy One. This is a rare and exalted occurrence. Kabbalah cites Chana's prayer as an example of such a moment.[8] The verse reads: "And [Chana] was bitter in spirit, and she prayed (על) to *HaShem*..."[9]

The Vilna Gaon interprets the word על in its literal sense, reading the verse as: "And [Chana] was bitter in spirit and her prayer reached (על) *beyond HaShem* [i.e., beyond the *partzuf, man*]."

The Vilna Gaon explains that Chana's prayer evoked levels of Divine providence that derive from the layer of pure grace, grades beyond the Blessed Holy One. He brings other examples of this type of prayer, and in each, the words על ה' mark its exceptional nature. Since this phrase does not appear in the talmudic passage

---

5. TB, *Bava Batra* 75b. See "Voice of the Bride," p. 260.

6. TB, *Zevachim* 46b; *Zohar* 3:5a; *Leshem*, HVS, ibid.

7. Our prayers are a substitute for the *korbanot*, which were offered only to the Tetragrammaton and not to other names of God (e.g., *Elokim*), as learned out by Leviticus 1:2, and codified in *Zevachim* 46b.

8. *Zohar* 3:79b (see Hebrew translation and commentary of *Metok Midvash*); R. Eliyahu ben Shlomo Zalman of Vilna (The Vilna Gaon, or Gra), *Biurei HaGra L'Agudat HaShas*, with the commentary of R. Avraham (Warsaw) p. 26, quoted in R. Eliyahu Dessler, *Michtav MeEliyahu*, 4:104.

9. 1 Shmuel 1:10.

quoted earlier, one can assume the moon is speaking to the Blessed Holy One (her spouse) and not to the Transcendent *One* above them both.

Part of the confusion surrounding the Holy One's identity comes from the disparity of level between ourselves and the moon. When *we* speak to the Blessed Holy One, we *are* speaking to a Transcendent aspect of God, relative to our standing here below. In contrast, the moon is the *Shekhinah*, herself, whose home is in the heavenly realms, the same as His.

This clarification of the Holy One's identity creates nothing less than a paradigm shift. Our story becomes a marital encounter instead of a theological debate. The moon is dissatisfied with her relationship and complains to her spouse. The sun responds by demanding that she diminish. She balks at the suggestion and tries to negotiate. He offers incentives and attempts to convince her that diminishment is really advancement. We never hear whether she consents to her fate or merely obeys, coerced by a lack of options.

The story ends with the Holy One engaged in a colossal effort of repenting, in his own words, "for making the moon grow small." This "transgression" is apparently so huge that it takes the entire course of history to mend its damage.

One must assume that the sun had options, at least theoretically. Otherwise, there is no concept of sin. The story itself offers no hint of what these choices might have been. Kabbalah provides clues.

As explained, the lowest two *partzufim*, called *man* and *woman*, duplicate the patterns of life on the physical plane. They gestate for nine months in the womb of *mother,* nurse for two years, and then begin a multi-phased sequence of growth. *Man* reaches his first stage of maturity at thirteen and *woman* at twelve.[10] The par-

---

10. R. Shalom Ulman, *Daat Elokim* (Jerusalem: Dafus Tfutza, 1983), *Tikun Partzuf Zu'n.*

allels between them and real men and women are obvious and intentionally so.[11]

One primary feature of man's life cycle is his journey from *katnut* (immature, narrow-minded, and self-centered consciousness) to *gadlut* (expanded, mature, and God-centered consciousness).

The terms *katnut* and *gadlut* roughly correspond to the sequential stages of personality development that psychology distinguishes as ego-identity versus self-identity.[12]

> **Ego-identity** is self-absorbed, survival-oriented, ruthless in its drive to avoid pain, and ignorant of its dependence upon the *whole*.

> **Self-identity** integrates both the conscious and unconscious layers of psyche into a higher unity that embraces all the facets of oneself. "Its capacity for self-criticism, and desire for truth release it from the fanatical self-obsession that characterizes the ego's preoccupation with self-preservation."

In its early stages of development, consciousness is limited to a narrow range of awareness that includes little more than its own needs and comforts. This is what psychology calls ego-identification. Slowly, as consciousness matures, it expands to include the unconscious and superconscious layers of psyche and acquires a capacity for empathy with perspectives outside itself. This sequence perfectly parallels the kabbalistic model of *man's* development from *katnut* to *gadlut*.

As explained in the "Relativity of Gender," when the original Adam split into *man* and *woman*, the conscious portions of Adam

---

11. Ramchal, *Klach Pitchei Chokhmah* (KPC), 115.
12. Erich Neumann, *The Origins and History of Consciousness* (New York: Bollingen Foundation, Inc., 1954), pp. 358–360. These are the definitions of the terms within a Jungian paradigm.

remained with *man* while its unconscious portions collected in *woman*.[13] Consequently, the kabbalistic model of developing *consciousness* applies particularly to him, for *man represents* conscious awareness in that paradigm.

Ramchal documents how the history of creation follows the developmental unfolding of *man*. For example, the Torah describes the early universe as one of "chaos and void." This, says Ramchal, reflects *man's* profound state of *katnut* at that time. As *man* evolved from *katnut* to *gadlut*, the conditions of physical existence similarly evolved.[14]

Ramchal portrays the *katnut* personality as judging, bad-tempered, irascible, cold, and incapable of bonded companionship.[15] He further notes that as long as *man* remains in back-to-back relationship with *woman*, he is at the developmental level of *katnut*.[16] Since this entire story transpires while sun and moon stand back-to-back,[17] the sun cannot help but react from his place of *katnut*, displaying all the personality distortions associated with that state.

One must conclude that, theoretically, if the sun were in *gadlut*, he would have responded differently. Other solutions to the moon's

---

13. *Ari, Etz Chaim, Heichal Zeir Anpin, Shaar Nesira* 1, translated here in "The Small Light to Rule by Night."

14. Ramchal, *Daat Tevuna*, pp. 135–146 (especially 140–146), as quoted in *Daat Elokim* 99–101 (especially 100); Ramchal, *Clalai Chokhmat HaEmet*, p. 22; as quoted in *Daat Elokim*, pp. 101–102; KPC 120–123.

15. Ramchal, KPC 52.

16. Ramchal, KCHA 23–24 (pp. 22a–24b); KPC 119; *Daat Elokim*, p. 137.

17. See Ari's description of *nesira* (pp. 82–87), which happens when mother infuses man with the lights of *chesed*. This causes *man's* and *woman's* backsides to become dissimilar, thus severing their backsided bond. Woman immediately collapses into diminishment, yet she and he are now free to turn and meet face-to-face. The sweetening of man's *dinim*, which occurs via the infusion of *chesed* that he receives from mother during the process of *nesira*, is what moves him from *katnut* to *gadlut*. In light of this sequence, see Ramchal, KPC 52, 121–135.

complaint must have been possible, had the sun been on a level of maturity to see them and choose them. We know that two kings *can* rule under a single crown, for that is the promised endpoint of the moon's ordeal.[18] This suggests that the sun could have found a way to accommodate the moon's complaint without requiring her to diminish. That would certainly have been preferable since, as we know from R. Elyashev, the moon's diminution set in motion a chain of cause and effect that is to blame for all the sin and evil in the universe.[19]

When the sun insisted that the moon grow small, he became responsible for all the negative repercussions of that decree, which are unfathomable in their vastness. No wonder it takes the whole course of history to mend the damage of that "sin." No wonder after nearly 6,000 years his *teshuva* is still not complete.

Yet how could the sun be expected to display the maturity of *gadlut* when he simply wasn't there? Other options might theoretically have existed in the universe, but they were totally beyond the sun's grasp, given his *katnut* level of development.

Nevertheless, for him as for us, sin carries consequences and requires atonement whether or not one could really have chosen differently at the time. *HaShem* takes all these extenuating circumstances into consideration and designs our *tikun* in the most gentle and compassionate way possible, which still gets the necessary cleansing and transformation done. In fact, the sin-offering that the sun "brings" to facilitate his atonement is an action specifically designated for *un*intentional transgressions.

Eventually, the sun will complete his *tikun* and repair the damage caused by his sin. Just as his transgression "caused the moon to grow small," so his repentance causes her to become great again.

---

18. *Ari, Etz Chaim*, MH 1:1. See p. 73.
19. *Leshem*, NH, which appears translated as chapter 5, "The Disparities of Gender Are the Cause of Evil."

A Baal Shem Tov teaching illuminates a kind of *teshuva* that must be similar to the sun's way of repenting "for making the moon small." Just as the sun's "sin" ultimately caused our own, so does his *teshuva* inspire our own. From the courage of his inner work and ceaseless soul searching, we, children of the moon, draw the strength to strive and grow and rise and shine.

TWO GREAT LIGHTS – REVISITED

GEMARA, CHULLIN 60B

רבי שמעון בן פזי רמי...

R. Shimon ben Pazzi pointed out a scriptural contradiction...

All the wisdom of the universe is contained in the Bible's first five books, for this is what it means that "God looked into the Torah and created the world."[20] Every fact originates in its holy text and "There is no truth except Torah."[21] It is impossible for something to be both true and not sourced in scriptural teachings. The time-honored mystery of *woman* and gender is no exception. The key to its *tikun* is sure to be found in the Torah's holy writ.

R. Shimon ben Pazzi identifies the place to start mining for answers. A snag in textual flow always signals hidden teachings. Like the "X" on a treasure map, there are sure to be riches buried beneath.

ויעש אלקים את שני מאורות הגדולים.

On the fourth day of creation **the Torah states, "and God made the two great lights."**[22]

---

20. *Zohar* 2:161b.
21. TY, *Rosh HaShana* 3:8.
22. Genesis 1:16.

In the kabbalistic system numbers have symbolic significance. In addition to their literal sense, they are also archetypes.[23] For example:

Zero represents the most pure and transcendent essence of Divinity, called *ein* (אין), or Blessed *NoThing*.[24]

One represents the fact of God as singular in relation to creation; that even with a vast universe of created things, there is nothing but God, and God is still one.

Two represents the appearance of polarities, oppositions, and paradox, of which gender is the prime example.

Three represents the fruit of two's generative union: man, woman, and child; thesis, antithesis, and synthesis.

Four represents the point at which this process snaps into an infinitely repeating cycle of generation and return. The "child" (*three*) finds a mate of its own (*four*) and a self-perpetuating system unfolds.

Etcetera.

HaShem created *two* great lights; not one, not three, not five, for with the number *two* begins the possibility of relationship, defined as "an association of two or more things."[25] With this numerical hint, scripture links the story of sun and moon to the mystery

---

23. This idea is beautifully explicated by Rav Yitzchak Ginsburgh, *The Hebrew Letters* (Jerusalem: Gal Aynai Publications, 1990).

24. A teaching that appears in many theological discussions is the distinction between two Hebrew words used to indicate God's oneness: יחיד and יחיד:אחד related to the oneness of God as expressed by the number *zero*; אחד to the oneness of God as expressed by the number *one*. *Zohar Chadash* 16; *Tikunei Zohar* 22.

25. *American Heritage Dictionary* (Boston: Houghton-Mifflin Company, 1994).

of gender. The Torah encodes its wisdom on this subject in the language of parable, for symbols convey their message straight to the soul, enabling them to bypass the intellect's blind spots and limitations.

The Torah's first clue is that both partners in this exemplary relationship started off "great." There is no hint of hierarchy between them or even a division of feature and function. Yet the same verse continues with a contradictory phrase:

וכתיב: את המאור הגדול ואת המאור הקטן!

It then states, "The great light to rule by day
and the small light to rule by night."

The Torah's second clue is that their equality does not last. A disparity suddenly appears. Only one light remains great while the other wanes small.[26] When the moon shifts in size, a dynamic element enters the picture. Their relative stature now changes with time. Are they equal or are they not? It depends on which slice of life one views when answering that question. What caused the moon to shrink in size? Why did her light ebb small? R. Shimon ben Pazzi tells what happened between the lines.

אמרה ירח לפני הקב"ה:

The moon addressed the Blessed Holy One . . .

The first step in cracking the Torah's code is to examine the char-

---

26. In physics and mathematics this is called symmetry breaking, and nearly every transition from one phase to another happens at the sacrifice of symmetry. Here the sun and moon were symmetrical in terms of size. In order for their system to move to a higher level – for *good* to become *very good* – their symmetry had to break. The moon shrank, which triggered a whole evolutionary progression that will culminate in the end of days with the net gain of positive transformation. For a lucid discussion of symmetry breaking as it relates to physics, see Michio Kaku, *Hyperspace* (New York: Anchor Books – Doubleday, 1994), pp. 209–213.

acters in this duologue: Who exactly is the moon, and what aspect of God manifests as the Blessed Holy One?

The Moon. Immediately, when *one* divided into *two*, gender appeared in the universe. This is necessarily so, since in order for these *two* to really be *two*, something had to distinguish them. In the physical world things are close when they are at the same address at the same time. In the spiritual realms (beyond space and time) things are close when they are similar and distant when they are different. The more features they share in common, the closer they are. If two things would be totally identical, they would instantly merge; they could not remain *two*, for their sameness would fuse them and nothing could override the force of that truth.

Consequently, even at the beginning, when sun and moon both shone with equal glory and the moon did not wax and wane, there still had to be something that distinguished them as sun and moon, masculine and feminine.

This question restated becomes: Which of the differences between *man* and *woman* are truly essential? Which go deeper than social conditioning?

This is an endlessly arguable question. For the purposes of this study a simple working definition will do. Biology, with its unambiguous distinctions between males and females, is the easiest place to look for a straight answer. On all other planes besides the physical (i.e., emotional, mental, and spiritual) the Rule of Interinclusion blurs the polarities of gender and frustrates the quest for sharp discernments. Conversely, there is no disputing the body's facts, which are blunt and universal.[27]

---

27. The Rule of Interinclusion also operates on the physical plane, yet its influence is more limited there. Even so, there, too, a continuum exists between the genders and each of these definitions has their exceptions; for example, there are women who cannot or do not want "to conceive, gestate, and give birth" and men who do not seek to impregnate, etc. Yet still the generalizations hold

Females possess the physical capacity (and drive) to conceive, gestate, and give birth.

Males possess the physical capacity (and drive) to impregnate by effecting intercourse.

The *moon*, as the archetype of this feminine modality, thus embodies the consciousness of producing offspring, a process that begins with an act of intercourse and extends for nine months thereafter.[28] One could say that the moon seeks union, not primarily for its own sake, but for the sake of producing something altogether new and beyond herself.[29]

The *sun*, as the masculine archetype, embodies the consciousness of union for the sake of disseminating seed, a purpose fulfilled in the moment of intercourse itself. One could say that he seeks union for its own sake, for the encounter and its bestowal, which define their meeting as a consummate one.

The Blessed Holy One – To whom is the moon directing her complaint? Is it the Transcendent *One* (Who outranks both "kings"), or is it her male cohort, the sun himself? Kabbalistic sources permit both interpretations.[30]

This ambiguity of identity between the couple's male half and the *One* that transcends them is significant and pervasive. The story

---

to a significant enough degree that the statements remain meaningful. See the introductory chapter called "Kabbalah," p. 8.

28. Though a child continues to need years of parental nurture, the parents can share this function completely. At our present stage of technological development, gestation is an exclusively feminine function. Though a mother also usually provides most childhood care, this need not be so.

29. All other gender associations are secondary to these: For example, a woman must *receive* seed to conceive and the mechanism by which she gestates a child from a fertilized egg is essentially *unconscious*. In general, a man must *consciously* participate in the act of intercourse and must *actively bestow* his seed to her.

30. Sometimes the Tetragrammaton refers to the transcendent totality of Divinity, sometimes to His more imminent expression as embodied by *man*.

of Adam illustrates this point and was discussed in the chapter "Gender Is Relative." To review: The first human being, called Adam, was a bi-gendered creature with male and female halves fused together like Siamese twins. *HaShem* severed their backsided bond and released them to meet as freestanding individuals. One half of this original Adam became man and one half became woman.

The distribution of attributes between these newly formed companions was not symmetrical. The conscious portions of the original Adam remained with *man*, while its unconscious aspects collected in *woman*.[31] This is why man maintained a continuity of identity throughout the process. If one defines *identity* as a conscious sense of self, then the "I" of that bi-gendered being, because it was conscious, stayed with man, and he retained the name Adam. The unconscious portions separated off into woman, and now, for the first time, assumed an identity of their own. Before, they were subsumed by Adam's conscious "I"; now they received a name unto themselves, called Eve.

As below, so above. Similarly, in the creation of sun and moon, the Transcendent *One* emanated from within Itself male and female polarities. And here, too, the male retains a continuity of identity with the original *One* that divided into two. Just as *Adam* refers both to the original bi-gendered creature and to the male person that later emerged, so is this true for *man* and *woman,* sun and moon. The term *Blessed Holy One* refers both to the *One* before there was two, and to the male half of the couple that emerged after that *One* divided into two.

The mysteries that unravel at the story's end seem most consistent with the opinion that reads this passage as a dialogue between sun and moon, and not she (moon) with a higher authority (see synopsis).

---

31. This is so by definition, for the *chassadim* are conscious lights and the *gevurot* are unconscious. See *Ari*'s description of *nesira,* pp. 82–87.

And yet, the fact that he retains the "name" that also evokes the Transcendent *One,* is not a semantic quirk. It shows that *man does* also embody the *conscious* will, vision, and wisdom of the Higher *One* that produced them. (She, by contrast, inherits Its unconscious will and vision. Her legacy is no less substantial, perhaps even more so, yet her wisdom takes years of cultivation to bear its fruit.)[32] By virtue of the sun's identification with its source, his voice does also resonate with an authority beyond himself.

רבש"ע, אפשר לשני מלכים שישתמשו בכתר אחד?

"Master of the universe, is it possible for two opposite-facing I-centers to unite in consummate union if they can only express one will between themselves?"

(רבש"ע, אפשר לשני מלכים ...)

Master of the Universe, is it possible for two opposite-facing I-centers to unite in consummate union if they can only express one will between themselves?

In the original division of *one* into *two* she embodied one set of traits and he their polar opposite. At this point sun and moon did not include aspects of the other inside themselves (except at a rudimentary level). Nowadays, in the era of *tikun* where the Principle of Interinclusion reigns, the primary bond between husband and wife occurs at their places of common ground: Her inner male binds to his masculinity and his inner female to her femininity. At the heart of their union lies a bond of identification.[33]

Since the story of sun and moon transpires *before* the era of interinclusion, these two kings could not identify with each other,

---

32. Based on the *Ari's* seven-stage model of feminine development, *woman* only comes into her fullness of *brains* toward the end of her life in stage 6. In real life, this is a gross generalization, but the demands of childrearing *do* generally keep women from developing that part of themselves in their earlier stages of life.
33. Rashaz, LT, *Parashat Matot,* p. 87, col. 2.

for they did not yet contain any of the other inside themselves.[34] Instead, their opinions always clashed. They embraced opposite poles of every paradox and found each other's positions incomprehensible. These two kings are accurately depicted as "opposite-facing I-centers."

(...שישתמשו...)

> Master of the Universe, is it possible for two opposite-facing I-centers to unite in consummate union if they can only express one will between themselves? One commonly accepted definition of "ושמתשי" is sexual intercourse and cohabitation, the universal symbols of consummate relationship.[35,36]

We know that Divinity, before creation, was lacking nothing, except, in some mysterious sense, the experience of actualized relationship, because there was no *other* with whom to relate. The history of creation is the life story of this cosmic "other" and its evolving relationship with God, its Creator. Since, by definition, God is only (and always) perfect, this relationship at the heart of creation must also be perfect.

The moon questions whether a consummate union (worthy of God's effort) can occur when the participating parties are opposite- facing I-centers who can only express one will between themselves. Without a capacity for empathy, can they ever build a mutually satisfying alliance? Can this design, as it stands, produce the ecstatic union that is the sole purpose of their existence?

---

34. It is more accurate to say that the interincluded aspects of each of them were so undeveloped and rudimentary that they were effectively inaccessible, though technically present.

35. This translation was first suggested by my *chavruta* Devorah Nov.

36. Reuben Alcalay, *The Complete Hebrew English Dictionary* (Israel: Massada Pub., 1965).

Underlying the moon's complaint is an unspoken vision of perfected relationship. She has expectations that are not being met. What is missing? The preceding chapters provide clues:

1. **Equality of stature.**[37] In a consummate relationship the partners match from the crown of their heads to the soles of their feet, which means they stand at equal height. Their equality of stature is a quantitative assessment. They possess an equivalence of attributes on every plane (physical, emotional, mental, and spiritual). Their distribution of strengths may vary according to gender (or not). The essential requirement is their equal value . . . truly (and not in name alone).

Equality of stature also requires equal access to resources (according to R. Luria). Each spouse draws his or her own autonomous flow of blessing from above without need of the other's mediating assistance. This mutual independence releases them to meet, for the first time in pure love, untainted by the subtle manipulations that always contaminate relationships of need.

A third feature of equalized stature is mutuality. To "meet" on the level of crown (the seat of will) is to share a perfect mutuality of desire.

2. **Eternally evolving.**[38] In R. Kook's language, an absolutely perfect relationship must include the possibility of perpetually deepening union.

3. **Fruitful.**[39] A consummate relationship is a generative one. It conceives new sparks and births them into the world, whether as actual children or expansions of consciousness.

---

37. *Ari, Etz Chaim, The Diminished Moon,* Chapter 3, here translated on p. 66.
38. *Orot HaKodesh* 2:529–531, translated as Chapter 6 on p. 173.
39. *Sulam, Zohar* 3:157a, translated as Chapter 4 on p. 99.

4. **Uncoerced.**[40] Each party must freely choose the other from a place of pure and authentic love. They marry, not because they have no options, not because they are scared to be alone, but because they want to know and be known by the other in every sense of that word.

The moon questions whether a consummate union such as this can evolve from the intensely polarized arrangement that is their present reality.

(... בכתר אחד?)

Master of the Universe, is it possible for two opposite-facing I-centers to unite in consummate union if they can only express one will between themselves?

The sun and moon began their partnership back-to-back, teaches R. Luria. They viewed the world from opposite perspectives and their natural responses always clashed. Their lack of freedom to occasionally break away and do their own thing intensified the strife. They were yoked together, forced to act in tandem at all times. With only one response allowed between them, each moment became a war of wills. The moon pondered: Can this design really produce the heavenly union that is the point of our existence?

She approached her spouse with her concerns: "Is it possible for two opposite-facing I-centers to unite in consummate union if they can only express one will between themselves?"

אמר לה: לכי ומעטי את עצמך!

He replied, "Go, and make yourself small."

The Blessed Holy One begins every one of His responses to the moon by bidding her departure. "Go..."[41]

---

40. *Leshem*, HDYH, MHY 3:4, translated as Chapter 5 on p. 137.
41. Twice He urges her "to *go*" in Hebrew and twice in Aramaic.

Go, and make yourself small...
Go, and you will rule by day and by night.
Go, Israel shall count by you the days and years...
Go, the righteous shall be named after you...

His language and its tone suggest several interpretations that might all be true.

1. One could read the phrase as a simple exhortation. The sun has asked something of the moon and wants it to be implemented at once, and so includes a call for alacrity in his request. "Go quickly, there is no time to wait. You must turn now to the task at hand." At each encounter, an obstacle lifts, which prompts a new call for speedy action.

2. The word לכי (Go!) is the command form of the verb הלך, which means "to walk, proceed, move forward." Perhaps the Holy One hereby alludes to the moon's role as the agent of transformation and forward motion.[42] She is the one that seeks union for the sake of birthing something new into the world. With these sharp words, He prompts her to remember who she is: "If your longing is positive transformation, then get on with it, despite its costs and inconveniences. Go, keep things moving. Do what you need to do, for you will never be satisfied with less than that. The need for progress is who you are."

3. It is possible that perfection (embodied by the sun) cannot bear the evidence of lack implied by the moon's report. He holds the pole of absolute perfection that precludes even the concept of improvement and perfecting. (See Chapter 6.) When the moon asserts a contrary reality, it

---

42. The explicit association of the root הלך with spiritual progress can be seen in a verse from Zechariah (3:7). "I will make you *walkers* amidst these *standers*."

threatens all that he represents. For this reason he requests her speedy exit. His words betray his discomfort with her dissatisfaction and the imperfection implied thereby.

אמר לה: לכי ומעטי את עצמך!

And He replied, "Go, and make yourself small."
The Holy One: "You are right! Two kings cannot rule under one crown, *except* if one first makes himself small. Then, at the end, when s/he grows back to full stature, they will share their crown without strife, for their separation and its ordeals will have transformed them. Furthermore, we both know that improvement cannot happen except via the shearing motion of 'descent for the sake of progressing to an even higher place in the end.'[43] You are the mistress of that truth, for you possess inside your bowels the wisdom of pregnancy, birth, and positive transformation. The consummate relationship you seek can and will be, but there is no avoiding its costs, which must be paid up front."

The very concept of relationship is paradoxical to its core. The joy of two uniting as one happens on many levels, but its most perfected expression occurs when both parties were really just parts of a single *one* all along. The greatest joy in the universe is the pleasure of becoming whole, of reuniting with the missing pieces of oneself.[44]

And yet, if the whole point is to become *one,* why did the Holy *One* decide to create *two?*

One obvious answer is that if the *One and Only One* had never

---

43. This statement is true in the universe as it is currently constructed. *HaShem* could have designed things differently, but the natural law that governs our world now includes this law.
44. *Leshem,* HDYH 2:4:17:6 (first word, *V'omek*).

split into two, there would be no relationship and no pleasure of reuniting. This is so by definition, for relationship is nothing but the "association of *two* or more things."

And these *two* must really be two. They must be truly distinct and fully autonomous entities, neither ruled nor controlled by the other.[45] Each must be free to choose according to his or her authentic truth. When one party controls the other, whether overtly or by remote control, they are not really *two*. Beneath the semblance of relationship there is only *one*, with a narcissistic extension that appears to be an "other" and creates the illusion of *two*.

The dilemma is obvious. A consummate relationship requires that its participants really be *one* and really be *two* at the same time. The paradox lessens if one expands the definition of relationship to include its pattern of change through time. It is really more accurate to view relationship as a dynamic sequence of development. When thus reframed, its contradictory elements appear as progressive stages in its life cycle.

The original paradox remains but its tension eases when one redefines relationship as "an association of two or more things *that follows a definite pattern of development.*"[46,47]

Phase 1   First, there is pure simple oneness without a trace of *two*. At this stage, *wholeness* lacks the possibility of transformation, for change requires encounter-with-*other* to rouse it to action. (This phase is generally hidden from view. It is the state of souls before they descend to the bodies of this world.)

Phase 2   Relationship requires two for its dance. Thus, the Holy

---

45. *Leshem,* HDYH, MHY 3, 4, and translated as Chapter 5 on p. 145.
46. This three-phase sequence of relationship beautifully parallels the Baal Shem Tov's teachings about the three stages of spiritual development. הכנעה (Submission), הבדלה (discrimination), המתקה (sweetening).
47. These three stages appear in *Zohar* 1:85b.

One conceals His oneness and manifests its opposite, which is two (or more). Gender then appears in the universe. (The three stages of back-to-back relationship that culminate in *nesira* explain how one divides into two, and how the moon's shrinking makes this happen.)[48]

Phase 3   Next begins the joyful and tedious process of revealing the hidden fact of oneness that was really true all along. Driven by a primal will-to-be-whole, each "half" seeks to join back with the other who was split from it. The closer they grow, the more complete they become, since really they are parts of a single *one*. The pleasure of their union is the pleasure of becoming whole. In the final stage *woman* stands equal and opposite to *man* and they meet for the first time as spiritual, intellectual, and emotional mates. (R. Luria's stages of front-to-front bonding describe this phase of their relationship.)[49]

Every relationship follows this path, though souls are bonded to varying degrees. The closer their roots, the more intensely they share this process. A minor connection may hardly register, while a marriage of soulmates may display this pattern in extreme.

It is clear from this definition that a couple must individuate before they can consummate (phase 2 must precede phase 3). And for this, each must have a kingdom completely their own. Two kings ruling under one crown are not yet fully *two*. In each decision one must forgo his will and accept the other's demands. Perhaps they alternate this role, or perhaps the same one compromises each time. Either way, a requirement of forced consensus stifles free will, thereby disabling a necessary precondition to selfhood.

And so the sun and moon agree: Two kings cannot unite in consummate union if they have not individuated from each other

---

48. See Chapter 3, pp. 79–87.
49. See Chapter 3.

fully. The scalpel that effects their severing, asserts the sun, is the moon's becoming small. Their kingdoms will then divide along natural boundaries and both will have a place where their will rules.

אמרה לפניו: רבש"ע הואיל ואמרתי לפניך דבר הגון, אמעיט את עצמי?

She answers Him, "Sovereign of the universe, because I spoke rightly must I diminish myself?"

The Moon: "Master of the universe, perhaps your assessment is correct and one of us must become small, but why does its entire burden fall upon me? Just because I sensed the problem first and voiced it aloud, why must I bear the full cost of its fixing?"

The moon, as the subconscious, is always pushing up the unrectified knots of personality and forcing the ego to face its flaws. The sun (as the conscious self) hates these humbling reminders and fights to keep their evidence repressed. The moon risks ruin when she speaks these truths, for they trigger an aggressive response by the ego (the sun's unrectified side)[50] to repress them and silence her... "Go! And make yourself small."[51]

And yet, the fact that it was the moon that first sensed the problem and strongly enough to mention it is significant. One who is dissatisfied with the status quo becomes more motivated to change it. The costs one is willing to pay for improvement reflect the intensity of one's discomfort with the present.

The moon's complaint proves her discontent and thus greater incentive to implement change. For her, the present is a dead end and this awareness prepares her to sacrifice for its correction. Discomfort is easier to bear when it is the route to a consciously chosen goal. This is what it means that "wisdom sweetens sever-

---

50. See "Synopsis" for a review of this concept and its sources.
51. The unrectified expression of the sun (or conscious self) is when it identifies with the ego, instead of integrating the ego into a more expanded and God-centered sense of self.

ities."[52] One who knows the purpose of his or her suffering and knows that it will bear positive results has a whole different set of tools to manage his or her pain. A promise of new life turns bitter into bittersweet, but only for those who actually experience their travails as pangs of birth. In this sense the moon *is* more equipped to handle the role of diminished one.[53]

אמר לה: לכי ומשול ביום ובלילה.

He replied, "Go and rule by day and by night."

The Holy One: "Your loss is only temporary and apparent. In truth your sovereignty will actually expand, for you will rule not only by night, but also by day."

The moon, who rules the unconscious depths of soul, exerts her natural authority over the night, the time of sleep and dreams and visions. In slumber the conscious mind retreats, leaving the moon to pilot the night ship: to integrate the day's events and set the morrow's tone.

And yet, in its quiet way, the moon also rules the day. Its steady flow of thought at the base of awareness, sometimes noticed, sometimes not, is what really sculpts the form of our lives. It is there that our most tenacious (though perhaps unwelcomed) desires exert their stubborn influence over our lives. A consciously asserted will is no match for the litany of beliefs and suppositions, mostly unconscious, that control our reflex level of response to the world.[54] Whether these habitual convictions be correct or mistaken, their force of repetition rules, and the tenor of our lives follows their lead.

---

52. *Zohar* 2:19b.

53. *Meor V'Shemesh*, MVS, *Parashat Korach* (first word, *V'hinay*).

54. "A growing number of researchers...agree that most behavior stems not from intentional choices but from mental activities triggered outside of awareness by features of the environment.... Conscious direction of behavior is important, but it takes place a small minority of the time." Bruce Bauer, "The Mental Butler Did It." *Science News* 156 (October 30, 1999): 280–282.

Only by enlisting the moon's cooperation can the ego implement the changes it seeks. The moon, in her smallness, does truly rule by day and by night.

אמרה ליה: מאי רבותיה, דשרגא בטיהרא מאי אהני?

She replies, "What is so great about that? Of what benefit is a lamp in broad daylight?"

The Moon: "Power is not the issue for me. Mutuality of relationship is my concern. Only because front-to-front relationship requires an equivalence of power does that enter into my complaint. The disparity of stature between the sun and a lamp makes a true meeting between them impossible. Even if their power is equal, their statures are not. In a consummate relationship the couple meets from the crown of their heads to the soles of their feet. The sun and a lamp do not even come close. The gap between them is so great that for most of their lengths a relationship hardly exists."

אמר לה: זיל, לימנו בך ישראל ימים ושנים.

He replies,
"Go! Israel will reckon by you the days and the years."

The Holy One: "Not only is the ceremonial cycle, with its marking of feasts and ritual practices governed by your monthly cycle...Not only is the (astrological) unfolding of heavenly influence placed in your domain[55]...but in direct response to your complaint, the yearly cycles of sun and moon will be synchronized to maintain a stability of relationship and equivalence of stature. The intercalation of leap years will assure the mutuality that you seek."

The Jewish calendar integrates both the lunar and solar cycles (unlike the Gregorian one, whose months of 30+ days do not con-

---

55. *Leshem*, HDYH, MHY 6 (first word, *V'hinay*).

sider the moon's rhythms). The Jewish year follows a lunar circuit. Each month begins on the new moon, and twelve months (354 days) comprise a year. The lunar cycle has 10 days less than its solar counterpart. Consequently, the two systems quickly diverge. One can observe this in the Islamic calendar, which only follows the moon. Its holy days fall in different seasons from one year to the next. Its new year may come in winter, and then years later in spring or fall.

The Jewish calendar adds a correction factor called a pregnant year, whereby every few years an additional month is added to the calendar.[56] A pregnant year has thirteen months instead of twelve (= 385 days). The whole point of this adjustment is to maintain stability between a lunar month and its solar season. In particular, it assures that the month of Passover (Nissan) always occurs in the springtime, as specified by the Torah.

The practice of adding a pregnant year is both a straightforward calculation and a deep mystery. According to kabbalah, its point is to maintain a stability of relationship between the sun and moon (*man* and *woman*) despite their differences in length.[57] By adding a thirteenth month every few years, their cycles stay synchronized and their seasons always match.

When the moon critiques the lack of parity between a "lamp" and the sun, the Holy One presents the calendar (with its pregnant years) as a way of maintaining an equivalence of stature despite their differing lengths and rhythms.

אמרה ליה: יומא נמי, אי אפשר דלא מנו ביה תקופותא, דכתיב והיו לאותות ולמועדים ולימים ושנים.

She replies: "The most basic unit of time is the **day,** which **is impossible to measure except by the** sun's **cycle** of rising,

---

56. One cannot create a leap year by adding days, for that would violate the moon's integrity. Her cycle defines the indivisible unit of *month.*
57. R. Gershon Chanokh Chenek, *Sod Yesharim,* especially Purim 2–3.

setting and rising again. The day is completely his domain. Nothing else enters into its calculation except the sun's presence or absence. Night is supposed to be my sovereign time yet I am not even always present then. For the unit of day (which includes a day and a night) I am irrelevant, a mere ornament.[58] Yet the Torah says, 'Let *them* be for signs and seasons and for days and years.' This means that on all three scales, seasons, days, and years, there is supposed to be a partnership between us. And yet, at the level of 'day' there is not even the beginning of a relationship between us."

זיל, ליקרו צדיקי בשמיך: יעקב הקטן שמואל הקטן דוד . . . הקטן.

Go. The righteous (*tzaddikim*) shall be named after you as we find, Jacob the Small,[59] Samuel the Small,[60] David the Small.[61]

The Holy One: "Your vision of consummate relationship seeks mutuality on all scales, including the unit of day. Granted, the twenty-four-hour literal day is defined by the sun alone. Yet the cosmic day (whose nighttime is *this world* and daytime is the world to come) defines its cycle by your absence and presence. Your diminishment conceals God and turns this 6,000 years into a cosmic night, and your re-emergence at the end-of-days turns its night into eternal day."

The terms *day* and *night* are both literal and metaphorical. In addition to the twenty-four-hour cycle of light and dark, these

---

58. Another example where "his" half of the couple retains their original collective name, for day = day + night.
59. (Amos 7:5). "Then I said O Lord God cease, I beseech Thee, how shall Yaacov stand? For *he is small*."
60. A renowned Sage called "the small" because of his humility.
61. (1 Samuel 17:13). "And David was *the youngest*. And the three eldest followed Shaul. But David went back and forth from Shaul to tend his father's sheep."

words also apply to the larger sequence of biblical history.[62] The first 6,000 years of the Jewish calendar (we are currently in 5760) are called "night," for God hides and spiritual darkness reigns. At some point between now and the year 6,000 (= 2240 C.E.), dawn will break. The seventh millennium (or world to come) must start by the year 6,000, and it marks the point of sunrise in the cosmic cycle of night and day.

Kabbalah anticipates a major shift in polarity at that time. Now, in *this* world, the *tzaddikim* are distinguished by their self-effacement before the Blessed Holy One. They embody the diminishment of the moon's ordeal to its extreme. Yet it is precisely their capacity to be "nothing" before God that ultimately makes them great. Others, who are less-than-righteous, refuse to grow small. Their misplaced pride will only detract from their stature when the world to come turns everything upside down.

In the seventh millennium the moon recovers her greatness and then surpasses her starting point.[63] The world to come is called "day," for God's light will shine then for all to see. That "day" will be like no other, for its sun will never set again. Its eternal splendor is the reward phase of history. Six thousand years we labor to serve God and in the seventh millennium we receive our paychecks with their eternities of blissful interest.[64] At some point in this longest "day" the moon will grow beyond the sun and she will shine to him.[65] The angels will direct their adorations to her (as embodied by her *tzaddikim*), for the moon will have supplanted the Holy One as the primary agent of Divine expression. All this

62. TB, *Pesachim* 2a.
63. Rashaz, *The Voice of the Bride*, here translated as Chapter 8.
64. TB, *Eruvin* 22a. "*This* world is for doing work, *next* world is for enjoying the earnings."
65. Rashaz, ibid.

the Talmud teaches by its perplexing passage:[66] "Now, the angels gather before the Holy One and worship Him with the formula of adoration that we imitate in our *Kedusha* prayer when we say, 'Holy, holy, holy is the Lord of hosts.'[67] There will come a time when the angelic hosts will recite 'holy, holy, holy...' before the righteous *tzaddikim* instead of to the Blessed Holy One."[68]

The moon thus achieves the parity she seeks, for while the sun rules our physical days, she rules the cosmic day.

חזייה דלא קא מיתבא דעתה ...

On seeing that she was not appeased ...

The Moon: "There is still a critical mismatch, a place that lacks parity. In terms of power perhaps we do balance out, yet there is still a lack of symmetry. While (perhaps) I share your greatness, you do not share my 'smallness.' In that place I am all alone. If that gap in experience remains we will never fully meet."

אמר הקב"ה: הביאו כפרה עלי שמיעטתי את הירח והיינו דאמר ר"ש בן לקיש: מה נשתנה שעיר של ראש חודש שנאמר בו לה'- אמר הקב"ה: שעיר זה יהא כפרה עלי שמיעטתי את הירח.

The Blessed Holy One said, "Bring an atonement for Me, for I caused the moon to forfeit her greatness, I made her **grow small." This is what R. Shimon ben Lakish meant when he declared, "Why** does *HaShem* change His language when He commands us to offer a he-goat on the new moon? A perplexing phrase appears here that does not occur elsewhere. **Concerning the new moon offering**

66. TB, *Bava Batra* 75b.

67. Isaiah 6:3.

68. The souls of the *tzaddikim* are rooted in the lowest *sefirah,* called *malchut,* which corresponds to the moon and the *partzuf, woman.*

the Torah writes, "A he-goat on the new moon *for the Lord?*" R. Shimon ben Lakish answers his own question: **The Blessed Holy One is saying** by this phrase, **"Let this he-goat be an atonement *for Me,* for the 'offense' that I have committed in reducing the moon."**

This final resolution includes two distinct elements:

- First, the Holy One commits to bringing a monthly offering, thereby conceding to the moon's request that He also diminish. A sacrifice, by definition, expresses the self-nullification of its bearer.
- Second, the particular type of offering the Holy One proposes is a sin offering, the most self-effacing of all the sacrifices.

A full appreciation of the Holy One's solution to the moon's complaint requires a familiarity with both animal sacrifices in general, and sin offerings in particular.

Offerings in General

To the uninitiated, the term *animal sacrifice* conjures an image of pagan cult worship. In fact, when performed according to the prescriptions and parameters of the Torah, it is a powerful ritual designed to turn the slaughtering of meat into a spiritually conscious act. Depending upon the particular type of sacrifice, certain portions of the animal are burnt on the altar and the rest get eaten.

In our computerized age of production-line butchers, the slaughtering of animals is a mechanical act. Efficiency is the sole consideration. There is no concern for how we justify this killing, and no symbolic statement is made. All is performed for the sake of food and profits alone. With all its technological sophistication, this is actually quite primitive. Though the slaughtering be in stainless steel warehouses with hygienic refrigeration, there is no honoring of life, no acknowledging of God, no trembling before the mystery of death. Stripped of its antiseptic veneer, there is an empty, mindless act of killing, the antithesis of all that "civilization" holds dear.

The Temple sacrifices were altogether different. Their whole point was to impress a jolting statement of truth upon the consciousness of all present and transform their relationship to God. Apart from the elevation offering, which was burnt completely, the slaughtering of animals that happened in the Temple was a profoundly conscious way of preparing food that would later be eaten by the individuals involved.

The Maharal explains the symbolic message of the sacrifices as follows:

> The point of a sacrifice is to show that *HaShem* exists at a level of inwardness that no other creature can touch. He transcends the physical world. Materiality cannot coexist at this core level of Divine existence [for matter is ephemeral, and only Eternity dwells there]. The message of the sacrificial offerings was this: The physical world has no actual or permanent existence except through its dissolution and reabsorption into Divine transcendence. There is *nothing* but the absolute unity of God.
>
> In the lower, and more superficial, realms there appears to be a multiplicity of creatures, but at higher levels this illusion dissolves and the real truth shines: There is nothing but the pure simple oneness of God into which all creatures must eventually return. The sacrifices reenact this hidden but truest of truths.[69]

The person bringing a sacrifice leaned on it with his full weight before it was slaughtered. The animal was a substitute for his own

69. Maharal, *Gevurot HaShem,* chapters 40 and 69.

life. If he was really sincere and felt the truth of God's absolute one-ness down to his bones, shouldn't he put his own body on the line? God says no, the human being must use this knowledge to do other, more essential work in the world. The ritual of animal sacrifice was a powerful and participatory drama that burnt the truth of Divine oneness into the cells of all who witnessed the act. As the animal transformed into light and heat, a visual statement was made: The physical world has no purpose as an end unto itself. It is only here to further God's will. The fate of all life and material existence is to vanish back into the Rootless Root of Divine being.[70]

It is said that animals longed to be sacrificed as Temple offerings. They would fight for the honor. They would drag their masters in tow through the courtyard, hurrying to lay their necks on the block. In this one moment they could accomplish transformations that take hundreds of lifetimes to complete. As a Temple sacrifice they became the very "stuff" of revelation. Their flesh, burning, permanently transformed the consciousness of all who looked on. Body transfigured into thought. The animal became the deepened awareness of God, which now permanently altered the lives of all experiencing this holy drama.

There are many types of offerings specified in the Torah. Dif-ferent animals, plants, and foodstuffs are used for each. Some are purely symbolic and some are practical aids to repentance. Some are daily and some are only for special occasions. Some are com-munal and some individual, some obligatory and some voluntary. The Torah only permits sacrificial offerings at the Holy Sanctuary in Jerusalem. Since the Temple is still in ruins, the obligation of animal sacrifices does not apply today and is thereby forbidden.

---

70. R. Eliyahu Dessler, *Michtav MeEliyahu* 2:195–196.

Sin Offerings in Particular

A sin offering is brought to enhance a person's repentance. It is the last step in a demanding effort to rectify wrongdoing. The Torah identifies three criteria when atoning for sins against God, and five for sins against people. This inner work is the essence of *teshuva*; the animal sacrifice merely supplements its effects.

The indispensable elements of repentance are as follows:[71]

1. Verbal admission before God that one committed a sin and that it was wrong.
2. Heartfelt remorse before God.
3. Resolve not to complete the sin again.
4. One must secure the forgiveness of the person harmed by apologizing again and again until he or she forgives.
5. One must recompense the person harmed for any loss or pain incurred by the sin.

Then, at the end of this process, one brings a Temple sacrifice to seal the effort. If the inner work has not been done, the sacrifice has no power to cleanse or transform. It becomes an empty gesture, void of significance. Conversely, repentance without animal sacrifice still heals and repairs.[72]

The Holy One could have chosen any offering to satisfy the moon's complaint, for every sacrifice requires its bearer to enter a state of self-nullification. The moon asks him to diminish and the sun goes one step further, he reduces *and* repents ... But for what? What is the offense he seeks to atone by his monthly sin offering?

One answer is as follows: The moon was correct. The sun did

---

71. Rambam, *Hilchot Teshuva* 1:1, 2:9.
72. Ibid., 1:3. This assumes that the Temple is not standing and the obligation no longer exists.

also need to diminish, and not just for their sake. All creatures must experience self-nullification at periodic intervals to remember that they are not God.[73] The sun had options, though, for diminishment takes many forms.

When the moon voiced her dissatisfaction, he could have put his ego aside (an excruciating form of self-nullification) and sought a way to satisfy her complaint that would have preserved her royal standing. After all, that is the sun's role. He received the lights of compassion and intellect for precisely this purpose. As the conscious self, his work is to transmute conflict into expanded awareness. When he encounters opposition, his challenge is to soften and stretch though his reflex be the opposite. That is how consciousness expresses *gadlut*. In contrast, the ego (in its *katnut*) meets opposition by scrambling to secure its position at top-center and to be right. The ego is a ruthless adversary, putting everyone down to preserve its post on top … "Go! Become small."

The sun's challenge is to hold integrity despite the ego discomfort it entails; to choose truth over vindication, compassion over counter-accusation, humility over victory. In this way the conflict catapults him to a higher consciousness with infinitely broadened horizons. Options appear that were never even glimpsed before. The main distinguishing feature of higher consciousness is its capacity to bear paradox, to hold contrary positions in a graceful tension that turns war into dance.[74]

Theoretically, had he been at a place of *gadlut*, the sun could have done exactly this. When the moon voiced her complaint, he

---

73. *Ari*, chapter 3.

74. This is a kabbalistic mystery of the *sefirah* of *daat* (knowing). *Daat* can even be defined as the capacity to bear paradox, for it is actually comprised of paradoxical elements – 5 *chassadim* and 5 *gevurot*. *Yeshuv hadaat* (inner peace) indicates the successful integration of these initially polar tendencies. See *Leshem*, HDYH 2:5:2.

could have stretched and found a way for them to work on their relationship as a team: to move forward, hand in hand, and solve their problems together. There *is* a way for them to share one crown, this we know, for it is the promised endpoint of their ordeal. R. Luria shows that in the end of days these same two kings will share their crown without strife.

Yet, though theoretically an option, the sun had not reached a developmental level where such a response was actually feasible. The whole concept of relationship was completely new to him. His inexperience (i.e., *katnut*) thus confined him to a much narrower range of behavior. The sun was given a test but lacked the tools to even see the higher option, let alone to choose it. Nevertheless, for him as for us, sin carries consequences and requires atonement, whether or not one could really have chosen differently at that time.[75]

The sun did not rise to the challenge posed by the moon's complaint. Instead, he tried to push the work of self-nullification off to her task list. There was no way his ploy would succeed. Every creature must pay these dues; there are no exceptions. Many try but always fail. A refusal to diminish lies at the root of every sin. Either one obeys spiritual law (itself a form of self-nullification) or defies it, and pays his or her dues in the purgation and repentance that always follow sin. No one skirts The Law for long.

Because the sun could not receive the moon's rebuke; because he shut her out instead of inviting her in with the generosity of spirit that is his higher calling; because he failed this test, the moon diminished and the inevitability of sin appeared in the universe.

Now he had to face an even more humiliating ordeal: He had to admit his mistake. He failed his test and the whole universe now suffers the repercussions of his error. When the moon accepted her

---

75. In fact, a sin offering is specifically for unintentional transgressions.

fate and agreed to step down, her backside became the root of evil and the font of its continued nurture from that point on. Everything that is wrong with the universe originates there, including sin. The possibility (and inevitability) of transgression began when the sun insisted that the moon grow small.[76]

The sun's plan backfired. He attempted to avoid ego discomfort and instead created a whopping dose of it. The sun has no option now but to face his shame and repent. "Bring a sin offering *for me*, for making the moon grow small." Yet *teshuva*, teaches Torah, not only repairs damage, but actually transforms the one who completes its inner work. When properly fulfilled, *teshuva* can bring the "sinner" to a higher level of perfection than was available to him before his fall.[77] In this way the sun's *teshuva* raises the whole world. Just as his avoidance of self-nullification is the root of all transgression, so is his sin offering the root of all repentance.[78] This idea is beautifully expressed by a teaching of the Baal Shem Tov:[79]

> A person completely free of blemish and sin would never encounter vice in the world. He would not see it in others nor even hear of its occurrence. Consequently, when a person witnesses wrongdoing (or even hears about it) he knows, beyond a shadow of a doubt, that that very same flaw exists, now, inside himself. Even if he is a *tzaddik* [and even presumably the Holy One Himself], the flaw is there, though in an infinitely more subtle form. He also knows that *HaShem* arranged the encoun-

---

76. *Chidushei Geonim, Shevuot* 4.
77. TB, *Brachot* 24b. "In the place where a fully transformed sinner stands, even a perfectly righteous *tzaddik* cannot reach."
78. R. Natan Sternholz (student of R. Nachman of Breslov), *Likutei Halachot, OC, Hilchot Rosh Chodesh*, Halacha 3, (4).
79. R. Yisrael Baal Shem Tov, *HaBaal Shem Tov al HaTorah, Bereshit* 127, *Ki Tissa* 9; R.Y.Y. Safron of Kamarna, ibid., *Parashat Shelach, p. 103a;* ibid., *Imri Peninim,* p. 208b.

ter between himself and the sinner to communicate to him, in no uncertain terms, that he must find the place inside himself that parallels the sin he witnessed and repent forthright. When the *tzaddik* completes the task of admitting his flaw, finding its expression, and repenting for it, he actually causes the sinner (whom he earlier witnessed) to repent as well. Their two souls are linked by the holy task they now share. On closer inspection, it even becomes clear that the *tzaddik*'s unrepented flaw (subtle though it was) actually caused the sinner's stumbling in the first place. Consequently, when the *tzaddik* now repents, this, too, influences the sinner, though now for good, and inspires him to repent as well.

Another story further illustrates this point:

The Tsemach Tseddek[80] traveled through the villages of White Russia with a small group of students. They stayed a few days in each town while the Rebbe answered questions, counseled, and gave blessings. One afternoon the Tsemach Tseddek excused himself and retired to his quarters. This was highly unusual, but the students assumed he needed a rest, and expected his return in an hour or so. When he didn't appear they went to see what the problem might be. They approached and heard the Rebbe crying and reciting psalms. One student was so overwhelmed by the Rebbe's weeping that he fainted. They returned to the group with their report and all recited psalms to support the Rebbe's efforts. They again approached his quarters, and found him engaged in afternoon prayer, but something was strange. The Rebbe was adding the special petitions that are only said for

---

80. The third Rebbe in the Chabad/Lubovitch lineage of Rebbes; grandson of Rashaz (R. Shneur Zalman of Liadi) who wrote the essay here translated, called "Voice of the Bride."

ten days a year between Rosh Hashanah and Yom Kippur when a person is particularly focused on repentance. Yet it was not that time of year. Later that evening, in synagogue, the Rebbe spoke on the power of tears, Torah, and psalms to cleanse the soul. He rested the entire next day and only returned to receiving visitors on the day following.

After some time a student asked the Tsemach Tseddek what happened that day. A wave of sadness crossed the Rebbe's face and he explained the following. "I learned this practice from my Holy grandfather and Rebbe, who heard it from his Rebbe, the Maggid of Mezritch, who learned it from the Holy Baal Shem Tov. When a person comes seeking advice for his problems and rectifications for his sins, I find the subtle point inside myself that exactly mirrors the blemish of his soul, and from that place of my own *teshuva*, I suggest a solution. On that day, a person came with a story, and I was disturbed by his words, repulsed even. I couldn't find any place inside that identified with his sin. This was frightening because the mirror never lies. The flaw had to be there, yet I was unaware of it. As long as it lurked in the subconscious depths of my heart, its influence would remain outside my control. *It* would stay the master of me rather than me being the master of *it*. I immediately conducted a personality inventory to find the flaw, and do *teshuva* for its concrete expressions in my behavior (subtle though they may be). By bringing that flaw into conscious awareness, I also brought it under my control. This is also the most powerful way for me to help the man whose story I heard, more potent than rebuke or even advice. My own *teshuva*, prompted by *his* confession, brought healing to him from the inside out. The souls of *tzaddikim* are connected to all the individuals of their generation and exert a constant influence on them. The *tzaddik*'s most subtle lapse in behavior (or even thought) can cause gross stumblings in those around him. The mirror never lies. I was the cause for this man's sin, and so I repented both for myself and for him. The more conscious one becomes, the more *teshuva* one must do."

This is the secret of the monthly sin offering where the Holy One repents "for making the moon small." He witnesses the "sins" of mankind, finds the infinitely more subtle shortcoming inside Himself that mirror their sins, and does *teshuva*, in part for being the cause of those sins. In this way, He lightens our burden and assists our efforts to become clean.

When the moon complained the sun had two options:

1. He could have pushed beyond his comfort zone, humbly considered the merits of her complaint, exerted himself in prayer, and sought a creative solution that preserved the integrity of both thrones. Had he been in *gadlut*, no doubt this is what he would have done.[81]
2. Instead (being in *katnut*) he chose a more defensive tack, protecting himself from the discomfort of her rebuke by putting her down. Let her be the one to diminish.

Strangely, both options achieve the same goal, and both take their toll of self-nullification to get there. Yet the first path is a short, direct, and scenic route, a joyful unfolding of life's possibilities. The second is a rocky road, with dead ends and bad smells, through wastelands and garbage dumps. It takes 6,000 years of sin and suffering to reach a designation that was moments away. The sun's lack of compassionate humility initiated a downward spiral of events that continues through today.

---

81. The Jewish vision of marriage is exactly this, as the Talmud says, "A man should love his wife like himself and honor her more than himself." TB, *Yevamot* 62b.

Yet just as the repercussions of his sin were enormous, the repercussions of his *teshuva* are infinitely more so. Day in and day out the sun repents, and his *teshuva* inspires our own. He observes our stumblings, finds the place inside that mirrors them, and repents. From the courage of his inner work and ceaseless soul searching, we, children of the moon, draw the strength to strive and grow and rise and shine.

The sun will succeed in his heroic effort to repair the damage of his sin, for the moon will again wax full. On that day *man* and *woman* will achieve the consummate union that is their pleasure and their purpose. The entire universe will celebrate their union in a blissful eternity shared by all.

DEBRIEFING

What Do We Know?

1. The moon addresses her complaint to the Blessed Holy One. According to kabbalah, that title generally refers to the *partzuf, man,* her spouse. This means that the conversation recorded in the Talmud between the moon and the Blessed Holy One is essentially a marital encounter between sun and moon, *man* and *woman.*

   Blessed Holy One = *man* = sun.

   Shekhinah = *woman* = moon.

2. *Man* and *woman* are oriented back-to-back throughout their dialogue, for their surgical uncoupling (*nesira*) is what initiates *woman's* diminishment and enables *man* and *woman* to then meet face-to-face for the first time.

3. The period of man's back-to-back union with *woman* coincides with the period of his *katnut* (immature, narrow-

minded, and self-centered consciousness). Consequently, in the conversation recorded by the Talmud, *man* is at the maturity level of *katnut*. His responses will necessarily reflect his developmental state.

4. *Man's* insistence that the moon diminish is a sin that requires the entire course of history for its repair. Every month, until the end of time, *man* "brings" (via his emissaries) a sin-offering to repent for his transgression.

5. The diminishment of the moon is the direct cause of all the sin, evil, and imperfection in the universe. Since it is *man* who insisted that the moon grow small, he becomes the responsible agent for all these things.

6. *Man's* developmental level made it nearly (if not totally) impossible to respond other than he did. His state of *katnut*, with its narrow-minded and self-absorbed view of the world, limited the options he could see, let alone attain.

7. Sin-offerings are prescribed by the Torah specifically for repairing unintentional sins. This is the offering that *man* "brings" (via his emissaries) as part of his own repentance process.

8. We know that it is possible for two kings to rule under one crown, for that is the promised endpoint of the moon's ordeal.

What Don't We Know?

1. We don't know what *man's* options were. We don't know how he should have responded to the moon's complaint. We don't know what could have happened had *man* been at the level of maturity called *gadlut*.

2. We don't know whether the moon actually consents to her fate or simply obeys for lack of options.

Logical Implications and Speculations

1. The Baal Shem Tov's teachings on the way *tzaddikim* do *teshuva* – what prompts them and how they serve the larger community – is a likely model for what it means that *man* repents.

2. If *man's* sin is that he "caused the moon to diminish," then his complete *teshuva* requires that he "cause the moon to again become great." *Teshuva*, by definition, repairs the damage caused by the sin and restores the system to its original state.

3. The dynamic relationship, illustrated by *man* and *woman*, applies on all scales, from the personal to the cosmic. On every level there is gender and striving for union. And on every level, consummation only occurs when male and female meet from the crown of their heads to the soles of their feet. All trace of diminishment must cease for *man* and *woman* to unite as one.[82]

As explained, we exist within a weblike hierarchy of relationships. Everyone is feminine in relation to those above, and masculine in relation to those below. The Zohar states: "The king, though supreme, is feminine and receptive to the Most Hidden One, and simultaneously, masculine and active toward the lower king. This bi-gendered status… characterizes the whole super-mundane world."[83]

The implications are profound. Everyone is in relationships where he or she is the feminine partner striving to realize an equality of stature with someone above in status, knowledge, or power. Similarly, everyone is in relationships where he or she is

---

82. *Daat Elokim,* pp. 143–150.
83. *Zohar* 2:4a.

masculine, providing the teachings, love, and resources for others to realize their full stature.

The principle of "measure for measure" applies without exception. The more kind and generous one is to those below, the more abundant will be the assistance provided from above. Conversely, the more grudging one is to one's "dependents" below, the more constricted will be the flow to him or her from those above.

If only we could integrate this truth to our bones: The rising of the feminine is a win-win situation. Its consummate union of equals is everyone's joy. This perfect marriage has been our (perhaps unconscious) yearning for 6,000 years, and from its realization flow all the promised blessings of the world to come.

10

PRAYER AS PRAXIS

R. Natan Sternholz on
the New Moon

from *Likutei Halachot*

כל עבודתנו בימים האלה לנסר את המלכות מז"א מבחי' אחור באחור ...
היינו לבנות את תפילה להקים את התפילה מנפילתה ... כי התפילה הוא
בח' מלכות ... יש שני תפילות יש תפילה שהוא למטה מהתורה והיא
טפילה לתורה ויש תפילה שהיא בח' אחד עם התורה ממש. וגם היא גבוה
מהתורה כי יש תפילה שמתפללים על צרכיו דהיינו פרנסה ובנים וחיים
ורפואה וכו' ... והיא למטה מהתורה וטפילה לתורה. ... אבל עיקר התפלה
השלמה היא כשאדם מתפלל על צרכי נשמתו בעצמו דהיינו שכל תפילתו
לזכות ליר`את ד' ועבודתו ית' ... ותפילה כזאת אינה טפילה לתורה. אדרבא
תפילה כזאת היא עיקר קיום התורה (...) והיא פרצוף בפ"ע) מאחר שמבקש
רק לקיים התורה שזה עיקר שלמות התורה. כי לא המדרש הוא העיקר
אלא המעשה ... וזאת התפילה היא שווה עם התורה וגבוה ממנה. כי עיקר
הכוונה בלימוד התורה הוא לקיים את התורה ... נמצא שהתורה והתפילה
שניהם שווים בקומתם. ואף גם התפלה גבוה יותר ... בבח' שני מלכים
בכתר אחד ...

The inner significance of our efforts to release *woman* from her
backsided bond to *man* ... all concerns the rectification of prayer,

323

for that is *woman's* primary mode of Divine service (as opposed to Torah study, which is *man's*). There are two types of prayer: one is lower than Torah study, and one is equal to it (and even higher). The former is the prayer of the diminished moon; the latter expresses her fullness of stature.

In lower prayer, one asks for material resources to maintain a quality of life that facilitates the service of God through mitzvot and Torah study. This prayer is lower than Torah study, for it serves as a means to study's nobler end. The ultimate goal here is study, yet for this one needs the material necessities that prayer provides....

In higher prayer, one asks for help in translating study into practice. One prays to be transformed by the Torah one learns each day, to turn its teachings into deeds, to embody its truths. This kind of prayer is not lower than Torah study; rather, the opposite. It goes beyond study, fulfilling the talmudic maxim "The real goal is not study, but action." Higher prayer accomplishes this goal, for it *does* turn study into action. Higher prayer is not an adjunct to scholarship, but a mode of service in its own right, equal to and even greater than study. In higher prayer the sun and moon are equals. In higher prayer these two kings do truly share a single crown.[1]

HaShem, let these teachings on *man* and *woman* culled from Your Holy Torah reverberate through the world and bring effects that are only good. May they open eyes, soften hearts, heal lives, dissolve obstacles, and strengthen truth in ways that serve You, and please You, and glorify Your name. Help us to meet conflict with humble compassion and turn its tensions into visions. "May You fill the flaw of the moon

---

1. R. Natan Sternholz (primary disciple of R. Nachman of Breslov), *Likutei Halachot*, OC, *Rosh Chodesh* 5.

that there be no diminution in her. Let the light of the moon become like the light of the sun and like the light of the seven days of creation as it was before it diminished, as Your Torah states, 'God created *two* great luminaries.'"[2] As individuals, couples, and communities, may our strivings to unite the moon with her beloved soon bear their fruit. May we rejoice together *this very day* in Your promised redemption.

BIOGRAPHIES

R. Yehuda Ashlag (*Baal HaSulam*, 1886–1955) was born in Warsaw and educated in chasidic schools. He was a disciple of L. Shalom Rabinowicz of Kalushin and of his son R. Yehoshuah Asher of Porissov. He also had a teacher of kabbalah whose name, he maintained, could not be divulged. R. Ashlag immigrated to Palestine in 1920 and settled in the Old City of Jerusalem, where he established a yeshiva named *Beit Ulpana leRabanim*. There he instructed his students in halacha and kabbalah. He is most known for his Hebrew translation and commentary on the *Zohar*, entitled *The Sulam*. He also wrote commentaries on R. Isaac Luria's *Etz Chaim* (called *Talmud Esser Sefirot*).

The Baal Shem Tov (*Besht*, 1700–1760) – R. Israel ben Eliezer, also known by the acronym the *Besht*, was the founder of the chasidic movement. He served as a teacher's assistant, elementary school instructor, and ritual slaughterer. After spending time in the Carpathian Mountains, he went through a spiritual metamorphosis and became an itinerant healer. After experiencing profound spiritual illuminations from heavenly teachers, he went on to become a charismatic leader who attracted many of the greatest

---

2. Standard Liturgy, *Kiddush HaLevana* (Monthly Prayer for Sanctifying the Moon).

scholars of the period. His close followers are the only recorders of his teachings, the *Besht* himself never authoring a text. His new mystical philosophy placed Kabbalah and prayer as the center of Jewish observance, through which one could come to an ecstatic awareness of the Divine Spirit in every aspect of the world. As the *Besht* and his followers came soon after the episode of Shabtai Tzvi, they met harsh opposition from traditionalists who feared another false messianic movement (excerpted from Pardes Project, OU, © 1996).

R. Kalonymous Kalman HaLevi Epstein (*Meor V'Shemesh*, **1751–1823**) was raised in Krakow, Poland. He distinguished himself at an early age with exceptional aptitude in Torah study and saintly qualities. He studied under R. Elimelekh of Lizhinsk and became his favored student. At R. Elimelekh's urgings he traveled to the courts of the Zlotchiver Rebbe, R. Zusha, the Apter Rav, and R. Levi Yitzchak of Berditchiv and spent time studying with each of these great chasidic luminaries. After R. Elimelekh's passing, he became a student of the Seer of Lublin. His commentary on the Torah, called *Meor V'Shemesh*, weaves together Kabbalah and chasidut into a wealth of psychologically insightful essays that are read and praised by chasidim and non-chasidim alike.

R. Shlomo Elyashev (*Leshem*, **1841–1926**) was born in a Lithuanian village called Zegar. He studied under R. Gershon Tanchum of Minsk and spent a number of years in Tels Yeshiva. After marrying, he moved to Shavel but refused to serve in the rabbinate, preferring to spend his days studying Torah in solitude. His works on kabbalah won him world renown and he became known as Prince of the *Zohar*'s Inner Teachings. In 1924, at the age of eighty-three, he immigrated to Israel and settled in Jerusalem. On the 27th of Adar, 1926, his soul passed to the next world and his body is buried on the Mount of Olives. All of his works bear as their main title *Leshem*

SheBo V'Achlama (the names for the three stones in the third row of the breastplate worn by the high priest). For this reason he is called the *Leshem*, after the first word of the title of his books. He is the grandfather of R. Yosef Shalom Elyashev, the world-renowned master of Jewish legal rulings currently living in Jerusalem.

R. Avraham Yitzchak Kook (1865–1935) was the first chief rabbi of what was then Palestine. R. Kook was perhaps the most misunderstood figure of his time. Born in Latvia of staunch chasidic and *mitnagdic* stock, he retained throughout his life a unique blend of the mystical and the rational. He was a thorough master of the entire halachic, midrashic, philosophical, ethical, and kabbalistic literature, which he brought to bear upon the contemporary scene. He saw the return to Eretz Yisrael as not merely a political phenomenon to save Jews from persecution, but an event of extraordinary historical and theological significance. R. Hutner once said that R. Kook peered down on our world from great heights and hence his perspective was unique. Over thirty volumes of R. Kook's writings are printed to date and many others still remain in manuscript form. There are a number of English translations, but these represent but a small fraction of his works (excerpted from Pardes Project, OU, © 1996).

R. Isaac Luria (1534–1572), known as the *Ari*, spent his adult years in Tzfat, Israel, with a small but select gathering of disciples. R. Chaim Vital is the most noteworthy among them. R. Luria taught his students orally, instructing them in his original system of theoretical kabbalah, as well as on how to commune with *HaShem* and with the souls of the tzaddikim. All this was accomplished by meditations on Divine names, and by *kavanot* (i.e., mystical reflections while studying or performing prayers and mitzvot). The *Ari* did not permit the propagation of his teachings during his lifetime and therefore was known mainly for his conduct and saintly qualities. After his death, R. Chaim Vital compiled several volumes of writings called *The Works of the Ari*. *Etz Chaim* is the most well known of them, and it is from there that the currently translated essay on the moon's diminishment appears. All of contemporary kabbalah builds upon the teachings of the *Ari*.

R. Shneur Zalman of Liadi (Rashaz, 1745–1813) was the founder of Chabad chasidut, and studied under HaMaggid Dov Baer of Mezritch, leader of the chasidic movement and student of the Baal Shem Tov. Under the Maggid, R. Shneur Zalman wrote and updated profound commentaries about the *Shulchan Aruch*. When the anti-chasidic movement was taking place in the mid-eighteenth century, R. Shneur Zalman went to Vilna and attempted to speak to the Gaon of Vilna to try to reach some kind of understanding between *chasidim* and *mitnagdim*. R. Shneur Zalman later published the *Tanya*, which was accepted as the written law of Chabad chasidut. His ability to explain even the most complex issues of Torah made his writings popular with Torah scholars everywhere. R. Zalman had a vast knowledge of mathematics and science as well. His son R. Shalom Dov Baer Schneerson became the leader of the chasidic movement after R. Zalman's death (excerpted from Pardes Project, OU, © 1996).

R. Shimon ben Pazzi (aka R. Simon, ~ 300 C.E.) lived in Lod, Israel, during the talmudic period. He was the prize student of R. Yeshua ben Levi, known for both his legal teaching and his mystical experiences. Many *aggadot* are said in R. Shimon ben Pazzi's name in both Talmuds. He was a close colleague of R. Elazar. R. Hekiyah, a student, gives over many teachings in his name.

R. Natan Sternholz (1780–1844) was a leading disciple of R. Nachman of Breslov. He transcribed almost all of his words and after the Rebbe's death laid the foundations of the Breslov chasidic movement. His own major works are *Likutei Halachot, Likutei Tefilot, Alim LiTerufah,* and *Yemei Maharanat.*

R. Chaim Vital (1543–1620) – R. Chaim was born in Eretz Yisrael, probably in Tzfat. He studied the revealed Torah under R. Moshe Alshech, and kabbalah under R. Moshe Cordevero. When the *Ari* arrived in Tzfat (from Egypt) in 1570, R. Chaim soon became his devoted student. The *Ari,* himself, expressed that his sole reason for emigrating from Egypt to Tzfat was to transmit his Torah to R. Chaim. It is amazing to remember that the *Ari* (who died in 1572 at the age of thirty-eight) studied with R. Chaim for less than two years. The impact of the holy *Ari* on subsequent Jewish history was incalculable, and that influence was only possible through the devoted work of R. Chaim Vital. R. Chaim wrote several works of his own, most notably a mystical commentary on the mitzvot called *Shaarei Kedusha* (*The Gates of Holiness*) (excerpted from Pardes Project, OU, © 1996).

Zohar – The *Zohar* is the central work of Jewish mysticism. Tradition ascribes its authorship to R. Shimon Bar Yochai and his students around the second century c.e. It first became known in the thirteenth century. The *Zohar* is actually comprised of several works and provides a mystical commentary on the Torah.

BIBLIOGRAPHY

HEBREW SOURCES

BIBLICAL

Tanakh (The twenty-four books of the Bible)
  5 – Torah (1313 B.C.E.–1273 B.C.E.)
  8 – Prophets (1273 B.C.E.–313 B.C.E.)
  11 – Biblical Writings (3760 B.C.E.–313 B.C.E.)[1]

RABBINIC

Babylonian Talmud (TB) (c. 505 C.E.)
Midrash Rabbah (c. 750 C.E.)
Midrash Tanchuma (c. 370–850 C.E.)
Midrash Tehillim (ancient)
Mishnah (c. 188 C.E.)
Palestinian Talmud (TY) (c. 400 C.E.)
Pirkei d'Rabbi Eliezer (School of R. Eliezer HaGadol, c. 100 C.E.)
Rashi (R. Shlomo Yitzchaki, 1040–1105 C.E.)
Sefer Yetzirah (attributed to Abraham the Patriarch, c. 1760 B.C.E.)

---

1. There are Psalms attributed to Adam (the first human being), as well as to Malkhitsedek and Abraham.

Sifri (attributed to Rav, c. 155–247 C.E.)

Targum Yonaton (c. 50 C.E.)

Torat Kohanim – Sifra (Rav, c. 220 C.E.)

Yalkut Shimoni (R. Shimon Ashkenazi HaDarshan of Frankfurt,
    c. 1260 C.E.)

Zohar (R. Shimon bar Yochai, c. 120 C.E.)

    Idra Rabba

    Idra Zuta

    Sifa d'Tsniuta

    Tikunei Zohar

MEDIEVAL AND LATER

Anaf Yosef, Etz Yosef (R. Chanoch Zundel ben Yosef, d. 1867)

Ari (R. Isaac Luria, 1534–1572)

    Etz Chaim (*Tree of Life*)

    Pri Etz Chaim (*Fruit of the Tree of Life*)

Baal Shem Tov on the Torah (R. Yisrael Baal Shem Tov, 1698–1760)

Beit Yaacov (R. Yaacov Lainer, c. 1820–1878)

Chidushei Geonim (compiled c. 1500 C.E.)

Ein Yaacov (R. Yaacov Chaviv, 1460–1516)

Heichal HaBracha (R. Yitzchak Yehuda Yechiel Safron of Kamarna,
    1806–1875)

Likutei Halachot (R. Nosson Sternholz of Breslov, 1780–1844)

Likutei Moharan (R. Nachman of Breslov, 1772–1810)

Maharal (R. Yehuda Loewe, c. 1512–1609)

    Chidushei Aggadot

    Gevurot HaShem

    Gur Arye

Meor V'Shemesh (R. Kalonymous Kalman Epstein, 1751–1823)

Metsudat David, Radbaz (R. David ben Shlomo ibn Abi Zimra, 1479–1573)

Mishneh Torah – Rambam (R. Moshe bn Maimon, 1135–1204)

Moshav Zekhanim (Tosaphists, c. 1100–1300)

Raavid on *Sefer Yetzira* (R. Yosef Ashkenazi, c. 1310)

Ramak (R. Moshe Cordevero, 1522–1570)
  Hakdama l'Sefer Yetzirah (Introduction to *Sefer Yetzirah*) *Pardes Rimonim* (*Pomegranate Orchard*) – PR

Ramchal (R. Moshe Chaim Luzzato, 1707–1746)
  Adir BaMarom (*Mighty in the Heights*) – AB
  Daat Tevunah (*The Knowing Heart*) – DT
  Derekh HaShem (*The Way of God*) – DH
  Klach Pitchei Chokhmah (*138 Entrances to Wisdom*) – KPC

Rashaz (R. Shneur Zalman of Liadi, 1745–1813) *Likutei Torah* – LT
  Siddur (*Tefilot MeKol HaShana*)
  Tanya (*Likutei Amarim*)
  Torah Or (TO)

Rif (R. Yitzchak Al-fasi 1013–1103)

R. Tzadok HaKohen Rabinowitz (1823–1900)
  Divrei Sofrim
  Or Zarua L'Tzaddik
  Pri Tzaddik
  Rasisei Laila
  Tekanat HaShavin
  Tzidkat HaTzaddik
  Yisrael Kedoshim

Shaar HaYichud (R. Dov-Ber Lubovitch, 1745–1813)

Shaarei Kedusha (R. Chaim Vital, 1543–1620)

Shaarei Ora (R. Yosef Gikatilla, 1248–1325)

Shulchan Arukh (R. Yosef Caro, 1488–1575) – SA

Sod Yesharim (R. Gershon Chonokh Chenekh Lainer from Radzin, c. 1839–1891)

Teshuvot HaBach (R. Yoel Sirkes, 1561–1640)

Vilna Gaon (R. Eliyahu ben Shlomo Zalman of Vilna, 1720–1797).

MODERN

Daat Elokim (R. Shalom Ulman, 1986. Bnei Brak: Dafus Tefutza)

Leshem (R. Shlomo Elyashev, 1841–1926)

   Drush Olam HaTohu (*Treatise on the World of Chaos*) – HDYH

   Hakdamot V'Shearim (*Preliminaries and Gates*) – HVS

   Sefer HaKlallim (*Book of General Principles*) – SHK

Matok Midevash, Translation and Commentary on Zohar (R. Daniel Frish, contemp.)

Michtav M'Eliyahu (R. Eliyahu Dessler, 1891–1954)

Orot HaKodesh (R. Avraham Yitzchak Kook, 1865–1935)

Sulam (R. Yehuda Ashlag, 1886–1955)

Torah Shelemah (compiled by R. Menachem Kasher, 1895–1983 C.E.)

Torah Temima (R. Boruch HaLevi Epstein, 1860–1949)

ENGLISH SOURCES

Bauer, Bruce. "The Mental Butler Did It," *Science News,* Vol. 156 (30 October 1999): pp. 280–282.

Ginsburgh, R. Yitzchak. *The Hebrew Letters* (Jerusalem: Gal Aynai Publications, 1990).

———. Unpublished Lecture Series on "The Fifty Gates of Understanding."

———. http://www.inner.org

Kaku, Michio. *Hyperspace* (New York: Anchor Books – Doubleday, 1994).

Neumann, Erich. *The Origins and History of Consciousness* (New York: Bollingen Foundation, Inc., 1954).

Schochet, R. Immanuel. *Mystical Concepts in Chassidism.* Appendix to the Hebrew-English translation of the *Tanya*: *Likutei Amarim, Tanya* (Brooklyn, N.Y.: Kehot Publication Society, 5740).

Steinsaltz, R. Adin. *The Essential Talmud*, trans. Chaya Galai (New York: Basic Books, Inc., 1980).

GLOSSARY

Amidah – (literally, "standing"). Another term for the *Shemoneh Essrei* (or Prayer of Eighteen Blessings). See *Shemoneh Essrei*.

Ari – R. Isaac Luria (1534–1572). Master kabbalist who wrote the essay here titled "The Small Light to Rule by Night," which identifies the seven stages of *woman's* life cycle. All subsequent kabbalistic writings on the feminine derive from this model. (See Biographies.)

Arikh Anpin – The lower *partzuf* in the *sefirah* called *crown*. It faces downward toward creation and generates a constant will-toward-good in the personality.

Atik Yamin (Atika) – The highest root of the soul. The innermost point of the *sefirah* called *crown*, which actually touches the Infinite Light and dwells in the pleasure and faith of that union.

Atzilut – The highest of the four planes of existence (physical, emotional, mental, spiritual) is called *atzilut*. It is the realm of pure archetypes and means, literally, "the world of emanation." (See Chapter 5, footnote 2.)

Back-to-Back Relationship – An immature and self-absorbed mode of relating in which neither partner ever really "sees" the other, except as an object whose sole purpose is to satisfy his or her own narcissistic needs. Adam and Eve's relationship before their *nesira* was back-to-back.

B.C.E. – Before the Common Era, and C.E. – Common Era. The Jewish way of interfacing with the calendar of the Christian world without using words that imply acceptance of its religious beliefs.

Bible – The twenty-four books of the Torah (5), Prophets (8), and Writings (11) that comprise the Jewish Scripture.

Binah – Third *sefirah*, called "understanding." The analytical faculty of mind. When *Chokhmah* encounters an insight, *binah* unravels this thought in breadth and depth, elaborating its implications and applications, thereby constructing a kind of visionary landscape that provides an extended context for the original seed idea.

Chasidut, Chasidism – (literally, "piety" or "loving-kindness"). The movement within Judaism founded by the Baal Shem Tov (1698–1760) which emphasizes unconditional love of the people Israel, and the fact that God's Presence permeates all levels of reality. It uses the inner dimensions of Torah to awaken the Jewish people to their collective inner self, and in this way, seeks to usher in the messianic era. The term *chasidut* is also used more generally to refer to an attribute or way of life that goes beyond the letter of the law.

Chassadim / chesed lights (generosities) – Lights of conscious awareness. The *chassadim*, when integrated, always inspire a generosity of spirit.

Chesed – Acts of kindness and generosity to those in need. It is the fourth of the ten *sefirot*, designating the Divine attribute of kindness and benevolence.

Chokhmah – The second *sefirah*, translated as "wisdom." The power of insight. The initial point where the potentiality of thought is first conceived. It is the second of the ten *sefirot* when counting from *keter.*

Circle Worlds – The first emanation of *sefirot* was as ten concentric circles. This arrangement was originally unrectified. It shattered, and our linear universe appeared in its place. The Circle World's nonhierarchical reality will eventually replace our own as the future ideal.

Daat – *Knowing.* The level of mind that connects the intellect to the heart and so represents the ultimate integration of knowledge into personality. When counting the *sefirot* as they express themselves through the conscious human soul, *daat* replaces *keter* as one of the ten. There is also a "higher *daat,*" which connects the right brain with the left and thus integrates the metaphorical and linear minds.

Dinim **(also called *gevurot*)** – These terms mean, literally, "severities" and refer to the dark knots of unrectified potential that are the driving force behind our universe. *Dinim* and *gevurot* are generally associated with unconscious lights and with the feminine. They originated in the World of Points.

Eden – Paradise. The term that describes the nature of physical reality before the shattering and fragmentation that followed Adam and Eve's sin. Eden is the state where *HaShem's* Presence visibly permeates reality, and all things are expressing their perfection and exist in a state of union with God.

Evil – Literally, "broken or unstable." The illusion of existence as separate and independent from God.

Front-to-Front Relationship – A relationship of true and healthy love. The couple bonds from mutual desire and shared vision. This possibility of relationship only arises after *nesira.*

Gadlut – (literally, "greatness"). Expanded, mature, and God-centered consciousness.

Gemara – The major component of the Talmud, the primary repository of the Oral Law. The *Gemara* analyzes, develops, and interprets the Written Torah in accordance with the explanations that were received simultaneously with its revelation by Moses at Sinai.

Gematria – Every Hebrew letter possesses a number value. The numerical total of the letter, word, or phrase is called its *gematria*. When words or phrases have the same *gematria*, they are understood to hold a special relationship to each other, and many secrets and meditations are based on the science of these equivalencies.

Gevurah – The fifth *sefirah*, translated as "might" or "justice," expresses itself in several ways. It meters the impulse to give, forcing it to adapt to the vessel's capacity to receive; it negates all that opposes the will of God; and it is the boundary-making, form-building power within creation.

Gevurot – See *dinim*.

Halacha – (literally, "walking"). The vast system of Jewish law derived from the Torah as received by Moses and explicated by the Sages, which defines the entirety of Jewish life. There is no area of experience that is outside the jurisdiction of halacha.

HaShem – (literally, "The Name"). It refers to God in general, though it specifically indicates the unutterable name (or Tetragrammaton), which emphasizes the transcendent, eternal, and compassionate attributes of God.

Hod – The eighth *sefirah*, translated as "splendor." *Hod* is the strength of wholehearted commitment to one's goals, even when their truth is beyond comprehension.

Holographic System – A holographic system is one where every sub-part contains information about the whole and every other sub-part within itself. Consequently, in a holographic system, it is possible to reconstruct the entire structure from any isolated component.

Hoshana Rabbah – (literally, "Great Call for Redemption"). The seventh (and last) day of Sukkot, marked by elaborate beseechings for rain and redemption. On that day congregants circle the table that holds the Torah scroll seven times.

Integrated Lights – Truths and understandings that have been apprehended by the mind or heart.

Katnut – (literally, "smallness"). A term referring to an immature, narrow, or constricted state of consciousness. This term applies both to an early stage in the normal course of human development; as well as to an age-inappropriate state of regression.

Keter – The highest *sefirah* and deepest root of the soul, translated as "crown." The place where the soul is hewn from the pure simple oneness of God. *Keter* joins God's will with man's will.

Klipah – (literally, "shell or husk"). A term that describes the way evil and impurity encase Divine sparks of good as a shell surrounds its fruit.

Kohen – Temple priest. The families descending from Aaron, Moses' brother, are assigned the responsibility of caring for the Temple and performing its religious rituals on behalf of the entire nation. In turn, they are supported by the people. Originally, the oldest son of every family was to fulfill this function of Temple service, but after the "sin of the golden calf" this privilege was withdrawn from the rest of the people and given instead to the tribe of Levi, and the sacrifices, in particular, to the sons of Aaron.

Kosher – Something that meets all the stipulations of Jewish law. In particular, it is used in relation to dietary requirements.

Lights – *Lights* are always equivalent to consciousness in kabbalistic writings. Each *sefirah,* or spark, is a *light* that transmits a particular insight or capacity for awareness.

Linear World *(Yosher)* – The universe as we know it, with *sefirot* organized along three vertical and parallel pillars. Hierarchical reality. Also called the World of *Tikun,* or *Barudim.*

Malchut – The lowest of the ten *sefirot* is called *malchut,* which means literally "royalty and kingship." It corresponds to the physical plane and represents the final stage in light's congealing into matter.

Man – Translation of the *partzuf* called *zeir anpin* (smaller countenance), which builds from the six *sefirot* from *chesed* to *yesod,* called the *midot* (or emotional attributes of soul). *Man* corresponds to the aspect of God called Blessed Holy One.

Man and *Woman* – Kabbalistic archetypes of male and female in their prime, as opposed to *father* and *mother,* which signify their later stages of life.

Mashiach – Though the Messianic Era will be the fruit of everyone's enlightened efforts, there will still need to be an individual (or couple) to coordinate this massive project of global harmonization. That is the role of *Mashiach.*

Messianic Era – The messianic era is a transitional time between *this* world and the next. It begins somewhere toward the end of the sixth millennium (we are now within the period of its likely beginnings) and will take us to the threshold of the world to come. It is the joyous stage of actualized perfection. Love of God, love of neighbor, and love of Torah reign.

Midrash – Third level of biblical interpretation in the model of

PaRDeS. Homiletical writings that explain the biblical text through the use of stories and sermons. The *midrash* often fills out a sparsely written biblical narrative, providing background, context, moral lessons, or legal implications.

Mishnah – First recording of the oral law compiled by Rabbi Yehuda HaNasi in 180 C.E. Primarily legalistic in content, the *Mishnah* consolidates the Oral Tradition as it had evolved from Sinai through the Second Temple period. It forms the basis of the *Gemara*.

Mitzvah, Mitzvot – The 613 commandments of the Written Torah. It is also used colloquially to refer, in general, to good deeds.

Mother – The higher (or elder) feminine archetype associated with the *sefirah* of *understanding* (*binah*).

Nesira (surgical uncoupling) – Tradition teaches that Adam and Eve were originally created as a single, bi-gendered creature with male and female halves fused together like Siamese twins. God then severed this bond, releasing them to meet face-to-face as freestanding individuals for the first time. This is how Jewish tradition interprets the biblical story of Eve's formation.

Netzach – The seventh *sefirah*, translated as "*victory, eternity, or endurance.*" *Netzach* is the power to overcome obstacles to the implementation of truth (which it conceptualizes in absolute terms).

Nikudim – See World of Points.

Nukva – See *woman*.

Or Ein Soph – Infinite Light. God's transcendent and primordial revelation. His simple, radiant, infinitely powerful light. The contraction that initiated the creative process caused this Infinite Light to become hidden within the circumscribed area that is the space of the created worlds.

Oral Law or Oral Tradition – The explanations and elaborations of the Written Law or Torah. These were also received by Moses at Sinai but passed from mouth to ear, teacher to student, master to disciple, until just after the destruction of the Second Temple. The first recording of the Oral Law was the Mishnah (180 C.E.), and this opened the way for all subsequent transcriptions of what ideally was to be a personal, verbal transmission of knowledge and information. Included in the category of the Oral Tradition are the Mishnah, *midrash*, *Gemara*, Talmud, and Kabbalah.

Pardes – (literally, "orchard"). Acronym for the four levels of Torah study: *pshat* (plain, literal meaning of the text); *remez* (hints and allusions in the text); *drash* (additional levels of meaning derived by verbal analogy); and *sod* (the esoteric, mystical dimension of the text).

Parasha – The Torah (Five Books of Moses) is divided into fifty-four sections, so that a portion is read in the synagogue each week and the entire Torah is completed each year. The fifty-four sections cover the possibility of leap years, when an extra month is added to the lunar year. Each portion is called a *parasha* or *sidra*. On non-leap years, certain *parashot* are doubled so that the entire Bible is still completed that year.

Partzuf / Partzufim – The set of six kabbalistic and human-like archetypes that coalesce into a family system, with each filling a unique role, for example: *father, mother, man, woman*. Equally frequently, these *partzufim* function as different "voices" or sub-personalities within a single individual.

Principle of Interinclusion – A distinguishing feature of our present universe is its holographic structure. Every piece contains something of every other piece inside itself. This is always true.

No matter how small the fragment, no matter how many sub-divisions one executes, the resulting particles always contain a complete set of the whole.

Pshat – The literal interpretation of scripture, its plot or story line.

Purim – Rabbinically instituted festival celebrating the miracle by which the Jewish people were saved from genocide during the Persian exile. Based on the Book of Esther.

Rabbi, Rav, Rebbe – Variations on a word that means teacher.

Rambam – Acronym for Rabbi Moshe Ben Maimon, a twelfth-century sage, scholar, and physician who made great contributions to Judaism's legal and philosophical heritage. Author of *Mishneh Torah* and *Guide for the Perplexed*.

Rashi – Acronym for Rabbi Shlomo Yitzchaki, eleventh century. The most important commentator on Bible and *Gemara*.

Remez (hint) – References to less obvious teachings that are based on idiosyncrasies of syntax or grammar.

Rosh Chodesh – New Month. The new moon, which is the first day of each Hebrew month, is observed with special prayers and more festive attire.

Rosh Hashanah – Jewish New Year. Occurs on the first day of the seventh month (Tishrei), which generally falls in September or October. It is a day of prayer, reflection, and repentance. It is further distinguished as the day for hearing the *shofar*.

Sefirah / Sefirot – The ten channels of Divine flow and emanation that link the Transcendent Light with Its evolving and apparently finite creation.

Seven-Thousand-Year Cycle of Biblical History – Tradition teaches that each creation day translates into 1,000 years of earthly history and the count begins from the appearance of Adam (a creature with specific spiritual capabilities that distinguish him from generic man, or *Homo sapiens*). The six weekdays are 6,000 years of refining ourselves and turning the world into a Temple that can hold and reveal the full Presence of God. This period culminates in the messianic time and then transitions into an entirely new era called the world to come, or seventh millennium and cosmic Sabbath. We are currently in the 5760th year of this cycle, as the Gregorian calendar shifts to its twenty-first century.

Shabbat – Sabbath. The seventh day of the week from Friday sunset to Saturday dusk. It is a day of rest from labor and business activity and it is specifically "creative" work (*malakha*) that is forbidden on Shabbat (i.e., the realization of an intelligent purpose by practical skill). There are thirty-nine categories of *malakha*, each with many details and particulars. For example, an observant Jew does not cook, light fires, sew, write, build, work in the fields, and many etceteras. In addition, Shabbat is a time to focus on the more spiritual dimensions of life.

Shekhinah – The feminine expression of God associated with the *partzuf woman*, wherein is concentrated all the Divine light that shines to the lower worlds.

Shemini Atzeret – (literally, "Eighth Day of Closure"). A holiday that immediately follows the seven days of Sukkot. The eighth day, Shemini Atzeret, is the simplest festival of the Jewish calendar. It, in itself, has no special observances beyond the standard celebratory meals that mark each holiday.

Shemoneh Essrei – (literally, "eighteen"). The group of originally eighteen, but now nineteen, blessings that form the core and backbone of Jewish worship. Under most circumstances the obligation to pray three times a day is only fulfilled by reciting the *Shemoneh Essrei*. This prayer is recited silently, while standing, feet together, facing Jerusalem.

Shulchan Arukh – (literally, "set table"). Authoritative guide to Jewish observance compiled by Joseph Karo (1488–1575).

Sod (secret) – Kabbalah. The mystical teachings embedded within scriptural text.

Soul – The spiritual essence of a person or thing; its life force and consciousness. To a certain degree, a creature's soul is apparent by its capacity to respond and interact with its environment and so to manifest a particular range of the infinite continuum of potentialities that exist within Divine consciousness.

Sukkot – (literally, "Tabernacles"). The fall harvest festival where Jews voluntarily exile themselves from the security of their homes and live for a week in fragile dwellings beneath the stars, to remind themselves of the impermanence of the material world. Special prayers are recited throughout that week and in the morning liturgy, congregants, in procession, circle the table that holds the Torah scroll.

Surrounding Lights – Truths and understandings that are too deep or great for the mind (or vessel) to grasp.

Talmud – The main repository of the Oral Tradition scribed in 499 C.E., which interprets and elaborates the Torah.

Tanya – (literally, "It has been taught"). The first word of R. Schneur Zalman's classic work on chasidut and the name by which it is commonly called.

Temple – (*Beit HaMikdash*). The Temple is considered a microcosm of the universe. Every element and all its proportions reflect the inner structure of creation. Similarly, the activities and ritual observances that take place in the Temple have profound mystical significance. There was one portable Temple called the *Mishkan*, constructed in the desert to accompany the Jews throughout their forty years of wandering. King Solomon built the first actual Temple of stone in Jerusalem in 996 B.C.E. Nebuchadnezzar destroyed it 410 years later, in 586 B.C.E. The Second Temple was built on the same site by Herod in 516 B.C.E. It was destroyed by the Roman army in 70 C.E. The Third Temple will be built in the messianic era.

Teshuva – (literally, "return)." Return to the service of God. The inner, all-consuming commitment to devote one's life to serving God. The process of lower *teshuva* involves acknowledging sins, regretting them, and committing to change.

Tetragrammaton – See *HaShem*.

This **world** – Our physical world, where all the laws of nature apply. The state of reality after eating from the Tree of Knowledge of Good and Evil and before the world to come.

Tiferet – The sixth *sefirah*, translated as "beauty" or "harmony." Situated on the central pillar, *tiferet* unites the selfless generosity of *chesed* with the self-preserving boundaries of *gevurah*. It harmonizes these two opposing impulses in accordance with the attribute of mercy and compassion. Its perfectly just, though sensitive, application of generosity and restraint is motivated, above all, by an abiding empathy with the innermost realities of one's fellow creatures and a genuine desire for their highest good.

Tikun – A word that means "rectification, healing, repair, perfection, elevation" ... all of these at once.

Torah – The first five books of the Bible revealed at Sinai. The word *Torah* often also includes the Oral Teachings and then denotes

into new light bodies wherein they experience an infinitely deepening ecstasy of relationship with God.

Worlds – Refers both to the four planes of reality: physical, emotional, mental, spiritual (see footnote on p. 137) and to the sequential stages in creation's unfolding (see map of the Unfolding of Worlds on p. 167).

Yesod – The ninth *sefirah*, translated as "foundation." *Yesod* is the bond, or channel, that actually joins the giver with the receiver, or the person to the world.

Yom Kippur – Day of Atonement. Climax of the ten-day period of repentance and rededicating one's life to God that begins with Rosh HaShanah. Observed as a fast day of prayer and deep devotion where we seek and are assured of pardon and forgiveness.

Zeir Anpin – See *man*.

the entire body of knowledge generated from the Torah by the Jewish people throughout history.

Tree of Knowledge of Good and Evil – The forbidden tree in Eden that represents a fallen state of consciousness where truth is twisted by emotional attachments and narcissistic needs.

Tree of Life – One of two trees at Eden's center and mentioned in Genesis 2:9. To eat from the Tree of Life is to extract the spark of eternal spirit from each moment by acting according to God's will. If one would eat only from the Tree of Life, one would not die.

Tzaddik/Tzaddikim – (literally, "righteous, perfect"). A person who has purged his or her entire being of all impurity and of every inclination (even subconscious) to act contrary to spiritual law.

Vessel – Kabbalah groups the world into lights and vessels, roughly paralleling energy and matter. Souls are lights and bodies are vessels. The earliest vessels formed from the outer layers of emanated light that congealed into sac-like forms that remained, even after their light withdrew. Vessels are feminine and generally associate with the *sefirah* of *malchut*. See "Kabbalistic Symbols of the Feminine," Chapter 1, p. 24.

Woman – Translation of *nukva*, the last of the six *partzufim*, built from the *sefirah* of *malchut*. *Woman* corresponds to the aspect of God called the *Shekhinah* or Divine Presence.

World of Points – The shattered world, also called the World of *Tohu* (*Chaos*), which preceded our universe and out of whose debris we are all built.

World to Come – The seventh millennium and period following the messianic era that marks an entirely new state of existence where physicality, as we know it, dissolves and souls are born

INDEX

STUDY OPPORTUNITIES
A STILL SMALL VOICE

Presents the Following Resources:

EATING AS *TIKUN*: This book notes that humanity's first error was an act of unholy eating (from the Tree of Knowledge), which means that only its opposite can fix it. All of life and all of history are training us for one end: to learn to "eat" in holiness, to not let the world's pleasures wrench our attention from God (even for an instant). The moment we get it the labor of this world will end.

EVOLUTIONARY CREATIONISM—Kabbala Solves the Riddle of Missing Links: The kabbalistic description of Eden's "fall" presents a scenario of crash and repair that is nearly identical to the account of prehistory derived from the cutting edge of modern physics, called Superstrings. A compelling and intellectually satisfying scenario emerges to explain the evolutionary history of the planet that is perfectly consistent with both Bible and science.

YOU ARE WHAT YOU HATE—A SPIRITUALLY PRODUCTIVE APPROACH TO ENEMIES: Enemies hold fallen slivers of our souls, estranged sparks that we do not recognize as pieces of our very own selves. The question becomes: How do we both protect ourselves and reclaim our sparks.

MEDITATION AND LEARNING RETREATS IN JERUSALEM: The goal of these retreats is to create an atmosphere that enables participants to access the full healing, guiding, and enlightening potential inherent in Shabbat. There is a wealth of "light" and bounty that comes into the world with Shabbat but for most people this remains an untapped resource. One sure way to harness its potential for healing and transformation is through the practice of retreat.

PRIVATE TEACHING, COUNSELING, AND SPIRITUAL GUIDANCE: In addition to her writing and classroom teaching, Sarah Yehudit Schneider is available for private study and counseling sessions.

RECORDED LECTURE SERIES: Sarah Yehudit Schneider has lectured widely both in Israel and the States. CDs and Mp3s on a wide variety of topics are available on the Still Small Voice website. For example: Prayer and Destiny; Free Will and Determinism; Judaism and Reincarnation; Messiah and the End of Days; The Secret of the Animals in the Garden of Eden; The Gift of the Oral Torah; What Is A Jew; as well as classes on most of the Jewish festivals.

A STILL SMALL VOICE is a correspondence school that presents classic Judaism as a powerful path of spiritual transformation. Its weekly lessons draw from all aspects of the Jewish religious tradition, from its most hidden and kabbalistic mysteries to its most basic principles of faith and practice. A year and a half of weekly lessons are currently available:

> **Prayer and Destiny** explores the mystery of prayer and how it is a potent tool for personal and spiritual growth (even more effective than visualization and affirmation). **20 weeks**.

> **The Enlightened Body** shows how the system of Jewish ritual practices is actually a powerful and penetrating spiritual path. **12 weeks**.

> **Synchrony** is an experiential exploration of the six constant *mitzvot*. Among the 613 religious obligations that comprise the Jewish path, six are meditations that one must hold in mind at all times. **13 weeks**.

> **Time Trekking** explores the deeper meanings behind the daily, weekly, monthly and yearly cycles of observance. **26 weeks**.

ENROLLMENT BENEFITS INCLUDE:

- weekly lessons of stimulating and practical insights into Jewish wisdom
- personal guidance through practical exercises that aid integration of the material
- timely holiday supplements
- answers to personal questions about lessons, and other topics of Jewish thought
- **time tested tools guaranteed to enhance peace of mind and quality life**

Chabad St. 90/16, Old City, Jerusalem, 9751648 Israel
tel: (02) 628–2988 smlvoice@netvision.net.il •
www.astillsmallvoice.org

ABOUT THE AUTHOR

Sarah Yehudit (Susan) Schneider is the founding director of A Still Small Voice, a correspondence school that provides weekly teachings in classic Jewish wisdom to subscribers around the world. Sarah is the author of Kabbalistic Writings on the Nature of Masculine and Feminine, published by Jason Aronson, Inc., in 2000, (available at www.astillsmallvoice.org/). In addition, she is the author of Eating as Tikun, Purim Bursts, and Evolutionary Creationism as well as numerous essays published in a variety of journals and anthologies.

Sarah Yehudit has produced and now works with a homeopathic remedy based on Kabbalah. It is designed to heal the deepest level of soul that was damaged by our collective participation with the Tree of Knowledge of Good and Evil.

Sarah Yehudit has a BA in Molecular, Cellular, and Developmental Biology from the University of Colorado in Boulder. Since 1981, she has lived in Jerusalem, followed an orthodox path of observance, and immersed herself in the study of mystical texts. In addition she completed the program for advanced study at Neve Yerushalayim

Seminary for Women. Sarah Yehudit teaches a variety of weekly classes in Jerusalem as well as offering private instruction to individuals seeking a more personal encounter with text.

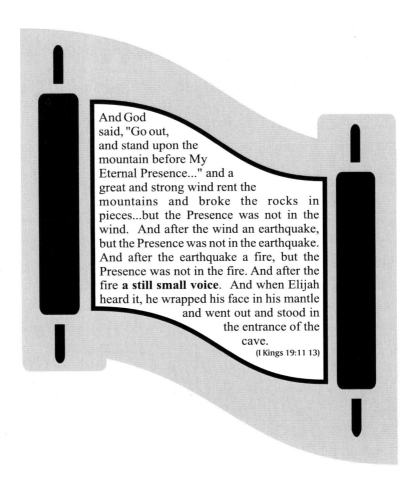

And God said, "Go out, and stand upon the mountain before My Eternal Presence..." and a great and strong wind rent the mountains and broke the rocks in pieces...but the Presence was not in the wind. And after the wind an earthquake, but the Presence was not in the earthquake. And after the earthquake a fire, but the Presence was not in the fire. And after the fire **a still small voice**. And when Elijah heard it, he wrapped his face in his mantle and went out and stood in the entrance of the cave.

(I Kings 19:11 13)